D0365491

POINT PARK
UNIVERSITY

Donated to the
Library by

Dr. W.H. Breslove

NATIONALISM IN FRANCE

MR 2 4 '06

NATIONALISM IN FRANCE

Class and Nation since 1789

Brian Jenkins

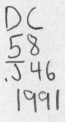

DC
58
.J46
1991

Barnes & Noble Books
Savage, Maryland

© 1990 by Brian Jenkins

ALL RIGHTS RESERVED

No part of this publication may be reproduced or transmitted, in any form or
by any means, without the written permission of the publishers.

First published in the United States of America 1990 by
BARNES & NOBLE BOOKS
8705 Bollman Place
Savage, Maryland 20763

Library of Congress Cataloging in Publication Data
Jenkins, Brian
Nationalism in France: Class and nation since 1789/Brian Jenkins.
p.   cm.
Includes bibliographical references (p.
ISBN 0 389 20943 0
1. France-Politics and government-1789-2. Nationalism-France-
History. I Title
DC58.J46 1990
320.5′4′ 0944-dc20

Printed in Great Britain

CONTENTS

PREFACE

In his remarkable essay on the nation, Stanley Hoffmann notes the absence hitherto of any systematic sociological history of French nationalism.[1] The present work was conceived with this deficiency in mind, though I would not pretend to combine the skills of historian, sociologist and political scientist in sufficient measure to make more than a tentative step in this direction. The task is indeed a formidable one, for it requires sustained theoretical reflection on the difficult concepts of nation and class through two centuries of social and political history.

The problems posed by such an ambitious enterprise have been stylistic as well as academic. It has not been easy to construct a text which focuses consistently on the central theme while at the same time situating the argument in its broad historical context. Those who are interested primarily in the theoretical issues raised by class and nation may find the historical narrative intrusive. Historians on the other hand, may well baulk at the level of generalisation involved, and may object that there are significant historiographical lacunae. In response I can only insist that the book does not purport to be either a theoretical treatise or a comprehensive history of the post-revolutionary period in France. Its focus is multi-disciplinary, and it represents an attempt at intellectual synthesis rather than a piece of primary research. Equally it makes no pretensions to 'scientific objectivity', a fraudulent concept in this context, and I have made no effort to disguise the political orientation and commitment which underpins my arguments. In full consciousness of the dangers of such an exercise, I hope that what follows will be judged on that basis.

The subject inevitably engages some of the issues raised by the current debate on the legacy of 1789, the necessary starting-point for any history of French nationalism. The liberal revisionist position, popularised by François Furet in France and endorsed by many commentators on this side of the Channel, has recently achieved ascendancy over the classical 'Marxian' approach to the history of the French revolution. Of course, ever since they occurred the events have been constantly re-interpreted in line with the prevailing ideological climate, and this most recent shift is no exception. However, the bicentennial celebrations have inevitably focused attention on what the Revolution has bequeathed to modern society, and this has engendered a retrospective moralistic tone which is inimical to serious scholarship. Evaluations of the Terror which make light of the historical circumstances which produced it, and spurious ideological analogies between Jacobinism and twentieth-century totalitarianism, do little to further our understanding of what took place.

My own particular concern, namely the development of the idea of 'nation', is equally prone to the distortions of this fundamentally ahistorical approach. A recent editorial in the British press, rightly acknowledging the Revolution as the birthplace of the democratic nation state, insists that the most complete expression of this idea is that of 'the people under arms' and reminds us that 'this destructive aspect of nationalism echoed throughout European history and met its Armageddon in the two world wars, which almost undid both France and Europe.' [2] As I hope to show, crude genealogy of this type is no basis for the study of a complex and multifarious concept which has been shaped and often transformed by the changing social and political context of two centuries of history.

ACKNOWLEDGEMENTS

The preparation of this book owed much to the inspiration and encouragement, not to mention the patience and forbearance, of others. Chronologically, my first debt is to the late William Pickles, onetime Reader in French Politics at the London School of Economics, whose knowledge and enthusiasm sparked my interest in French history. Much later I had the good fortune to arrive in the School of Languages and Area Studies at Portsmouth Polytechnic, where the work of Eric Cahm and Vladimir-Claude Fišera among others had laid the foundations for a vigorous tradition of academic research. Their initiative in launching the British Research Group on Socialism and Nationalism was vital to the development of my own research interests, and the friendships and intellectual exchanges bred by that venture have been of lasting value. There are many other names I could cite in this context, notably Roger Thomas, Ken Lunn and Robin Okey. In particular, I must single out Günter Minnerup, with whom I collaborated on an earlier book and whose ideas on the theoretical problem of the 'nation' have been a constant reference-point for my own reflections on the subject. Needless to say, however, neither he nor any of the other colleagues I have mentioned can in any way be held responsible for what appears in the pages that follow.

The pressures under which we all work in the Polytechnic sector make it hard to sustain research interests. In this respect, I must also acknowledge my debt to all those involved with the Association for the Study of Modern and Contemporary France and its quarterly Review, which has done much to stimulate academic activity in the field of French Studies. I also wish to express my gratitude to Tony Chafer, Bob French and all my colleagues in the French Department at Portsmouth Polytechnic, without whose co-operation and encouragement I would not have found the time to embark on this enterprise.

Finally, I would like to thank all those friends who have put up with my antisocial tendencies for over a year, and above all my wife, Julia Vaughan, whose tolerance went beyond all reasonable bounds.

1

INTRODUCTION:
NATION AND NATIONALISM

> The theory of nationalism represents Marxism's great historical
> failure.
>
> (Tom Nairn)

We live in a world of nation states, some of which have existed as
independent and well-defined territorial units for centuries, while many
have only achieved political sovereignty in the last thirty years. When
the United Nations was founded in 1948 it counted forty-eight members
– today there are 160. In the course of two centuries the idea of nation has
gradually established itself as the key legitimising principle of statehood
everywhere, and it is therefore not surprising if the related term 'nationalism' has become one of the most overworked epithets in the
political vocabulary. It is applied to independence movements and to
established states, to ideologies of both internal integration and external
aggression, to the widely differing contexts of nineteenth-century
Europe, anti-colonial liberation struggle and contemporary separatist
'micro-nationalism'. It may be the vehicle for the interests of the state or
for the aspirations of the 'people', for doctrines of emancipation or
repression, and it is all too easily used as a sloppy euphemism for what
might more appropriately be classified as chauvinism, racism, jingoism,
imperialism or, in a rather different vein, simple native patriotism.

This rather casual use of the term in everyday speech is not
necessarily reproduced at the level of political theory, where it is at
least recognised that the term must be qualified in a variety of ways in
order to distinguish between what are clearly very different ideologies
and movements. Left, right, bourgeois, revolutionary, bureaucratic,
populist, anti-colonial and imperialist are among the many comple-
ments commonly used to provide a greater degree of precision.
However, the suitability of the noun itself 'nationalism' in these

1

varying contexts is rarely questioned, and this is not simply a matter of semantic convenience. Behind it lie certain crude theoretical assumptions which have blunted the concept so that its utility as a methodological tool has been seriously impaired.

The main schools of thought that have coloured the historical debate on the 'national question' have been liberalism and Marxism.[1] In so far as any theoretical approach brings with it certain assumptions, it is relevant to note that both these positions are, in their different ways, inspired by universalist principles and aspirations. The tradition of Enlightenment thought, with its emphasis on the rights of man and the freedom of the individual, looked to the liberating power of reason as a force which would transcend the narrow parochialism inherited from the age of feudalism. Marxism rejected this 'bourgeois idealism' in favour of the emancipatory mission of the industrial working class, but it remained equally convinced that history was working to undermine the 'artificial' vertical divisions of humanity, this time through the vehicle of international proletarian solidarity. It is understandable, therefore, that theorists of both persuasions have approached the phenomenon of nationhood with an instinctive mistrust. The proliferation and persistence of nation states has often been viewed a priori as a problem, an obstacle on the anticipated path of human development, the very antithesis of a longed-for 'internationalism'.

Both approaches have thus been preoccupied with the task of explaining why national consciousness has taken root and survived in a world where such narrow loyalties appear increasingly anachronistic. Both have assumed that the source of the explanation lies in the fact that nations do indeed 'exist' as objective social realities, brought into being by underlying historical forces (with the corollary, of course, that they will continue to exist as such until the onward march of history decrees otherwise). For liberal theorists this process of nation formation is conceived largely in cultural terms, drawing on concepts of ethnicity, linguistic unity, collective historical experience and 'communities of fate'. Marxists, on the other hand, have tended to see the emergence of nation states in terms of changing modes of production and, more specifically, the rise of the bourgeoisie. As the body of theory has evolved in response to new circumstances, there has been a substantial interchange between the 'cultural' and the 'economic' strands,[2] and this is not altogether surprising given the methodological affinities between the two approaches. Both are fundamentally deterministic. The processes of cultural differentiation in the one case, or economic homogenisation in the other, 'produce' nations, which in turn engender 'nationalism'. The latter is conceived in the broadest possible terms, as a body of sentiments derived from membership of the nation. Apparently any movement or ideology which deploys the imagery of national identity may be properly described as 'nationalist', for by promoting a sense of nationhood it is prolonging the survival of what both liberals and Marxists tend to see as an historical anachronism – the nation state.

Such a broad definition of nationalism is, of course, extremely unsatisfactory. There are few political movements that do not try to appeal to the specific social, historical and cultural experience of their national community. Is this single bland common attribute to be regarded as more important than what might divide such movements – ideals and values, social bases, political goals, their aspirations for this 'national community'? And is there really no distinction to be made between movements and ideologies which place the concept of 'nation' at the very centre of their designs (self-determination, the preservation of sovereignty, territorial expansion, economic autarchy) and those which simply seek to concretise their political message by using the myths, symbols and folk-memories of their own national culture?

The approaches to which we have referred offer no real basis for exploring the complex relationship between 'nation' and 'nationalism'. Starting from the assumption that nations objectively exist, they have above all been concerned to identify the forces that have allegedly brought nations into being. This has led them to see nations as culturally or economically determined entities, rather than, as we would claim, human artefacts whose study belongs to the realm of *politics*.

TOWARDS A THEORETICAL PERSPECTIVE

This book is not primarily a theoretical work, and this introductory chapter can do no more than summarise an analysis that we have developed at greater length elsewhere.[3] In response to the cultural and economic determinism of much of the classical debate on the national question, we would advance three initial propositions.

The first one may seem superfluous, for Marxists and indeed most liberal theorists would acknowledge that 'nations' are indeed a strictly historical phenomenon. However, in some 'cultural' approaches to the question that emphasise the importance of ethnicity, language and territory, there is a tendency to dig rather deep in time for the origins of nationhood, so the point is still worth making.[4] Namely, nations are not timeless, natural entities. They were preceded by other forms of social and geographical organisation – tribes, *gentes,* fiefdoms, vast territorial empires – whose legitimacy was based on profoundly different principles from those of the modern nation state. Recognition of this is an essential starting-point for any discussion of the issue. The failure to do so leads to an indiscriminate use of the terms 'nation' and 'nationalism', which blurs the distinctions between state, race, ethnic group, locality and national community.

The second point is directed more specifically at the cultural explanations of nationhood. There is no doubt, of course, that ethnic, linguistic or territorial solidarities along with a shared historical experience have often provided the 'raw material' from which nations have been built. They have also helped, though rather inefficiently, to shape national frontiers. They have furthermore led to prolonged academic and political debate as to which precise combination of criteria should be the yardstick for measuring whether a particular nation exists,[5] and this rather fruitless pursuit highlights the weaknesses of this deterministic approach. Quite simply, nations do not pre-exist as culturally-defined entities, they are 'called into being' by political action. The criteria developed by the cultural perspective, even when combined with economic-territorial considerations, are largely irrelevant to the analysis of the nation-building process in much of the Third World for example, and this reflects their Euro-centric bias. But a more fundamental point is our contention that ethnic and linguistic communities that never develop the desire to constitute their own states are not nations. It would never occur to anyone to regard the Italian-speaking citizens of the United States as a nation, whereas the French-speaking citizens of Canada do invite consideration as such. Nationhood can only be expressed through the existence of a nation state or through a movement to build such a state. To summarise the point in terms we have employed elsewhere, 'the theoretical problem of the nation belongs neither to the sphere of culture and linguistics, nor that of economics and geography' but to that of politics.[6]

This emphasis on the centrality of politics to our understanding of the nation is equally crucial for our third proposition, which challenges another more rigorous determinism, namely the economistic approach evident in classical Marxism. According to this view, nations are the by-product of bourgeois economic interests, and emerge spontaneously through the capitalist quest for wider markets and the role of a common language as a vehicle for commodity exchange. On this assumption, movements to build nation states are the agents of an already powerful and coherent bourgeoisie that has a clear conception of how that state and its founding ideology will be used as instruments of class domination. Thus, both before and after the founding of the nation state, nationalism is no more than an ideological tool in the hands of the bourgeoisie.

While this analysis at least recognises the historical specificity of nationhood, it rests on an excessively economistic interpretation of the transition from feudalism to capitalism in Europe, that complex and uneven process which straddled several centuries. This question requires lengthier development than our earlier propositions, but it is hoped that what follows will be of more than just methodological interest, for it focuses on a period that was crucial for the nation-building process in France itself.

The decay of the European Old Order, which spanned at least four centuries from the Reformation and the Renaissance to the Russian Revolution and the First World War, proceeded at different speeds and assumed different forms across the continent. The process is inseparable from the spread of capitalist economic relations and the rise of a 'bourgeois' class, but the primary and determining influence accorded to the transformation of 'productive forces' by classical Marxism leaves too many questions unanswered. At worst such an approach is crude and simplistic, and at best, where an attempt is made to relate the changes in economic substructure more closely to those in the political and cultural superstructure, the arguments become so tortuous as to smack of sophistry.

Within feudalism two major forces were working to undermine the structures inherited from the medieval period. First, there was the rebellion of the peasantry against serfdom, often related to the struggles of religious reformation movements, which with varying degrees of success across the continent was modifying the social hierarchy in the countryside. In the long term, by releasing the rural labour force from the master–serf relationship, this process was laying the basis for future capitalist development. More immediately, how-ever, the effect was to undermine the status of the petty aristocracy and slowly to transcend the particularism of feudal society. This trend was reinforced by the centralising tendencies of the feudal monarchy itself which, by weakening the political autonomy of the local nobility and subordinate principalities, provided a new focus for the aspirations of all social classes. Not least among these was this selfsame aristocracy, whose resistance to royal absolutism was frequently to become a rallying point for the political ambitions of other groups in society.

Secondly, against this background, the gradual formation of a bourgeois class over a period of several centuries is partially explained by the growth of simple commodity production, the use of money, the commercial development of isolated urban centres and great ports. But equally relevant is the religious Reformation, the secularisation of learning, the development of printing, the spread of universities, the flowering of art and science in the Renaissance. Together these forces were combining to produce a heterogeneous intermediate layer of functionaries, lawyers, men of learning, entrepreneurs and financiers, raised above the common level by wealth or education, sometimes aspiring to noble status or landed property, but collectively representing a leaven of change within feudal society.

By the late eighteenth century, such categories had not in the most of Europe achieved the collective identity which merits the title 'class'. Except in the case of England, and to a lesser extent Holland and France, capitalist economic relations were not yet sufficiently developed to provide a focus for bourgeois class consolidation. The structures and attitudes of this incipient bourgeoisie cannot therefore be explained in terms of shared economic interests, but rather in terms of a convergence of economic, social and political aspirations, each enjoying relative autonomy. Once this is accepted, it is no longer an anomaly to find that some of the best promoters of 'bourgeois' political interests were liberal aristocrats, that certain 'bourgeois' categories were happily integrated into the structures of the *Ancien Régime,* or that capitalist entrepreneurs were not necessarily the motor of revolutionary change in France.

An aristocracy that was gradually losing its feudal character, a bourgeoisie still in the process of formation, a peasantry slowly emerging from serfdom, an urban populace that was far from being a 'proletariat', this was the social context in which the principle of nationhood made its historical debut. It is therefore simplistic to see the establishment of nationalist movements and nation states in the nineteenth century as the work of the bourgeoisie only, let alone as a simple expression of its 'economic' interests. Indeed, the very success of the concept of 'nation' lies in the fact that it was a distinctly 'political' formula, capable of mobilising behind it a variety of contradictory social and economic aspirations.

The principle of nationhood emerged from a struggle to redefine political sovereignty in term of representative institutions claiming to incarnate the collective will of the people. On the one hand, this implied the rejection of the traditional feudal bases of royal authority, and the imposition of legal and constitutional constraints on the power of the crown. On the other hand, it also required the suppression of feudal rights and of the corporate privileges of a society of orders, the establishment of a community of citizens enjoying, in principle at least, equality before the law. As we have seen, a variety of forces were paving the way for this challenge to the Old Order, but the pace of change varied widely across Europe. In social and economic terms, the relatively developed north-west (England, Holland, France, Belgium) was in marked contrast to the territories to the south and east, while the vast Tsarist and Habsburg empires were still almost medieval in character. It was above all in England and France that the legacy of political centralisation had forged a sense of territorial identity, reinforced in the former case by Britain's island location, and these were therefore the prototypes of the modern nation state.

In England the struggle against royal authority and aristocratic privilege in the seventeenth century culminated in the bloodless Revolution of 1688, when the crown was finally subjected to constitutional and parliamentary control. However, a gradual convergence of interests between aristocracy, gentry and commercial bourgeoisie meant that this challenge could be successfully mounted without invoking the active support of the lower classes. Moreover, since feudalism had by this time been largely dismantled, the deep social antagonisms bred by the French *Ancien Régime* a century later had already been defused in the English context. Clouded by religious issues, the events which finally imposed constitutional monarchy did not decisively divide the country's social elites, did not trigger agrarian unrest or call into question an entire social order. The 'Glorious Revolution' never needed to invoke the principle of 'nation' as a source of legitimacy because the issues were resolved in the upper echelons of the social hierarchy.

By contrast, as we shall see, the process set in motion in 1787 in France gradually brought to a head all the major social and political contradictions of *Ancien Régime* society. The liberal sections of the aristocracy and bourgeoisie were driven to form a radical alliance with the lower classes, both rural and urban, and from this revolutionary political coalition emerged the modern political concepts of nationhood and nationalism. It was the French Revolution which first raised the ideal that political authority should rest not on supernatural notions of divine right, tradition or on the imperatives of foreign conquest, but on *popular consent*. The continental *Ancien Régime* of vast empires, petty principalities and the patchwork of feudal particularism provided neither the territorial nor the organisational basis for the structures of democratic control implied by this principle which, in the wake of the revolutionary and Napoleonic wars, found its expression in movements to establish sovereign nation states.

This ideal of self-governing nationhood raised the aspirations of all social classes, and lent to these early nationalisms a popular democratic dimension which was often misinterpreted in classical Marxism. The utopian vision of a new egalitarian order based on the 'general will' may have been sentimental in historical terms, but it cannot simply be dismissed as an ideological smokescreen for 'bourgeois' interests. To do this is to project the class divisions of mature capitalism retrospectively onto a much earlier social configuration. Nationalism, with its emphasis on the formal equality of a nation's citizens beyond class differences, emerged at a stage when the process of capitalist class differentiation was not very far advanced. The 'bourgeoisie' and the 'popular classes' were not yet fully aware of their mutual antagonism or capable of imposing class-conscious leadership on the democratic movements, and the Old Order was thus challenged in the name of a heterogeneous 'people'.

Nationalism, as it first emerged in Europe, might thus be defined as

a political movement or ideology dedicated to establishing by secession, unification, or revolution, a national state which will unite all individuals sharing a particular set of criteria of nationality (ethnic, cultural, historical) under a common regime based on the notion of popular sovereignty.[7]

In this original democratic sense, nationalism has been reproduced more recently in the context of anti-colonial liberation struggles and the 'separatist' movements of Western Europe. As in the original European model, here too it appears to correspond to a distinctive phase in the evolution of class relations, and to fill a vacuum between capitalism and socialism. In the Third World, a weak local 'comprador' bourgeoisie and the socially disparate masses were drawn together in anti-imperialist nationalist struggle, neither being sufficiently developed to undertake this task on their own. In the case of the new 'separatisms', the objective class relations would seem to be less significant, though the changing class structures of advanced capitalist society merit further analysis in this respect. More crucial here, however, is the subjective factor of ideological disillusionment, as the crisis of 'bourgeois' politics and the failures of socialism lead submerged nationalities to seek a new state terrain for their frustrated democratic aspirations.

It is beyond the scope of this chapter to develop these analogies any further, but one thing at least is clear. In neither of these cases can nationalism be explained in terms of the interests of an indigenous national bourgeoisie, and similarly little light is shed on the process by the alternative preoccupation with cultural definitions of nationhood. The territories of the Third World 'nations' are the artificial by-products of colonialism, while the 'micro-nationalisms' of Europe have in some cases lain dormant for generations before acquiring a new vigour in the last twenty years.

If nationalism appears to fit this particular social and ideological configuration, then clearly we should be cautious about the use of the term in the quite different context of mature capitalism and the established nation state. To return to the nineteenth-century European model, the unity of the nationalist movements was undermined as the social antagonisms generated by capitalism became more acute. This was evident even in cases where statehood had not yet been achieved. In the struggles for German and Italian reunification, the democratic popular nationalism of Freiligrath or Mazzini is in marked contrast to the subsequent militarist nationalism of Bismarck or the liberal-capitalist nationalism of Cavour. And in an established nation state like France, the nationalism of the young French Republic is starkly at odds with that of Louis Bonaparte some sixty years later. The revolution-ary-democratic and the bourgeois-liberal strands of the national ideal diverged, the former moving towards working-class socialism while the latter developed into the conservative ideology of 'integral nation-alism' and imperialist chauvinism.

There are two mechanisms at work in this process of transition. At the social level the growth of capitalist class relations tends to break the sentimental unity of the democratic movement by forging a new awareness of the antagonisms of class society. At the political level, once statehood is achieved the whole focus of nationalism changes, and the word 'nation' takes on a new instrumental form. It becomes in many cases a rhetorical device, or as some would have it a 'secondary ideology',[8] rather than a concrete political concept associated with the goal of self-government. Political movements in established states will inevitably appeal to the specific cultural horizons of their citizens, but other ideological considerations will dictate the nature of this appeal. Those on the left will tend to cultivate the legacy of common democratic struggle, while conservatives will stress the values of order and unity which sustain the state and the social system. In both cases the word 'nation' is used to provide a wider legitimacy for ideologies generated by class antagonism.

This is not to say that the issues of self-government, independent statehood and political sovereignty which lie at the heart of nationalism automatically disappear from the agenda once the nation state has been established. States exist within an international environment where the threat of war, conquest or neo-imperialist domination continue to raise the issue of self-determination. However, even these situations are often clouded by the fact that states may cultivate the threat of external interference for purely internal purposes.

This discussion serves to highlight the variety of differing contexts in which the term 'nationalism' is commonly used. As we have already indicated, much of the literature on the subject simply cuts through the political complexities of the question by adopting a deterministic view of the nation and an insufficiently discriminate definition of nationalism. My proposition that the problem belongs to the realm of politics implies an attempt to unravel these complexities, but still within a determinedly historical framework. My starting-point, however, is that nations are created by nationalism rather than the other way round, and that the genesis of nation-building movements has always been the desire to establish self-governing communities. If nationalism has often been treated as synonymous with patriotism, chauvinism, imperialism or racism, this imprecision stems from two fundamental methodological flaws. The first is the failure to appreciate the specificity of the modern national idea, and consequently the tendency to equate it with other concepts like state, race or homeland. The second is the failure to relate the evolution of the national idea to the changing political and social-class context of a given community, the tendency to treat it in linear terms as part of the history of ideas rather than in dialectical terms as an expression of the political contradictions implicit in class society.

It would be unreasonable, of course, to propose that the term 'nationalism', which enjoys such wide currency in common parlance and among historians and political scientists, should be used more discreetly. Indeed, for the purposes of what follows, any attempt to limit the use of the term solely to those cases that we have cited would appear decidedly artificial. However, the semantic problems must not be allowed to detract from the main thesis, namely that nationalism has become a portmanteau expression with little theoretical precision, and that its many usages cannot be treated simply as so many variations on a

single theme. They reflect profoundly different historical circumstances and profoundly different articulations of the national idea, as
we hope to show in the case of France.

NATIONALISM IN FRANCE

French history is a particularly propitious field for the development of
the arguments we have summarised above. We are dealing with a
country which for a century before the Great Revolution had enjoyed a
clear territorial identity, had established a powerful centralised state,
and whose inhabitants were slowly beginning to acquire a degree of
collective consciousness. As we have suggested earlier, France was in
this respect a key prototype of the modern nation state. But it was not
yet a 'nation', a concept which had little or no political currency before
1789. In a society based on 'orders' and on the divine right of Kings, the
French people were 'subjects' not 'citizens', the inhabitants of a
territorial unit rather than conscious actors in their own history. The
day that Louis XVI was forced to assume the title 'King of the French'
rather than that of 'His Most Christian Majesty, the King of France'
was a momentous one in the history of the modern national idea.

The French did not become a 'nation' in the seventeenth century
when the monarchy centralised and unified the country on a feudal
basis, nor in the course of the eighteenth as the forces of economic and
cultural homogenisation began to forge a greater sense of collective
identity. They did so when events turned them into political actors in
their own right, and when the democratic movement against autocracy
and privilege invoked the principle of the sovereignty of the people
over their territory. In the case of France, the issue was not clouded by
the need to define new frontiers through secession or reunification,
which was of course the task that faced subsequent nationalist
movements in continental Europe. In these latter cases the goal of self-
government was often obscured by the 'cultural' emphasis on building a
sense of nationhood. In the French Revolution, on the other hand, the
essence of the national idea, that of popular sovereignty and self-
government, was posed in its most unambiguous terms, and it was this
political concept whose contagious effects were to redraw the map of
Europe in the course of the nineteenth and early twentieth centuries.

As the concept of nation was born in France, it is perhaps not
surprising that the word at least has never been far from the centre of
French political discourse ever since. The Revolution of 1789 did not
conclusively establish all the institutions associated with the modern

bourgeois state, let alone the more radical forms of democracy envisaged by the popular revolutionary movement. Through the years of political and constitutional upheaval between 1815 and 1870 the democratic movement repeatedly articulated its aspirations in terms of the struggle of the oppressed 'nation' against the political and social elites, and even after the birth of the socialist and labour movement the revolutionary tradition remained a rich storehouse of 'national' myths and symbols that were readily deployed. On the right too, the Bonapartist legacy had adapted the idea of nation to its own distinctly authoritarian purposes, and at the end of the nineteenth century the right at large was to adopt and further modify this heritage. In two hundred years of history marked by war, defeat and occupation and by revolution, revolt and *coup d'état,* the issues of national sovereignty and political legitimacy have repeatedly been posed in acutely conflictual terms. In no other country in the world has what is commonly referred to as 'nationalism' found such varied expression, even to the extent that in the last twenty years France, like Britain and Spain, has fallen prey to the 'separatist' struggles of its own submerged nationalities. But to understand these historical ramifications we must return to the birthplace of the national ideal in the French Revolution itself.

2

THE FRENCH REVOLUTION
AND THE BIRTH OF
NATIONALISM

> The principle of all sovereignty lies essentially in the Nation. No
> body, no individual can exercise authority unless it comes
> expressly from this source. . . . Law is the expression of the
> General Will. All citizens have the right to contribute to its
> formation, either personally or through their representatives.
> (Declaration of the Rights of Man, articles 3 and 6)

The continuing fascination of the French Revolution for contemporary
historians reflects its status as an event of international rather than
purely domestic importance. Its unfolding drama was both rehearsal
and catalyst for the social and political transformation of Europe in the
nineteenth century. Liberals emphasize the Revolution's precocious
contribution to the development of the democratic ideal, while
Marxists see the events as a peculiarly vivid demonstration of class
conflict in the transition to bourgeois society. Furthermore, by drawing
the masses onto the political stage the revolution assumed a popular
character which still fires the radical imagination and which offers
unique insights for those who seek to understand the forces that have
shaped the modern world.

There is, however, one aspect of this rich legacy which, though
frequently acknowledged, has rarely been elaborated upon – namely the
Revolution's decisive role in the advancement of the political concept of
'nation'.[1] It has not, perhaps, been sufficiently recognised that the
newly-proclaimed principle of 'national sovereignty' was central to the
class dynamics of the Revolution, and eventually to the process which
undermined the *Ancien Régime* in the rest of continental Europe.

This chapter will focus primarily on this neglected element, and the
events of the revolutionary period will be treated thematically rather
than chronologically. However, as a preliminary it will be necessary to

address some of the orthodox interpretations of the Revolution in order to elaborate our own approach more clearly. The classical debate on the period has opposed Marxists and so-called 'revisionists', the one school insisting on the 'bourgeois' character of the Revolution and the other arguing that the concept of 'class' is of little value for understanding what took place.[2] As indicated in our opening chapter, the position we have adopted falls somewhere between the two, for while we would challenge the view that the Revolution was purely an expression of bourgeois interests, we nonetheless see 'class' as an essential explanatory factor.

The class structures of late eighteenth-century France have already been touched upon briefly, and there is of course a voluminous literature on the subject.[3] Though the country was by this time experiencing the first effects of technical innovation in the manufacturing sector, the economy was essentially based on agriculture and traditional crafts. The overwhelming majority lived in the countryside, and some 80 per cent of the working population were engaged in farming, mostly at subsistence level. Manufacturing was as much a rural as an urban activity, dominated by artisans, peasant craftsmen and small masters, and though textile mills were springing up in some towns, there were very few large industrial enterprises. Commerce, finance and usury remained the most lucrative areas of capitalist activity, but the ownership of land and of seigneurial rights were by far the most important sources of wealth.

The identification of a genuine 'bourgeois' class is problematic for a number of reasons. First, the economic definition of class runs up against the hierarchy of privileges implicit in the 'society of orders' and the seigneurial system. Nobles could engage in certain commercial and industrial operations without loss of rank, and many of them had been promoted into the nobility from the upper echelons of the Third Estate. At the same time, wealthy commoners often owned large estates and could acquire seigneurial rights. 'Class' thus cut clean across legal 'rank', and the image of a privileged landed aristocracy ranged against the commoners of the commercial and industrial bourgeoisie is hard to sustain.

It is within the Third Estate, however, that most Marxist historians tend to look for the contours of the 'bourgeoisie', but this poses just as many problems. Among the wealthy, those whose income was generated by genuine capitalist activity in industry, commerce and finance were heavily outnumbered by landowners (themselves often *rentiers* rather than genuine *entrepreneurs*), lawyers, officials and the members of intellectual, scientific and artistic professions. Similarly, those who lived off the profits extracted from trade and manufacture were in the vast majority small artisans, working alone or with a handful of paid employees in small workshops. Large-scale manufacturing enterprise was rare, and even in the key field of textiles the 'putting-out' of contractual labour to cottage industry was more common than the concentration of the workforce in mills and the development of genuine wage labour.

While this heterogeneous social bloc of the wealthy, educated but under-privileged may be regarded as a 'bourgeoisie in the making', it had little awareness of itself as a distinct 'class' within the Third Estate. Its varied economic, social and political aspirations had not yet fused into a coherent ideology geared to strictly capitalist values. The industrial sector was still in its infancy, and the environment of the small workshop with master, journeyman and apprentice often working side by side for incomes that were not widely different did not favour the development of capitalist class antagonism. Social relations within the Third Estate can best be understood in terms of graded hierarchy of ranks and strata rather than in terms of clear class divisions. The grievances aroused by the undoubted inequalities between 'commoners' were as likely to be expressed in rivalry between town and country, between Paris and provinces, between hostile trade guilds, between peasants and vagrants, as between rich and poor. Most crucial of all, however, was the growing resentment against royal absolutism and the privileged orders, and when these issues came to a head between 1787 and 1789 the momentum for change proved capable of uniting the socially disparate Third Estate into a genuine collective force.

THE MECHANICS OF REVOLUTION

It was the 'aristocratic revolt' against the King's successive attempts to impose economic reforms by means that were perceived as arbitrary which paved the way for the summoning of the Estates General in May 1789. While many aristocrats, both reactionary and liberal, shared with the middle-class representatives of the Third Estate a desire to limit the power of the absolute monarchy, this potential coalition fell apart on other issues. The crisis in the state's finances called into question the unequal privileges and obligations of a 'society of orders', and the unwillingness of sections of the nobility and the ecclesiastical hierarchy to abandon their status as privileged estates opened up a 'second front' in the revolutionary process. When the Third Estate's deputies, in defiance of the two senior orders, transformed themselves on 17 June 1789 into a 'National Assembly' with powers to devise a constitution, they thereby announced their intention of redefining royal authority in terms of 'national consent' rather than on the basis of a narrow compromise between social elites such as had been devised in England a century earlier. The Declaration of the Rights of Man and the Citizen and the suppression of 'orders' laid the foundations of French nationhood.

These developments were, however, more than just an expression of the reforming zeal of enlightened aristocrats and Third Estate *notables,* for by mid-1789 the 'popular' classes had been drawn into the chain of events. The political breach that had been opened by the conflict between the three orders, and by the Third Estate's self-identification with the 'nation' mobilised social aspirations on a broad front. Peasant unrest provoked by a series of bad harvests was now directed into a frontal assault on the seigneurial system, feudal dues and excessive royal taxation, and when in mid-July 1789 the King tried to intimidate the National Assembly, the decisive intervention of the Paris populace in defence of 'their' representatives ensured that thereafter the urban *sans-culottes* were a force to be reckoned with. The great wave of legislation in August 1789 – equal fiscal liability for all, the suppression of venal and hereditary offices, the abolition of feudalism, of provincial and urban privileges and, effectively at least, of seigneurialism – must be seen within this context. Popular demands went beyond the intention of some 'reformers', but the former had to be accommodated in order to stabilise the situation and to forge a social bloc that could resist attempts to turn the clock back.

As the King and the former privileged orders increasingly made common cause against the Revolution, threatening both civil and external war, so the battle-lines were constantly redrawn between those who sought a compromise which would halt the revolutionary process, and those who believed that only by continued popular mobilisation could the Revolution make its achievements irreversible. The successive ascendancy of different political factions in the transition from the constitutional monarchy to the Jacobin Republic of 1793 reflected a complex interaction of classes and class fractions, but to see this simply in terms of conscious bourgeois manipulation of the popular movement is misleading. In many respects there was a genuine convergence of sentiments and interests, and though the political leaders of the Revolution, even in its most radical phase, were almost exclusively drawn from the ranks of the relatively wealthy and educated, many of them saw themselves (and were seen) as the liberators of a whole people rather than as the nucleus of a new social and political elite.[4] There was no cohesive bourgeoisie carefully plotting its path through the revolutionary minefield, subtly directing its foot-soldiers in an assault on the *Ancien Régime*, painstakingly constructing institutions that were tailor-made for bourgeois domination. Rather it was the revolutionary process itself that began to clearly define the contours of that bourgeoisie, to give it self-recognition, to demarcate its interests from those of both the former privileged orders and the subordinate classes. If the institutions founded by the Revolution were to serve the long-term interests of the bourgeoisie, this was not so much because they were designed exclusively for this purpose, but rather because it was historically impossible in class terms for them to assume anything other than a bourgeois form.

If the Old Order rested on corporate privileges and arbitrary authority, it was natural enough that the Revolution should invoke against it the principles of individualism. The Declaration of the Rights of Man and the Citizen, the bedrock on which so much revolutionary legislation was founded, promised to liberate the individual from the political, social and juridical shackles of the *Ancien Régime* and raised the ideal of the free-thinking citizen playing an active role in the community of the 'nation'. Even the specific protection it gave to 'property' cannot be seen as simply 'bourgeois' in a country of land-owning and land-hungry peasants, small masters and aspiring journeymen. If in the process of demolishing feudal and corporate privileges, the trade guilds and the communal rights of the landless and semi-landless countrymen were also swept away, it would be dishonest to cite such measures as proof of far-sighted capitalist calculation. For many radicals this was part and parcel of the attempt to restructure society on the basis of free and equal citizenship. In the immediate task of dismantling the Old Order and demolishing the most visible agencies of oppression and injustice, there was a genuine convergence of class interests, sustaining the myth of the 'unity of the Third Estate' and the illusion of the 'general will'.

Though there were, of course, bourgeois elements who from the start saw the Revolution more clearly in terms of class advantage (just as there were others who regretted the passing of the *Ancien Régime*), the 'bourgeois' character of the Revolution cannot be explained in these terms. It was the dynamics of the revolutionary process itself which hastened the appearance of class contradictions, which gradually established the limits beyond which the new privileged strata would not accommodate popular democratic demands, and which laid the foundations of a more self-conscious, if not yet fully ascendant, bourgeois class. Liberty, equality and the rights of man, the generous vision which had united the revolutionary movement, was to founder on the emerging structures of capitalist class society. The 'liberation of the individual' became the 'individualism of the liberated', liberty became economic liberalism, equality and the rights of man were translated into the bourgeois fictions of 'la carrière ouverte aux talents' [5] and the 'rule of law'.

THE BIRTH OF THE 'NATION'

As we have suggested, the class structures of capitalist society were in a very early stage of maturation in late eighteenth-century France, and it was the political struggles of the Revolution that laid bare the class antagonisms of an emerging capitalism. In social and economic terms this was a precocious development, for a further forty years were to pass before capitalist interests were sufficiently strong to shape a political regime in their own image.[6] In this respect, as in so many others, the French Revolution was a prophetic event, confirming the relative autonomy of the political domain within its broader social and economic context.

This reassertion of 'politics' leads us back to the central question of 'nation' and its relation to class, for it was the immature level of social class differentiation which allowed the concept to take political shape in 1789. The process was set in motion early in that year during the preparation for the meeting of the Estates General, with the Third Estate delegates being chosen, albeit by an indirect procedure, on a fairly wide franchise. This, and the drawing-up in each district of *cahiers de doléance*,[7] inevitably raised the level of popular political consciousness and fed expectations that these delegates would be truly 'national' representatives. The really decisive moments, however, came in June 1789, when the irreconcilable differences between the three orders led the Third Estate to forgo the co-operation of the nobility and clergy and to assume the title of 'National Assembly' on 17 June. When, three days later, faced with the threat of royal dissolution, the Assembly swore the celebrated 'Tennis Court Oath' resolving not to disband until it had established a constitution, the sovereignty it assumed drew its legitimacy from the nation at large. The lawyers, magistrates, landowners and businessmen delegated by the Third Estate were no longer petitioners to the royal court or junior partners of the privileged orders. They had been driven by events to identify themselves as the collective voice of the nation.

Initially the invocation of this new principle did not imply a threat to the existence of the monarchy, nor indeed did it envisage the active participation of all citizens in the political process. The notion of government by consent certainly implied constitutional and parliamentary control of the crown, just as the concept of national sovereignty implicitly challenged aristocratic and seigneurial privilege and the whole society of orders. At this stage, however, it was not assumed that these reforms were incompatible with the survival of the monarchy itself, nor was it assumed that the principle of government by national consent required a wholesale democratisation of the political process. The events of mid-1789, however, drew the masses onto the stage and initiated a popular dynamics which was to characterise the whole revolutionary period. This was due in part to the millennarian expectations which the summoning of the Estates General had raised among the common people, but popular intervention was decisively hastened by the conflict between the three orders, and the King's eventual support for the privileged estates as exemplified by his attempt to disband the 'National Assembly' with the threat of military force in July. It was this fear of aristocratic and royal reaction which drove peasants into open revolt against the seigneurial system in late July, and which on the fourteenth of the same month drew the Paris people onto the streets to protect the National Assembly and save the Revolution.

The ideal of national unity which inspired this process, culminating in the Constituent Assembly's momentous legislation in August, should not be seen as an illusion or a sham. As the *cahiers de doléances* reveal, there was a broad agreement between all three orders on constitutional questions and the curtailment of fiscal immunities, and many enlightened nobles and clerics shared the Third Estate's commitment to individual liberties, freedom of opinion, religious toleration and the suppression of aristocratic privileges. Neither is it accurate to see the abolition of feudalism and seigneurial rights as something imposed on the Constituent Assembly by the peasant rebellion, for as the *cahiers* again show, the urban bourgeoisie, despite its strong landholding interests, was even more likely to demand the abolition of serfdom and seigneurial dues than were those from the rural areas.[8] The social bloc which demolished the *Ancien Régime* was thus cemented not simply by

19

reluctant concessions, but often by a convergence of interests, and even on occasions by a generosity of spirit.

As Lyn Hunt has indicated,[9] the Revolution set itself the task of national regeneration, involving no less than the creation of an entirely new moral and political order. This wholesale abandonment of the past required the development of a new symbolism, imagery and rhetoric, and the concept of nationhood was to be central to this heroic enterprise. In her words:

> There were no recognised birthrights of the 'freeborn' Frenchman to sustain and animate revolutionary rhetoric. Instead the French harkened to what I will call a 'mythic present', the instant creation of the new community, the sacred moment of the new consensus. . . . 'The discourse of the Revolution about itself' revealed an effort to form a new Nation on the basis of a new consensus. The language of ritual and ritualised language served the function of national integration. It expressed the need for social solidarity.[10]

There was no room in this vocabulary for 'words associated with the Old Regime, names tainted with royalism, aristocracy or privilege.' [11] By the autumn of 1789, she records, *'Etes-vous de la Nation?* had become the watchword of National Guard patrols.' [12]

However, if the task of overthrowing the *Ancien Régime* had forged a sentimental unity in which ethical issues temporarily submerged the deeper antagonisms within the Third Estate, the problems of constructing a new order were to prove more divisive. The nation which had been called into being was too heterogeneous to remain united in the process of consolidation which followed. The distinction drawn between 'active' and 'passive' citizens in the form of a property franchise,[13] peasant hostility to those seigneurial dues that still remained, measures like the abolition of the guilds and later of workers' coalitions, began to demarcate the 'bourgeois' from the 'popular' revolution. These antagonisms were inevitably aggravated by the continuing economic and financial crisis and the growing sense among the subordinate layers of society that the Revolution had not fulfilled its promise to transform their conditions of existence. At the same time the attempt to secularise the state through the Civil Constitution of the Clergy was a major factor in providing the counter-revolution with an embryonic popular base.[14]

In many respects, nonetheless, the multiple conflicts which radicalised the movement from 1791 to 1794 were caused as much by the struggle to defend what had already been achieved as by differences over long-term objectives. With the emigrated nobility massing foreign armies on the frontiers and counter-revolution fermenting in the provinces, the threat of civil and external war made continuing popular mobilisation essential. The price of this was, however, more than many of the moderate leaders of 1789 were willing to pay, and the Revolution passed into more adventurous hands. In the process the concept of 'nation' itself was gradually redefined. The idealised image of a unified Third Estate rallying behind its organic elite was replaced by the more combative, democratic symbolism of tried and trusted patriots struggling to defend the 'general will' against the combined efforts of 'traitors' and *emigrés* and the whole reactionary weight of *Ancien Régime* Europe.

The behaviour of the King was decisive in this respect. Despite his attempts to resist change from the outset, the belief that Louis XVI could be detached from the privileged orders and transformed into a genuine representative of the nation died hard, not least among the popular classes. His dealings with *emigrés* and foreign monarchs, his attempted flight to the frontier in June 1791, his continued use of the royal veto against revolutionary legislation finally forced the issue of deposition and the establishment of a Republic. With the election of the Convention in September 1792 and the referendum on the Constitution of 1793, the Revolution sought the democratic legitimacy it now needed as the drift toward war and civil war gathered pace. This new climate of political idealism and economic hardship in turn mobilised the more radical sections of the *sans-culotte* movement, whose increasingly egalitarian demands forced the Republican government to envisage laws against food hoarders, fixed prices for grain, public works, and an intensification of the revolutionary purge. In the process the relationship between the Jacobin leadership and the popular movement was stretched to the limit and the boundaries of the 'bourgeois' Revolution were finally reached. The Great Terror was conducted not only against 'counter-revolutionaries' but also against 'undisciplined' radicals, and though it justified itself in terms of the revolutionary ideal of the 'general will', it must also be seen as an attempt at stabilisation. The politics of terror served, however, both to alienate the moderates in the Convention and to 'demobilise' the popular movement, and paved the way for the bourgeois *reprise en main* in July 1794.

In the course of this radical phase of the Revolution, the principle of 'national sovereignty' was finally equated with 'popular sovereignty'. The inherent democratic logic of the Third Estate's appeal to the nation in 1789 had worked itself through. The *cahiers de doléances* had placed their trust in the generosity of the 'great'; the Constitution of 1791 still invited 'passive citizens' to have faith in the representative character of a parliamentary elite; the *sans-culottes* of 1793 reached beyond the forms of liberal democracy in their demands for popular government and the direct accountability of 'their' deputies.

In this process the class divisions and power relations of emerging capitalism had set firm limits to what could be achieved, but nonetheless the powerful political concept of nationhood had been launched. After centuries in which authority was invested with supernatural legitimacy inciting passive and fatalist obedience, the nation state would turn subjects into citizens and raised the prospect of 'government by the people'. For nearly a hundred years thereafter the French left drew its ideological sustenance from the image of the oppressed 'nation', the repository of democratic ideals, held in check by a ruling class whose allegiance to Catholicism, *Ancien Régime* Europe or to international capital made them enemies of the national interest. The 'nation' thus invoked could be the sentimental *pays réel*[15] of February 1848, as socially disparate as the Third Estate had been, or the combative vanguard of the Paris Commune. In either case the *patrie* was the free and equal nation summoned up by the French Revolution and subsequently thwarted in its democratic mission by selfish class interests and ideological manipulation.

THE FRENCH REVOLUTION AND 'NATIONALISM'

It was this potent association of nationhood with democracy which was to make 'nationalism' the key agency in the collapse of the *Ancien Régime* in the rest of continental Europe over the ensuing century. The message of liberty and equality proclaimed by the Revolution, and the example it offered of popular struggle against tyranny, had profound international reverberations, both for those who were inspired by it and for those who feared the danger of contagion. With the onset of war, the Revolution became more than just a distant event known by reputation alone, for its ideas were borne across Europe in the wake of France's victorious armies. The universalist claims of the Rights of Man were translated in 1793 into the concrete objective of bringing 'fraternity and assistance' to oppressed peoples, and the abolition of feudalism and seigneurialism in conquered Belgium announced the Republic's intention of dismantling the entire Old Regime of Europe.

This message was, of course, substantially diluted as the revolutionary armies of 1793 were gradually transformed by domestic events into the Imperial Army of Napoleon. Though the democratic *élan* was lost however, the social and political structures of the Bonapartist state still bore the hallmarks of bourgeois revolution, and the whole period of territorial conquest and political disruption substantially weakened the Old Order that was restored in the settlement of 1814–15. The most significant legacy of these twenty years of war was, however, that it had awakened a deeply subversive sense of nationhood which was to redraw the map of Europe over the next hundred years.

If France became a nation through an attempt to democratise its institutions *within existing national frontiers,* in the rest of Europe the problem was posed in different terms. The awakening desire to impose legal and constitutional constraints on political authority could find no clear focus in vast territorial empires on the one hand and petty principalities and statelets on the other. The sense of collective identity necessary for the challenge to autocracy thus cut across the territorial structures of the Old Order, feeding on a sense of linguistic, ethnic or historical community and thus paving the way for German and Italian unification and for the dismemberment of the Tsarist and Habsburg empires. The principle of national sovereignty bequeathed by the French Revolution was, in this new context, inevitably overlaid with a strong cultural emphasis. Though clearly inspired by the democratic goal of self-government, the territorial demarcation of new nation states on a constitutional basis required first the development of a national consciousness which would transcend feudal particularism and challenge the old structures of imperial authority.[16]

The class bases of this nation-building process were even less clear-cut than they had been in France, for much of the rest of continental Europe capitalist economic relations were far less advanced. The middle strata in society had not yet developed the characteristics of a genuine bourgeois class centred on commercial and industrial interests, and the further east we go the more dubious becomes the proposition that the formation of nation states was related above all to the capitalist quest for wider markets. Even if such interests had been powerful enough to dictate the course of events, why should they have espoused nationalism when, as in Austria and Russia, large multi-national empires offered even wider commercial opportunities? Nationalism, here as in France, must be seen rather as the political solution to the growing contradictions of the Old Regime, mobilising the socially diverse victims of feudalism, petty autocracy or imperial domination in a struggle to create new institutions that would be more responsive to their various, and often contradictory interests.

Thus while the French Revolution and its aftermath had played a major role in awakening European nationalisms, these various movements did not reproduce the specific class alliances of the French example. In 1848 the German middle classes were unwilling to risk revolutionary mass mobilisation and, by the time Bismarck and his Junker army brought about German reunification from above, German capitalist interests had abandoned the ideal of the national state in favour of a customs union. The Italian bourgeoisie only fell in behind the national movement after Garibaldi's successes, while in the economically backward Austrian and Russian empires nationalism was largely the province of middle-class intellectuals and functionaries, of an impoverished local gentry and aristocracy, of threatened artisans and traders, with the peasantry providing the main popular base.

These examples confirm even more conclusively than the French case how misleading it is to equate the formation of nation states with the economic interests of an indigenous national 'bourgeoisie'. By the time that French capitalism was strong enough to leave its mark on the political institutions of the Louis Philippe regime, fully forty years after the Revolution, in most areas of Eastern Europe the 'national' capitalist class was so embryonic and dependent that it was quite unable, and often unwilling, to play a significant role in the separatist movements. The key role of the middle classes in the nation-building process was more often played by lawyers, officials and journalists than by commercial and industrial entrepreneurs, and these former elements were generally not equipped to impose class-conscious leadership on the nationalist movements. Nationalism thus emerged in a phase when the *Ancien Régime* in Europe was sufficiently eroded to be overthrown, but when the bourgeoisie was insufficiently developed to impose its hegemony on the *volonté générale*. Hence the powerful democratic impulse which lay at the heart of the national deal.

Nationalism was 'bourgeois' only in so far as it could not transcend its historical limitations. Once the deadwood of the Old Order had been cleared away, the new nation state did indeed provide an ideal framework for bourgeois class consolidation and eventual hegemony, not primarily in terms of markets, but above all as an arena within which it could come to control the political process, legitimate its rule and reshape a national culture in line with its own values. When the early Marxists began to address the 'national question' at the end of the nineteenth century, this pattern was already well advanced in certain established nation states, including France. The revolutionary concept of 'national sovereignty' which had brought them into being was now being reworked into a ruling-class ideology of conservative 'integral nationalism' and imperialist chauvinism. Many Marxists thus committed the error of equating this repressive integrative ideology within established states with the struggles of nationalist movements still fighting for independent statehood in the Central and East European empires.[17] To do so was to confuse two entirely different phases of historical class development, and to bequeath to later socialists the orthodox view that 'nationalism' in all its guises was essentially a bourgeois ideological mystification.

It is hoped that the historical approach of this book will allow us to avoid this confusion. However, as a preamble to what follows it is necessary to make some brief methodological distinctions. First, and this is the central point, it would be wrong to assume that the 'national question' as we have defined it had been resolved in France thanks to the Revolution. It was not until 1870, with the coming of the Third Republic, that the principles of democratic legitimacy became a solid institutional reality, albeit in the 'formalist' bourgeois sense. Until then, the French democratic movement found it natural to invoke the oppressed 'nation' against the country's social and political elites. It was only when the *political* lines of division came to correspond more closely to the class antagonisms of maturing capitalism that this consensual vision of the nation became more difficult for the left to sustain.

Second, the Revolution's work was also incomplete in another way. Despite its wide popular impact, large sections of the population, especially in the more remote rural areas, remained deeply parochial and traditionalist in their attitudes and did not begin to think of themselves as members of a national community until the end of the nineteenth and the early years of the twentieth century.[18] This aspect of the nation-building process, whose mechanisms were economic as much as political, has important implications for the evolution of the national idea in that particular period.

Finally, it is nonetheless important to recognise that the Revolution did indeed mark a watershed in the development of popular political consciousness. Thereafter it was increasingly difficult for any regime in France to rely on the deadweight of moral passivity, social deference and political ignorance. Legitimacy came to depend more and more on at least some token of popular consent, and less and less on notions of tradition, custom and the divine origins of human authority.[19] In this context the rhetoric of 'nation' became an option for conservatives as well as for democrats, but as long as Catholicism and royalism remained effective agencies of order the right was loth to flirt with a concept which had such deep-seated democratic associations. When, however, at the end of the nineteenth century, doctrines of so-called 'integral nationalism' did indeed begin to mark the ideology of conservatism, they built on a pre-existing body of ideas with which we have yet to deal. This was the curious hybrid of 'Bonapartism', whose origins lie of course in the Napoleonic era that brought to an end the decade of revolution.

3

STATE AND NATION
UNDER NAPOLEON

Sovereignty resides in the French people, in this sense; that everything, absolutely everything, should be done to ensure its well-being and its glory.

(Napoleon Bonaparte)

THE REPUBLIC OF THE DIRECTORY

If the 'heroic' period of the Revolution from 1789 to 1794 launched the ideal and the rhetoric of democratic nationhood, the years from the fall of Robespierre to Bonaparte's 'coup' in 1799 were characterised by political stalemate and disillusionment. The Great Terror itself had demobilised the *sans-culotte* sections, and with the fall of the Jacobin regime in July 1794 the new *Thermidorean* leadership of moderate Republicans moved quickly to crush the popular movement and to repeal the more radical measures introduced under Robespierre. In the words of Denis Woronoff, '4 Prairial Year III is one of the crucial dates of the revolutionary period. The people had ceased to be a political force, participants in history. They were now no more than victims or spectators.' [1]

The repression and purge of Jacobin leaders swiftly followed, and when the new constitution was proclaimed in September 1795 it reintroduced the distinction between 'active' and 'passive' citizens through a property franchise, and restored the system of indirect elections. Although this admitted more people to the vote than under the 1791 constitution, the electoral colleges were actually more restrictive in character, and open only to the richest sections of the bourgeoisie. [2] The principle of universal suffrage proclaimed in the 1793 constitution was thus rejected in favour of a return to the principles of 1791, and a bicameral legislature was set up alongside an executive of five 'Directors'. The constitution was preceded by a Declaration of Rights and Duties which made it clear that the democratic and egalitarian aspirations of the 1793 constitution (the 'Code of Anarchy' as its critics called it) were now to be replaced by the principles of property and liberty. With the advent of the 'Directory' the *juste milieu* of bourgeois opinion reasserted itself, chastened by the radical excesses of earlier years.

The new regime proved incapable, however, of establishing any popular legitimacy. The diluted republican principles on which it rested were unlikely to arouse intense enthusiasm, indeed they were designed to appeal to those who craved peace and stability. This ambition might conceivably have been realised had the regime allowed some form of organised politics to flourish, but instead the leaders of the Directory not only failed to organise their own supporters but, in Lyn Hunt's words, 'refused to allow the formation of any organised opposition and purged the legislature whenever the left or the right seemed to win the elections.' [3] At the same time they were unwilling to break with their liberal principles to the extent of winding up elections altogether or establishing an openly authoritarian state. The image of the Directory was soon that of an unprincipled, negative, opportunist regime in which the narrow political class of the *pays légal* was cut off from the *pays réel*.

This is not to deny, of course, that the regime faced formidable problems both at home and abroad. The Jacobins succeeded in re-establishing their strength after the defeat of Thermidor, and at the same time the counter-revolutionary movement gathered pace and made the royalists an even greater threat. The genesis of mass politics between 1789 and 1794 had left a legacy of ideological intensity, bitter rivalries, myriad local grievances, a host of scores to settle, and in such circumstances it was not easy to hold the middle ground, let alone to recover the lost unanimity of the early days of the Revolution. A weak government and an unstable legislature faced a succession of attempted 'coups', royalist uprisings in the provinces, continued agitation over issues like inflation, conscription and the status of the Church, and yet, paradoxically it might seem, elections were characterised by chronic levels of abstention. This reflected the growing disillusionment of the primary electors at the unrepresentative nature of the electoral colleges and the purges conducted against opposition deputies. Widespread discontent thus had few channels of political expression, and as disaffection increased so the centrifugal tendencies in directorial society gathered pace. The 'common vision' which had once united the revolutionary movement had been lost.

In this context it is not surprising that the rhetoric of 'nation' which had unleashed such potent aspirations now had a somewhat hollow ring to it. A concept which was first derived from the unity of the Third Estate, and which then became the watchword of the democratic republicans and the popular movement, carried little conviction in a chronically divided regime which had set out to marginalise the Jacobins and effectively to exclude the people from the political process. The words nation and *patrie* had of course by now become part of the 'ritualised language' of the Revolution, and the Directory saw the whole symbolic paraphernalia of republican speech, costume and calendar, and the celebration of revolutionary *journées* and military victories, as a vital means of binding people to the Republic. Such rites had now lost their popular spontaneity, however, and had become what might anachronistically be called part of the 'ideological apparatus' of the regime. Discussing the role of festivals under the Directory, Woronoff concludes: 'This ritual, which quickly became ossified and almost incomprehensible, transformed the festival into a mere spectacle whose success varied but from which, however, all popular participation was excluded.' [4]

The latter point returns us to the question of 'class' in relation to nation. It has become commonplace to regard the period of the Thermidorean regime and the Directory as the reassertion of moderate bourgeois leadership over the revolutionary process, as a return to the principles of 1789–91. However, the relationship between the wealthy and educated middle classes and the rest of the former 'Third Estate' had been transformed in the meantime. In the early days of the Revolution the liberal bourgeoisie had appeared to be the 'organic elite' of the people, the spokesman of the nation. Now it had acquired, through bitter experience, a deeper sense of its own class interest and identity, and the bond of trust which had once made it the natural focus of popular aspirations had been decisively broken. The lower orders of society were now prey to growing apathy and disillusionment, some increasingly tempted by the counter-revolution's exploitation of the religious issue, some retaining their faith in the millennarian aspirations of the democratic Republic, but few able to see the Directory as the incarnation of any of the great principles that had divided the country since 1789. The concept of nation had lost its mobilising power in a community that was politically exhausted and socially divided.

In the light of this it might seem paradoxical that the main field in which the regime enjoyed some success was in the prosecution of the war. It is, of course, true that the energy and resources expended in military enterprise did nothing to alleviate domestic problems, and that the growing autonomy granted by a weak regime to some of its leading generals in the field contributed to its eventual downfall. More significant for our theme, however, is a subtle change in the nature of the national mission which continued to inspire France's victorious passage across Europe. The theme of bringing 'fraternity and assistance' to the oppressed peoples of Europe in a war against tyranny everywhere inevitably carried less conviction under the opportunist bourgeois Directory than it did in the heady days of 1793. Symptomatically, French intervention in Switzerland in support of the 'patriots' and a liberal constitution in early 1798 also involved the annexation of the territories of Mulhouse and Geneva for strategic and economic reasons. As Woronoff has put it, 'the young [Swiss] Republic was from the outset the victim of a policy in which "missionary" intentions combined with imperialist designs.' [5] The pattern of looting, requisitioning and extortion that came to characterise the French occupation of 'liberated' territories inevitably alienated the local population and led to the embarrassing incidence of popular uprisings against the liberator. The imposition of conscription in Belgium by General Jourdan in 1798 sparked off a major peasant revolt, but this could easily be represented as the work of the counter-revolution and Catholic reaction. More ironic was the uprising of Italian patriots in Turin in February 1799, calling for the liberation and unification of Italy, which turned the imported Jacobin doctrines of national sovereignty and self-determination against all occupiers, including the French.

This is not to say, of course, that these aberrations only occurred under the Directory, for it would be naïve to assume that the previous 'Jacobin' regime had had full control of its military personnel. Furthermore, the doctrine of 'fraternity and assistance' proclaimed by the radical republicans, however noble its intentions, may itself be seen as a kind of veiled imperialism with its image of France as the liberator and educator of less enlightened peoples. However, if the armies of 1793 were driven, partially at least, by political zeal and a sense of mission, those of the Directory undoubtedly owed less allegiance to the civil regime, which had after all deliberately set out to moderate such passions. It would seem likely that loyalty to military commanders and the prospect of plunder may have somewhat displaced political fervour in the motivation of the troops. As for the regime itself, it would appear that the quest for military glory and economic advantage through an imperialist policy of expansion had begun to take shape well before Bonaparte's seizure of power.

BONAPARTISM: PROBLEMS OF DEFINITION

If the rhetoric of 'nation' found few echoes in the divided and disillusioned society of the Directory, the regime established by Napoleon Bonaparte after his successful coup of 9 November 1799 was to make this vocabulary the key agency of political mobilisation. Indeed, of all the ideological traditions that have emerged in France over the last two hundred years, none has been so consistently identified with an appeal to national identity as the phenomenon of Bonapartism. It is certainly true that systematic use was made, both under the Napoleonic regime and under the second Bonapartist Empire some fifty years later, of a whole range of ideas that are commonly associated with so-called 'nationalism' and, as we indicated in our introductory chapter, we do not intend to engage in a semantic debate as to when and whether that term is appropriate. It is our intention, however, to argue that the invocation of nationhood by Bonapartism differs in almost every respect from the ideology that fired the early revolutionary movement. In its definition of the nation it substituted state for people, bureaucracy for democracy, passive obedience for active citizenship. The principles of self-determination and the 'equality of nations' were perverted by imperialist designs, and the whole emancipatory ideal implied by the equation between nation and people vanished behind the imperatives of order and discipline.

To recognise the vital distinctions between these two doctrines is not, of course, to suggest that there are no historical or ideological links between them. As we shall see, Bonapartism sought to reconcile some of the principles of the Revolution with more traditional values, and the new concept of nationhood was given pride of place in this attempted synthesis. Inevitably then, there are superficial parallels in the imagery of nation developed by democratic republicanism on the one hand, and Bonapartism on the other. Neither is it surprising, given the political immaturity of the community at this stage, if many indeed saw Bonaparte's nationalism as an extension of earlier republican ideals rather than as a decisive break with them.

The history of ideas is not, however, a simple linear evolutionary process, for it is subject to metamorphosis and distortion. To take a later example, fascism would have been unthinkable without the prior existence of socialism, and indeed it borrowed some of the latter's precepts in order to pervert them, but this does not establish a direct relationship between the two. Similarly Bonapartism was a creature of the age of democracy, whose values it proceeded to deform for its own authoritarian purposes, but it remains historically and politically distinct. Tenuous ideological affinities are of little account once attention is turned from the abstract discussion of ideas to the world of historical realities. Then it becomes hard indeed not to recognise the obvious distinction between the revolutionary nation that sought to mobilise popular democratic aspirations against the established social elites, and a regime which sought to reconcile all classes and to liquidate conflict by equating the nation with the will of a plebiscitary dictator.

The special character of Bonapartism can only be appreciated by examining the historical context in which the regime was first established. Class and class conflict is an essential dimension in this, and Marxists have generally seen Bonapartism as the product of a situation of class deadlock, where in order to preserve their social and economic hegemony the bourgeoisie are willing to surrender their direct political leadership to an 'exceptional state' of a populist authoritarian type.[6] This analysis, which builds on the work of Marx himself in relation to the regime of Louis Bonaparte some fifty years later,[7] is for that reason of questionable value as regards 1799, irrespective of its merits in the later case. It would be hard to substantiate the proposition that Bonapartism follows a state of 'equilibrium' between bourgeoisie and working class, which is the drift of Marx's argument in 1851, for a number of reasons. Capitalist development had not yet produced anything resembling a genuine working class at the end of the eighteenth century, and even if we regard the *sans-culottes* as the precursors of such a class, we have already indicated that the regime of the Directory had effectively expelled the people from the political process and undermined their capacity for mass action. The riots of May 1795 were the last great popular *journées* of the revolutionary period.

It is true of course that the radical middle-class Jacobins still enjoyed some popular support both in the towns and in the countryside, but it is generally recognised that a far greater threat to the survival of the Directorial regime came from the royalists and the counter-revolution.[8] This suggests an alternative interpretation of the nature of the class deadlock, namely that it was one which opposed the bourgeois revolution to the former privileged estates of Church and nobility. However, in classical Marxism a situation of equilibrium between bourgeoisie and landed aristocracy produces a very different kind of 'exceptional state', namely the absolutist monarchy! While this proposition is of considerable interest because, as we shall see later, it encourages speculation on the links between royal absolutism and Bonapartism, it is becoming clear that Marxist typologies of the state are insufficiently flexible to deal with the social and political complexities of this particular period.

The Marxist approach to the study of the revolutionary period in France is not so much 'wrong' (for it contributes much to our understanding of the broader historical context of change) as insufficiently precise to throw light on the complex details of the process. The realm of politics must be accorded its proper autonomy, and once this is done the nature of the underlying class dynamics itself becomes clearer. The Directory did indeed collapse under the weight of its own contradictions. In the words of one historian, it was 'a liberal system which could survive only by violating its own legality.' [9] This was a measure of its real and imagined fragility. The threat of the counter-revolution was concrete enough, as witnessed by the continuing war and civil war, the climate of conspiracy and a series of attempted royalist coups. The parallel fear of Jacobin insurrection had less substance, but this 'anarchist obsession' of the new property owners is no less significant. It reflects the fact that the so-called bourgeoisie, although it had achieved a greater sense of class identity in the fires of revolution, was nonetheless not yet able to impose its leadership on the nation.

The class stalemate was thus infinitely more complex than traditional Marxism has recognised. It involved a still heterogeneous bourgeoisie that remained divided as to the kind of regime it wanted, a declining aristocracy that still wielded considerable ideological influence, especially among the peasantry, thanks to the religious issue, and an urban populace which despite its increased political consciousness was not yet an independent force in the political arena. In a society where modern class divisions were still immature, political cleavages inevitably cut across social divides. For this reason, the nature of the impasse that the revolutionary process had reached in 1799 only becomes intelligible at the political level.

THE BONAPARTIST STATE

In the words of H.A.L. Fisher in his classic lectures on Bonapartism, 'Bonaparte came, as he said, "to close the Romance of the Revolution", to heal the wounds, to correct the extravagances, to secure the conquests.' [10] The regime he established reflected an extraordinary 'fusion of opposites' [11] in which the rival concepts and interests thrown up by the factional politics of the preceding decade were integrated into a new synthesis.

Power did not simply fall into Napoleon's hands in November 1799; indeed the coup was very nearly bungled, and though many politicians and the least politicised sections of public opinion were resigned to the need for a *dictature de salut public,* the future of the regime remained uncertain. Legitimacy was won in part by the early success in establishing political stability and order, and in restoring peace both at home and abroad. However, Napoleon recognised that in the long term his regime required a more absolute and permanent legitimacy, a degree of moral authority. The quest for this was central to the institutional development of the regime and to its policies. Ironically, given Napoleon's well-known contempt for the *idéologues,* the task of assuaging passions and reconciling rival doctrines was profoundly ideological.

The hybrid character of Bonapartist ideology is aptly illustrated by the fact that the regime invoked all three of the forms of legitimacy defined by the sociologist Max Weber.[12] That Napoleon's authority rested partially on charismatic qualities is axiomatic, but his assumption of the title Emperor in 1804 and his efforts to found a dynasty correspond more closely to what Weber saw as traditional bases of legitimacy. Finally, the (largely empty) concessions made to the principles of popular sovereignty and parliamentarism, the major reforms of the administrative system, the codification of law, all confirm that Napoleon was equally intent on establishing what Weber called legal-rational legitimacy.

These observations, however, offer only a limited perspective on the Bonapartist synthesis, which can be more fully appreciated if we consider the various political traditions he was seeking to reconcile. These may of course be presented in terms of a simple dichotomy: 'the opposition of *Ancien Régime* and Revolution, of absolutism and Jacobinism, of Divine right and popular sovereignty, of the use of force and the rule of law, of Napoleon's temperament and his experience as a revolutionary.' [13] As we have seen, however, the political realities of the revolutionary period were more complex than that, and the social and political antagonisms it provoked cannot be reduced to a simple polarity of positions as suggested in the quotation above. At least three distinct sources of inspiration can be discerned in Bonapartism.

First of all there is the theme of popular sovereignty and social egalitarianism, new radical concepts given concrete form by the participation and politicisation of the lower orders in the revolutionary process. Henceforth no regime could afford to take popular acquiescence for granted – consent had to be actively sought. As one author has put it, 'a new element – the sovereignty of the people – radically changed the nature of the political equation.' [14] Napoleon was quick to recognise the importance of the trappings of popular consent, which were institutionalised in the form of the plebiscite. Though this classic device of personal power was devoid of democratic content in a regime which stifled civil liberties and political debate, the illusion of direct democracy was sustained by the inspirational qualities of Napoleon's leadership, his undoubted successes and his self-identification as the incarnation of the general will. His mistrust of bourgeois parliamentary assemblies, his egalitarian distaste for the privileges of birth and station, his appeal to a missionary idealism which still survived in the ranks of the army, all of these were capable of striking a chord with even the most radical and politicised elements of the popular classes, who had lacked leadership and inspiration since the days of the Terror.

Second, we must turn to the image of Napoleon as the man who completed and consolidated the work of the bourgeois revolution. Here, undoubtedly, we are dealing more with solid achievement and less with the symbolic realm. The decisive reforms of 1789 – equality before the law, the abolition of feudalism, suppression of venal and hereditary offices, freedom of enterprise – were safeguarded. The three great legal codes enshrined the principles of private property and family authority, and the administrative structures of modern France were conclusively established. The embryonic public education system reflected both the social elitism and the meritocratic individualism of bourgeois ideology, and the introduction of the notorious *livret*[15] for workers reinforced the capitalist bias in labour relations which had already been established by the ban on workers' unions in 1791.

This legacy of consolidation and modernisation, which laid the foundations for the emergence of a fully-fledged bourgeois state later in the nineteenth century, nonetheless had its price. This was the sacrifice of the civil liberties and representative principles which the liberal middle-classes had considered central to their enterprise in 1789, and to which the bourgeoisie of the Directory had continued to pay lip service. As we have reported, the latter regime felt obliged periodically to abandon these principles and to violate its own constitution in order to protect a weak executive against factious assemblies. Napoleon showed no such ambivalence. If the Directory had resisted 'organised politics', Bonaparte simply repressed 'all political activity worthy of the name'[16] through rigorous censorship, a ban on meetings and associations, sweeping police powers and the imprisonment of political offenders. If the Directory had rigged elections and purged the legislature, Napoleon ensured that the token assemblies he established were so unrepresentative and impotent that the all-powerful executive would never need recourse to 'illegal' measures. The senate, chosen by the head of state, had its role limited to safeguarding the principles of the constitution and to nominating the members of the two other assemblies from lists of candidates filtered through a complex system of indirect elections. The Legislative Assembly could vote but not debate, the Tribunate could debate and not vote, but even the latter's rhetorical flourishes were used to justify its eventual abolition. In the words of Fisher, 'at the close of the Empire every source of friction had been carefully eliminated from the working of the central machine.' [17]

This image of a politically and administratively centralised state inevitably invites the analogy of the absolutist monarchy which had been dismantled in 1789, and this brings us to the third wellspring of Bonapartism, namely the counter-revolution. This area is fraught with contradictions, for there is no doubting Bonaparte's hostility both to the Bourbons and to the former privileged orders. However, as one author has put it, 'both his instinct and his education drove him towards monarchy. In 1806, the word "subject" replaced that of "citizen".' [18] By this time, of course, Napoleon had been proclaimed Emperor and his dynastic ambitions were soon to become apparent. In the wake of his military conquests, he placed his brothers and sisters on thrones and showered principalities and dukedoms on his favourites. New honours and decorations were established, and eventually an 'imperial' nobility. The laws against the *emigrés* were gradually relaxed and then lifted altogether, and increasing religious toleration culminated in the *Concordat* with the papacy in 1802. While the ecclesiastical property confiscated by the Revolution was not to be restored, and the state retained the right to appoint bishops, Catholicism was given protection as the religion of the majority of Frenchmen.

There was in all this, no doubt, a measure of pragmatism and even personal vanity. It was natural enough, however, for a dictator embarking on a career at the end of the eighteenth century, to see the hereditary principle and the power of organised religion as essential ingredients of political order and stability. The novelty of Bonapartism was that these traditional themes were wedded to myths of direct democracy and popular sovereignty on the one hand, and to the modernising ethos of bourgeois individualism on the other.

BONAPARTISM AND THE NATION

An ideology which drew on such contradictory sources required a central integrating force, and this was supplied by the appeal to nationhood. The former consensus, whose disintegration in the years 1794-9 had deprived the word nation of its powerful symbolic appeal, was now reimposed from above. A felicitous phrase – 'la nation organisée' [19] – conveys the forced nature of this rebirth of the national ideal. Its essence was 'order', the elimination of factional rivalries, the stifling of debate, 'making life safe and easy for the ordinary householder who was content to let the great world of politics go its own way.' [20] If the call to nation in 1789 had turned subjects into active citizens seeking their own emancipation, ten years later loyalty to the nation implied obedience to the state, respect for the Church, pride in the army, commitment to the leader.

Napoleon was able to effect this dramatic reversal thanks in part to the climate of resignation and the sense of impasse which had let him into power. This allowed him the leeway to neutralise and then conciliate the royalist and Jacobin factions, to reduce parliamentary assemblies to impotence, to centralise and strengthen the state apparatus. However, a community which had undergone the intense political experience of the previous ten years could not be seduced simply by Bonaparte's judicious manipulation of political elites. The age of ideology had dawned and, as we have already indicated, Bonapartism had a decidedly original contribution to make in this respect.

The essence of the Bonapartist view of the nation was its deep antipathy for factional rivalries, for internal debate and dissent. This inevitably reassured those who were exhausted by a decade of fear and insecurity, especially property owners and peasants. At the same time, notions of order and discipline appealed to the supporters of the counter-revolution, and many royalists nursed the hope that Bonaparte's coup was the prelude to the restoration of the monarchy. Finally, however, Napoleon's impatience with factious assemblies and the political class of the Republic struck a chord with the remnants of popular radicalism, the partisans of direct democracy embittered by the 'betrayals' of their parliamentary leaders.

The suppression of political activity left a vacuum, however, and the new 'nation' needed to be given a more positive sense of its own identity. Before examining how this identity was constructed ideologically, it is vital to take account of one salient historical fact, namely that France was a state, a territorial entity, a great continental power *before* it was ever a nation in the modern sense. Now, we have already seen that the principle of self-government and active citizenship which lies at the heart of nationhood was one aspect of the revolutionary heritage Bonaparte found it impossible to accept. It was inevitable, then, that in his search for the bases of national unity he would look back beyond the Revolution to the institutions and values which had provided stability in earlier times.

The rehabilitation of the Church and the recognition of the continuing moral force of religion as an agent of order was crucial to this. Napoleon was not a religious man, but he clearly appreciated the ideological power of faith. Indeed, he regarded it as a key agency in the development of a collective national identity. While for republicans the nation was the product of active popular intervention in history, for Napoleon it was rooted in timeless tradition and the patient submission of the subject: 'Religion is a part of destiny. With the soil, laws, manners, it forms that sacred whole which is called *La Patrie,* and which one must never desert. The principal charm of a religion consists in its memories.' [21] The ten-year revolutionary assault on the Church had not broken the hold of Catholicism over the majority of the community, and indeed the religious question was the main catalyst of the counter-revolution. In appropriating religion to the service of the state, Bonaparte was able to win the approval not only of reactionaries but also of the many erstwhile supporters of the Revolution who had been driven into sullen silence or outright hostility by the excesses of republican anti-clericalism.

Even more important was the equation effected by Bonapartism between nation and state, and here the pre-revolutionary legacy is equally apparent. The absolutist monarchy had long been intent on welding the community into a coherent unit of government through its centralisation and refinement of the administrative machine, and many of the abortive reform proposals of its final years looked in the direction that Napoleon was later to take. Indeed, the latter's achievements in this sphere built as much on the work of the absolutist monarchy as on that of the Revolution. The long tradition of a strong centralised state, sustained by the myth that the sovereign was the neutral guarantor and arbiter of corporate rights and privileges, had inevitably left its mark on French political culture, and Bonaparte was both a product and a beneficiary of such attitudes.

However, the Revolution had radically changed the foundations of state legitimacy, and authority had to be justified in new terms. The new political nation was not willing to accept a purely abstract equation between state and national interest – the relationship had to be more visible and concrete. The head of state himself, of course, was crucial in this respect, for both his charismatic qualities and the institution of the plebiscite allowed him to identify himself with the general will. Other features were equally important, however. The recruitment of public officials and military commanders was influenced by the meritocratic principles of *la carrière ouverte aux talents,* and this lowering of the social barriers to public employment made the state appear more representative, thereby compensating for the total absence of free political debate. The willingness of Napoleon to accept the co-operation of all those who would rally to his cause, placed former royalists and regicides, Girondins, Jacobins and Thermidoreans side by side in the institutions of government, creating the illusion of a politically neutral state machine dedicated to serving the national interest. Secondary and higher education too was stripped of factious content, with mathematics, medicine and the physical sciences given pride of place over the dangerous disciplines like history, and the political and moral sciences. Denied its right to independent political existence, the nation was invited to recognise its own featureless image in the mirror of the state.

Finally, it would clearly be impossible to comprehend the Bonapartist view of the nation without reference to its military dimension. France was in a state of war for much of the Napoleonic period, and this inevitably had considerable repercussions for civil society. The quest for military glory was essential to the 'heroic' character of Bonaparte's leadership and was a key agency of internal unity. Military affairs dominated the work of government and military discipline conditioned the conduct of public administration. Furthermore, the voracious appetite of the military machine for men and materials made active popular participation (anathema to Bonaparte in every other realm but this), an absolute necessity.

The identification of the nation with the foreign policy of the state and the prestige of its armies is yet another area where Bonaparte was building on a long tradition. Well before the Revolution France was a major continental power with worldwide influence and a glorious military past. Its strategic interests were well-defined and no doubt many of its inhabitants identified sufficiently with their 'homeland' to feel a sense of pride in its achievements. Napoleon too was able to draw on this simple apolitical native patriotism, and there was undoubtedly a heavy dose of classical *Realpolitik* in all his military and diplomatic moves. Some have seen the spectacular conquests that built the Napoleonic empire as aimed above all at the construction of a continental coalition against maritime England. Others see it as a policy of territorial aggrandisement inspired by a desire to emulate Alexander or Charlemagne, or by the vanity of dynastic ambition. Many, however, attribute a political mission to Bonaparte's conquests, and see them as an, albeit ambivalent, culmination of the missionary zeal of the young Republic. The political dimension seems undeniable, given the changes that he wrought in the occupied territories, but its precise character is predictably complex. Indeed, Napoleon's legacy in Europe reflects the contradictions of his domestic regime.

In many respects, the soldiers of the Grand Army could still feel they were the liberators of the oppressed from tyranny. The essential principles of 1789 – abolition of feudalism, civil equality, freedom of enterprise, religious toleration – were proclaimed in the conquered territories, along with the central provisions of the Napoleonic codes (trial by jury, equal inheritance, legalised divorce). At the same time major administrative reforms based on rationalism and meritocracy spread the enlightenment message and broke down social barriers. Set against the creaking despotism of the continental empires, Frenchmen inevitably saw themselves as the agents of progress.

There was, of course, a darker side. The regimes of the Napoleonic empire had a parasitic quality, and their institutional arrangements were tailored to the needs of the occupier. Their constitutions created powerless legislatures and nominated executives, which were insulated from popular opinion by the absence of free elections and the suppression of political liberties. If Napoleon regarded the French as incapable of exercising political rights wisely, he was even less likely to offer such privileges to the other peoples of Europe.

This of course raises serious doubts about the nature of Bonaparte's undoubted contribution to the development of nationalism in Europe. As we have seen, he was not disposed to be sympathetic to the idea of self-determination, which is the very essence of the aspiration to national sovereignty. It was strategic considerations rather than sympathy with the principle of nationality which largely inspired the various settlements which cut Germany off from Austria, united Italy under a single administration and set Poland against Russia. That the Napoleonic interlude, with its modernising thrust, undermined the hold of the Ancien Régime empires cannot be denied, but Bonaparte no longer carried the democratic message of 1793 with its call for the equality of nations and the right to self-government. Indeed, in many areas, particularly in Germany, the reaction *against* the alien influence, spoliation and repression of the French occupation was itself a major factor in promoting a sense of nationhood.

CONCLUSION

The Bonapartist conception of the nation exchanged the active citizen for the passive subject. Nation was no longer the assertion of democracy from below, it was an organising principle imposed from above, repressive, integrative, stressing the imperative of obedience and loyalty to institutions. In short, the nation was no longer the people, it was the state.

It is nonetheless true that Bonaparte was able to tap some of the idealism that had fired the early years of the Republic, especially through his military exploits, and the fact that his hostility to the Old Order placed him, for many, on the side of enlightenment and progress. This was increasingly the case as the Napoleonic legend was reshaped in line with Bonaparte's St Helena writings, where the popular, revolutionary, Jacobin and even 'liberal' dimensions of Bonapartism are retrospectively accorded pride of place.[22] Under the Restoration and Orleanist monarchies there was certainly some overlap between republican and Bonapartist circles, which shared certain preoccupations.

This testifies to the ambiguities of Bonapartism, to its seductive qualities in an exhausted and divided society where the level of political education, though precociously high, was still relatively immature. The essence of the Bonapartist dictatorship is to be found, however, in its major domestic achievements, notably in the field of administration and law. The instruments of this were a meritocratic elite based on the fusion of the old and the new,[23] but whose core was made up of 'disenchanted republicans who preferred a stabilising modernisation to the upheavals and uncertainties of widespread political participation.'[24] The bourgeois conquests of 1789 had to be consolidated and, after ten years of conflict and uncertainty, the liberal dimension of the revolutionary heritage was seen as the most expendable part. The bourgeoisie was not yet sufficiently developed, or self-confident, to take the risk of trying to legitimate its aspirations through representative institutions.

The most significant long-term legacy of Bonapartism, however, concerns its reworking of the concept of nation into an ideology of integration and control. Bonapartism proved that through the appeal to nationhood it was possible to invoke older traditions of ethnic, cultural and territorial identity and of the sanctity of the state, all of them profoundly conservative in their implications. Bonapartism showed in fact how the rhetoric of nation could be pressed into the service of the dominant classes, and in this respect it foreshadowed the narrowly exclusivist and chauvinist ideology that was to serve the interests of the fully-fledged capitalist state later in the nineteenth century.

4

THE NATION DENIED:
FRANCE 1815–48

As all constitutions are in their principles divine, it follows that Man can do nothing in this domain unless he leans on God, whose instrument he thereby becomes.

(Joseph de Maistre)

Political rights, far from being based on the principle of equality, are based on that of inequality: political rights are of necessity unequal, and unevenly distributed.

(*Moniteur universel,* 6 October, 1831)

THE RESTORATION MONARCHY

The Napoleonic regime had provided a framework for the partial reconciliation of old and new elites and for the consolidation of the major bourgeois reforms of 1789. However, for fifteen years free debate and representative institutions had been stifled, and the fall of the empire revived the *notables'* taste for politics. The Charter of 1814, with its invocation of civil equality, liberty and property, fitted this new mood. It guaranteed an independent judiciary, a free press and religious toleration, restored parliamentary institutions, and extended voting rights only to those 'responsible' property owners who paid at least 300 francs in annual taxes. This blend of liberalism and elitism had considerable attractions for a liberal bourgeoisie which hoped to continue its peaceful conquest of power more freely than the authoritarian empire had allowed.

However, some details of the Charter gave reason to doubt the sincerity of its commitment to liberal constitutionalism. It was deemed to have been granted as a royal concession by a King who was in 'the nineteenth year of his reign'. It restored the *fleur de lys* flag and re-established Catholicism as a state religion. The monarch was deemed to

43

be unaccountable, and he alone could initiate and promulgate laws: the legislature was reduced to the role of passing the law, without the right of amendment. Indeed, the legitimacy of the monarchy seemed to draw as much on *Ancien Régime* traditions as on the principles which Louis XVI had reluctantly accepted some twenty-five years earlier.

The possibility that the return of the King might open the doors to aristocratic and clerical reaction was quickly confirmed by the social climate of the First Restoration. However, this in itself laid the ground for Napoleon's dramatic flight from Elba in April 1815, and the ease with which he won the country over and re-established his authority revealed how far the tide of royalism and counter-revolution had retreated in favour of a growing acceptance of the principles of 1789. This inevitably raises the question of how, after Waterloo, the monarchy was restored with so little opposition, and why the former privileged orders were able to reassert their influence to such an extent under the Restoration. After twenty-five years of revolution, republic and empire, the results of the 1815 elections to the Chamber of Deputies are astonishing, however unique the circumstances. Ninety per cent of those elected were royalists, nearly half were former nobles, and one fifth were returning *emigrés*!

Clearly political circumstances in 1815 left little room for manoeuvre. Years of war culminating in final defeat had exhausted the country, and the restoration of the Bourbons reflected the preferences of the victorious monarchies and autocracies of *Ancien Régime* Europe. There is some truth in the allegation that Louis XVIII returned to the throne 'in the baggage train of foreign powers'. However, the settlement would not have recommended itself to the statesmen of Europe if it had not been socially and politically feasible, and no explanation can dispense with some analysis of the balance of class forces that made such a solution possible.

Numerous studies have shown how the aristocracy was able to salvage some of its wealth, status and influence after the Revolution. By a variety of strategies it had retained or bought back part of its land, had transformed seigneurial dues into rents, and in some cases had adopted entrepreneurial farming methods or invested in industry. The gradual reintegration of *emigrés* under Napoleon was completed under the Restoration, and it is suggested that 60 per cent of the 670 richest families in France in the 1820s were still *Ancien Régime* aristocrats.[1] The years of political upheaval and war had brought industrial stagnation, which prevented the bourgeoisie from exploiting the liberal economic reforms of the Revolution. As a result the aristocracy had retained a significant social base, strong enough to allow it to reassert its political influence once the fortuitous circumstances of 1815 had presented the opportunity.

It was assisted in its ambitions by the attitude of the bourgeois *notables* who, having long since abandoned the path of revolutionary mass mobilisation in favour of a more elitist strategy, had placed their hopes in the regime's respect for the spirit of the 1814 Charter. Their illusions were soon shattered when the 'White Terror' of 1815–16, which saw ultra-royalists in the rural Midi wreak revenge on republicans and Bonapartists, was condoned by a government which itself instituted censorship, purges and other security measures against the accomplices of Napoleon's '100 days'. After four brief years of more conciliatory policies, the regime fell increasingly under the influence of the ultra-royalists in the 1820s, with the tightening of press controls and the rigging of elections against the liberals. The aristocracy was allowed to colonise the administration, the army and indeed the Church, where after 1815 nearly 80 per cent of those appointed to the episcopate were aristocrats.

Catholicism itself enjoyed a similar revival as the Church secured an increased state budget, won control of educational administration, set up its own secondary schools and strengthened its influence over primary education. The medieval and ecclesiastical pomp of Charles X's coronation in 1824 symbolised the new alliance of 'throne and altar', and in the same year the death penalty was restored for sacrilege. The annual number of ordinations trebled, and though the growth of ultramontanism with its allegiance to Rome was scarcely to the liking of government, the monarchy could not afford to dispense with the enormous ideological authority that religion continued to exercise.

The former privileged orders did not regain this influence simply by default, nor were they content to count on popular fear and deference. Ultra-royalism developed a strong populist flavour which played on a variety of accumulated peasant grievances. Not least of these was widespread resentment against an urban-based professional and commercial bourgeoisie which had bought the lion's share of the *biens nationaux,* enclosed common land, monopolised local offices and generally turned the revolutionary land settlement to its own advantage. For many peasants, the development of capitalism blighted their dreams of land acquisition and social advancement, and made them increasingly dependent on the merchants and financiers of the towns. An equal hostility was often felt for the state, which during the Revolution and empire had subjected them to taxation, regulation, purges, conscription and above all its official anti-clericalism.

In certain regions of the country, especially those where religious faith was strongest and where the rural habitat restricted sociability and access to the wider world, the royalists were successful in cultivating among the peasantry a nostalgia for an idealised version of the Old Order. The social paternalism of 'natural' elites was set against the materialism of bourgeois self-interest, the values of traditional community against the disruptive effects of capitalism, the concept of organic self-governing regions against the overweening bureaucracy of the state, the comforting security of religious belief and ritual against a threatening changing world.

The impact of such ideas is hard to measure in a country where all but 90,000 individuals were excluded from the electoral rolls. However, there is clearly a danger of exaggerating their influence. Governments under the Restoration tolerated the 'White Terror' but often repressed the activities of liberals, Bonapartists and republicans. It would be wrong to assume that counter-revolutionary sentiments were in the popular ascendancy purely because they were more visible, and the fate of the First Restoration had given ample recent evidence of deep and widespread hostility to the *Ancien Régime* and all its trappings.

Even more important in this respect is the fact that, as we have already indicated, the liberal bourgeoisie was unwilling to take the risk of appealing for popular support. Its increasing consciousness of its own class interests under the Directory and the empire had weakened the social and political ties which had once bound it to the rural and urban popular movement. Without this support, the bourgeoisie was as yet insufficiently developed as an economic and social force to wrest political control from the aristocracy, especially in such unfavourable circumstances as those of 1815.

However, as time went by things moved in its favour, as indicated by the growing strength of the liberal opposition in the Chamber of Deputies. The restoration of peace in 1815 for the first time allowed French businessmen and entrepreneurs to take advantage of the liberal economic reforms of the Revolution, and the consequent acceleration of industrial development, though far from spectacular, both enriched and expanded the bourgeois class. This steadily tipped the scales in favour of a more dynamic *grande bourgeoisie* which was increasingly impatient with the archaic nature of the Restoration regime.

As in 1789, however, it was the intransigence of a reactionary aristocracy, this time personified by Charles X, which made confrontation inevitable. In August 1829 he decided to challenge a liberal-dominated assembly with the appointment of an ultra-royalist government including several ministers with notoriously reactionary pasts. Deadlock led prime minister Polignac to call new elections, which merely served to increase the liberals' parliamentary representation. In a further assertion of his executive prerogatives, the King used the emergency powers granted him by the Charter to introduce ordinances suspending freedom of the press, dissolving the newly-elected Chamber and further amending the electoral process. This blatant abuse of the spirit of the Charter was suicidal in the changed climate of opinion. Within days insurrection became revolution, and only a week after the proclamation of the ordinances, Charles X abdicated.

Diverse social and economic grievances, given focus by an upsurge of popular anti-clericalism, ensured that the liberal opponents of the regime would enjoy support from the lower orders, especially in Paris and other major towns. The most striking aspect of the 1830 'revolution', however, is the ease with which the new leadership was able to manipulate this popular discontent, to impose the solution of the Orleanist monarchy and subsequently to repress the peasant and artisan agitation which had brought it to power. The *grande bourgeoisie* had finally displaced the old elites, and largely on its own terms. In Roger Magraw's phrase, 'despotism shifted from chateau to Stock Exchange.' [2]

THE NATION 1815–30

It is scarcely surprising that the word nation and all its associations were almost totally absent from political discourse under the Restoration. A regime which excluded the vast majority of the adult male population from political life, which appealed to pre-revolutionary values, which felt sympathy for the *Ancien Régime* autocracies of Europe and indeed intervened on their behalf under the white flag to defeat the Spanish liberals, could feel nothing but indifference or antipathy for the idea, whether in its revolutionary or in its Bonapartist guise.

The Restoration never set out to legitimate its authority on a representative basis. The Charter was a royal concession rather than a contract, and parliamentary control of the King was a dead letter. Indeed, it is difficult to find a historical analogy for the monarchy of 1815–30. It has no parallels with the constitutional regime of 1789–92 which made Louis XVI 'King of the French', nor did it make the equation between state and nation which lent legitimacy to

Bonapartism and, in a different way, to the modernising absolutism of Louis XIV.

The ideology of the regime was in fact a rearguard action against economic and social change, in which the ultra-royalists set the pace. Indeed, the only 'modern' element was precisely this recognition that in the post-revolutionary era such values could not be taken for granted, but required active ideological expression. The symbolism of Charles X's coronation looked back beyond Louis XIV to the medieval period. The theocratic ideas of de Bonald and de Maistre saw the King as no more than 'God's representative', rejected the enlightenment and depicted society as an organic natural order. The ultramontane bias of the religious revival viewed the state with suspicion and looked to Rome for authority, while in a re-enactment of the aristocratic revolt of 1787–89 the provincial nobles raised federalist and regionalist aspirations. If the absolutist monarchy had sought to subdue the aristocrats, the Restoration saw them recolonise the state, the army and the Church.

It is equally fruitless to search for the revolutionary rhetoric of popular nationhood and self-government among the liberal opposition, or among the *idéologues* who vainly clung to the 1814 Charter. Such language implied mass mobilisation and insurrection, and this was considered neither desirable nor necessary by the bourgeois *notables*. They had no intention of unleashing the democratic aspirations of 1792, and when the Restoration's clerical and illiberal excesses gave them the opportunity for a change of regime, they were careful to offer the people specific targets for attack rather than invoking the dangerous catchwords of equality and fraternity. The themes were liberal-constitutionalist and anti-clerical, and the urban popular classes, threatened by economic depression and technical innovation but politically inexperienced after thirty-five years of enforced quiescence, 'carried through a revolution on behalf of their exploiters.' [3]

THE ORLEANIST MONARCHY

If the Restoration of 1815 had disappointed the liberal bourgeoisie, the Revolution of 1830 was equally disappointing for republicans, and for those liberals who had hoped that the transfer of power would be a prelude to popular reform. Agitation in July 1830 had spread from Paris to other major towns, and had been sufficient to arouse fears abroad that the new regime of the 'King of the barricades' would export the revolution and encourage the nationalist aspirations of Italians,

Belgians and Poles. When it became clear that the regime was determined to restore order and to make no further concessions, popular frustration fuelled continuing unrest between 1830 and 1832, exemplified by attacks on the clergy, by food riots and demonstrations, and by strikes like the famous revolt of the Lyons silk workers in late 1831.

However, for the majority of the former liberal opposition there had been no revolution, simply a reaction to the previous regime's constant abuse of its own constitution. Indeed, the new Charter of 1830 did not substantially depart from the spirit of its predecessor, with its guarded concessions to press freedom, its retention of a two-chamber legislature, and a minimal extension of the suffrage which doubled the electorate to around 200,000. The key difference, however, lay in the underlying principles of executive authority. Louis Philippe's accession was consecrated not by medieval and ecclesiastical ceremony, but by an oath of loyalty to the Charter in the presence of the legislators. The King's legitimacy was thus seen as based on consent, on a contract between him and the elected representatives. He was no longer to enjoy the emergency powers to which Charles X had had recourse in July 1830, and this reduced his executive independence. Furthermore the spirit of the new Charter was confirmed by events. The King's early attempts to intervene personally in government were nipped in the bud, and as power passed increasingly to his ministers so the principle of a degree of responsibility to the Chamber of Deputies was established.

The significance of parliamentary control was, however, substantially diluted by the thoroughly unrepresentative nature of the elected Assembly. The limited property suffrage, now also extended to the formerly non-elective departmental and municipal councils, ensured a high degree of consensus within the 'political class', and this was reinforced by the repression conducted by Casimir Perier's government in 1831-2. The administration was purged, newspapers were confiscated and the Lyon silk workers' insurrection was put down by force. Such measures effectively eliminated both republicans and Bourbon legitimists from positions of influence, and the latter suffered a further blow when the hereditary principle in the Chamber of Peers was abandoned in favour of government patronage. As a result, divisive social and constitutional issues were wiped off the political agenda of the regime's narrowly-based parliamentary institutions. In Tudesq's words, 'no longer was there room for sentiments and illusions in political life, which became a matter of rationality and self-interest.' [4]

The classical historical view of the 1830 revolution and the regime it established has identified the process with the rise of a *grande bourgeoisie* which now had sufficient economic and social influence to tip the political scales in its favour and fashion the political system according to its own class interests. Contemporary witnesses as diverse as Marx, Guizot and de Tocqueville saw events in this light, and historians of varying persuasions have been influenced by this perspective ever since. A revisionist challenge has, of course, been mounted, largely by British and American scholars, and the main substance of this case hinges on arguments about the 'retarded' nature of French economic development during this period, and thus the absence of a cohesive and dynamic bourgeois class. However, more recent historiography has raised serious empirical and conceptual doubts about the work of these revisionists, and the classical approach has been largely rehabilitated.[5]

Though France was second only to Britain as an industrial power in the period under consideration, it would be futile to deny that, in comparison with the later experience of many other countries, the French industrialisation process was slow and uneven. The survival of a large peasant farming sector and of artisan-style manufacturing created a dual economy where only a small minority were in the front line of technical progress. In the 1830s the aristocracy was still strongly represented among the rich, land remained the principal source of wealth, and the average bourgeois was often more attracted by a career in the public service or the liberal professions than by the world of business.

However, the evidence of substantial economic development between 1815 and 1848 is undeniable. Growth averaged 3.5 per cent each year from the mid-1820s to the mid-1840s, and overall industrial production increased by 30 per cent in the same period.[6] In particular sectors like the railways, and among some leading firms in textiles, coal and metallurgy, there were major advances in investment and technology. Similarly it is a mistake to equate landed interests in these years with an aristocratic *rentier* mentality, for in many areas of the country capitalist priorities were penetrating agriculture. Indeed, the distinction often made by the revisionist historians between the *milieux* of industry, land, finance and bureaucracy is an artificial one for, as Magraw puts it, there was a 'constant osmosis' [7] between them in the Orleanist elite. The period saw the emergence of great bourgeois dynasties like the Periers, the Laffittes, the Foulds and the Hottinguers, whose wealth was derived from a range of financial, industrial and agricultural interests, and whose members also rose to high rank in politics, the civil service or the liberal professions. At the same time the percentage of nobles in the Chamber of Deputies, in the prefectoral corps and in the office of mayor declined dramatically.[8]

Central to this process was the class cohesion brought about by common social and ideological values. There were, of course, disagreements over issues like foreign policy and attitudes to the Church, and it would be ludicrous to expect to find a total concordance of economic preferences within a bourgeois class whose very *raison d'être* was competitive and individualist self-interest. There was conflict between the proponents of protectionism and those of free trade, and Marx himself saw a distinct clash of interests between a financial and railway oligarchy and a weaker lobby of industrial capitalists.

However, underlying these disputes there was a genuine ideological convergence, aptly summed up in politics by the notion of the *juste milieu* which sought to hold a middle course between the dangers of republicanism and reaction. The key values of 1789 were given their full bourgeois resonance – individualism, private property, equality before the law, religious toleration – and the regime claimed to have completed the Revolution. There would be no return to the clerical excesses of the Restoration nor to the egalitarian excesses of the radical Republic. For Orleanists, the monarchy, divested of its mystique, became a set of institutions guaranteeing order and limited representative government. Anti-clericalism was toned down by 'Gallicanism', a practical recognition of the utility of the Church as an agent of social discipline. Guizot's famous public education law of 1833, which ended the Church monopoly in primary education, nonetheless saw moral and religious instruction as an essential element of the syllabus.

It was Guizot again who encapsulated the social and political philosophy of Orleanism in the notorious phrase *'enrichissez-vous'*. Only wealth and education could secure for the individual the right and the capacity to play a role in public affairs, hence the tax qualification for voting. Furthermore, since the Revolution had established the principle of civil equality and had abolished venal and hereditary offices, every individual was deemed to have a chance of making his way in the world provided he had the energy and the talent. The 'social question' simply did not exist.

There can be little doubt that legislation and government policy responded to dominant bourgeois interests in these years. The state relaxed the laws on bankruptcy and joint-stock companies, encouraged mergers and industrial investment, and undertaxed the rich. It promoted the construction of railways, roads and canals, tightened the laws against workers' combinations, repressed strikes, and generally backed employers in labour disputes. No other regime in French history has appeared to correspond so closely to Marx's famous definition of the capitalist state as an executive committee for the management of the collective affairs of the bourgeoisie.

In reality, however, Marx's dictum does not fit the case. France under the July Monarchy was dominated not by a 'class' but by a fraction of a class, the *grande bourgeoisie*. It was not only peasants, artisans and workers who found themselves excluded from representation and influence, but the broad ranks of the middle classes too. The owners of medium and small-scale businesses, provincial doctors and lawyers, a host of individuals with property, education and social aspirations, were denied a political voice, and saw their interests neglected and their careers blocked by a narrow clique which monopolised power and patronage.

What divided the *pays légal* from the *pays réel* was not strictly speaking a matter of class. The principles of private property enjoyed wide acceptance in the ranks of the middle class and the peasantry, and collectivist ideas had as yet made little headway among urban workers. Indeed, capitalism had as much to fear from legitimists who harked back to pre-industrial values as from the small socialist sects inspired by the doctrines of Saint-Simon, Cabet, Fourier and Proudhon. Given the security of its economic and social position, why did the upper bourgeoisie risk popular opprobrium by refusing to move towards a more democratic political system?

The reluctance of the Orleanist elite to make concessions in this direction was more than just a matter of selfish and short-sighted opportunism. Memories of 1792–4 had divided the expanding ranks of the bourgeoisie between those for whom any extension of democracy carried with it the threat of social revolution, and those for whom access to the political process was a necessary condition of further social advancement. Not for the first nor for the last time, the ideological divisions bred by the Great Revolution weighed heavily in the balance, and the persistence of these prejudices was lengthened by the relatively slow pace of industrialisation. Faced with a parochial and politically unpredictable peasantry, enclaves of aristocratic reaction and the dangerous egalitarianism of the urban workers, the ruling bourgeois groups were unwilling to take the risk of political democracy. Bourgeois values had not yet penetrated and reshaped society at large, and the capitalist elites were not yet ready to attempt to legitimate their authority on a liberal-democratic basis.

THE NATION 1830-48

The identification of the Orleanist regime with the 'nation' could never be more than an empty formula. It rested on Louis Philippe's responsibility to a parliament of *notables* who in turn represented that tiny proportion of the adult population who were deemed capable of reflecting on public affairs. Whereas conservative Britain had one elector for every 25 inhabitants after the Reform Bill of 1832, 'revolutionary' France had one for every 170 inhabitants.[9] In a country where egalitarian notions of popular sovereignty and active citizenship had been raised at the barricades only to be flouted, the elitism of the July Monarchy was a provocation. As the gap between the political preoccupations of the *pays légal* and those of the *pays réel* widened, so the ideal of democratic nationhood again began to exercise its appeal on the opponents of the regime.

Of course, the defeated legitimists, for all their new-found populism, still had no place for the nation in their catechism of ideas. Ultramontane, federalist, paternalist, their sympathies lay abroad and in the past, and their support was largely in those rural areas which had remained insulated from the economic and political changes that were reshaping national life. Indeed, their loss of power in 1830 led many to emigrate in imitation of their fathers forty years earlier, and René Rémond records the existence of a kind of legitimist 'international', where supporters of the Bourbons, the Stuarts and the Spanish Carlists intermarried, conspired and fought for each others' lost causes.[10]

It was, then, above all on the left that the concept of nation began to revive. The social conditions for this have already been explored, for as we have seen the class bases of potential opposition to the regime were extremely broad. It encompassed the diverse ranks of the disfranchised middle classes, urban artisans and workers alienated by the brutalities of capitalism, and a peasantry threatened by agrarian crisis. In this context, the generous vision of the democratic nation united in its multiple grievances against a narrow ruling elite had considerable attractive power, recalling the solidarity of the Third Estate in 1789.

Of course, fifty years of capitalist development and political strife had made this kind of class alliance even less viable than it had been at the start of the Great Revolution. However, the sentimental appeal of the idea, fuelled by the moral generosity of romanticism, republicanism and utopian socialism, masked the underlying class antagonisms, especially when the events of 1848 unexpectedly provided a focus for a revolutionary challenge to the regime.

There were, in fact, diverse forms of opposition to the main governing majority between 1820 and 1848, both inside and outside parliament. The so-called 'dynastic opposition', which remained committed to constitutional monarchy, shared with the moderate republicans a pragmatic liberal concern to appease the democratic aspirations and the anti-clericalism of those who had helped carry the 1830 revolution through. The more radical republicans were barely represented in parliament, and operated underground through a network of organisations co-ordinated by the *Société des droits de l'homme*. The movement also had spasmodic contact with the various socialist sects and with the craft-workers' co-operatives, but not with the rump of the Bonapartist movement, whose dynastic ambitions were discredited by two rather farcical attempts in 1836 and 1840 to repeat Napoleon's 'flight of the eagle'.

Given this diversity, it is perhaps not surprising that nationalist sentiment under the July Monarchy was above all fired by issues of foreign policy, which served to conceal the internal antagonisms of the domestic opposition. Indeed, the discontent generated by such issues fed as much on the Napoleonic legend as it did on the Jacobin ideal of exporting the Revolution. The pacifist policies favoured by both Louis Philippe and Guizot, with their acceptance of the 1815 settlement and their cultivation of English friendship, aroused deep popular hostility and were criticised by de Tocqueville as potentially fatal for the regime. Indeed, nostalgia for France's former missionary role and for foreign policies that challenged the European Old Order in support of national independence struggles, was one of the main rallying points for parliamentary and extra-parliamentary opposition in general.

The precise blend of Bonapartism and republicanism in all this is hard to ascertain. What is beyond doubt, however, is that such sentiments were opportunistically exploited by politicians who not only had no stomach for war, but who also had no desire to apply at home the democratic principles of nationhood they claimed to support abroad. This applies not only to the dynastic opposition but also to Adolphe Thiers who, during his two periods of office, courted popularity by backing the Spanish liberals against the Carlists, and having Napoleon's ashes transferred to the Pantheon. A surer measure of where he really stood was to be found in his statement of opposition to universal suffrage: 'National sovereignty, understood as the unlimited sovereignty of the broad masses, is the most erroneous and the most dangerous principle for society that can be evoked.' [11]

It was in the values of republicanism that the truest expression of the national ideal of popular sovereignty was to be found, and when the Revolution broke in February 1848 it was republicanism that was to become the natural rallying point for all forms of opposition to the regime, from liberalism to socialism. Fraternity has been seen as the sentimental keynote of February, along with faith in the moral power of ideas and in the efficacy of human institutions as agents of social reconciliation. Utopian socialism, popular romanticism and democratic idealism all paved the way for this myth of national solidarity, which disguised the underlying class antagonisms of the revolutionary movement.

The work of the great historian, Jules Michelet, and in particular his *Peuple* (1846) and his *Histoire de la Révolution française* (1847), exemplifies the curious blend of ideas which converged in the revolutionary nationalism of 1848. For him, France was a country with a universal destiny, *la patrie universelle*. Drawing on a religious romanticism which identified Christianity with *l'égalité fraternelle*, and which sat somewhat uneasily alongside the traditional anti-clericalism of the left, Michelet identifies the Great Revolution of 1789 with God's 'second coming' and France's gift to the world. It was a revolution not of the bourgeoisie but of the people, not of class conflict but of humanitarian ideals.[12] The notion of the 'global unity of the revolution' was central to the republicans of 1848. It drew a veil over the antagonism of class interests, explained away the Terror as a necessity of circumstance, reconciled the bourgeois and the popular revolutions, and focused on the idealism of the unfulfilled republican dream.

5

NATION, BONAPARTISM AND SOCIALISM: FRANCE 1848–71

> The name Napoleon is a complete programme in itself: it stands
> for order, authority, religion, the welfare of the people within;
> without, for national dignity.
>
> (Louis-Napoleon Bonaparte)

THE REVOLUTION OF 1848

Political elitism and corruption, economic recession and agrarian crisis, frustrated aspirations and, according to Lamartine in 1847, simple 'boredom' with an unimaginative and opportunist regime, helped to undermine the July Monarchy. The events which paved the way for insurrection were, however, surprisingly banal. The banquet campaign organised since mid-1847 by the dynastic opposition, involving the drinking of toasts in favour of electoral reform, was scarcely revolutionary in intent, and it had aroused little public interest. Comparison with the campaign around the Estates General in 1789 would suggest the aphorism of 'history repeating itself as farce', and yet it was the banning of a banquet called in Paris for 22 February that set the insurrection in motion. After two days of street fighting, with the middle-class National Guard unwilling to support the troops and successive changes of prime minister failing to appease the demonstrators, Louis-Philippe abdicated.

Collective idealism and emotional solidarity are, of course, part and parcel of any revolutionary process, especially in the early phases of success. In the immediate aftermath of February's 'beautiful revolution' (Marx's dismissive phrase) middle-class talk was all of a new era of justice and social harmony, and the moderate republicans who led the new provisional government were persuaded by pressure from the street to offer ministries to two radicals and two socialists. The regime conceded freedom of the press and association, and by granting manhood suffrage extended the electorate from some 200,000 to nearly eight million. It also raised more radical hopes by reducing the working day, by setting up the Luxemburg commission to propose further social reforms, and by establishing national workshops for the unemployed. Though the latter proved to be glorified charity workhouses, for a while they were mistakenly seen as the basis for the producer co-operatives Louis Blanc had envisaged in his *Organisation du travail,* the fulfilment of the principle of 'the right to work'.

The February Revolution revived the sense of democratic nationhood which had first been stirred in 1789, and gave it more concrete expression in the form of republicanism. Republicanism, as Marx acknowledged, cannot be identified as the ideology of a specific social class. Predicated on the notion of the formal equality of the nation's citizens beyond class differences, and seeing the common exercise of political rights as the essential basis of a harmonious, democratic social order, it was the logical expression of the revolution-ary ideal of nationhood first raised in 1789. The leading role in the provisional government of the poet Lamartine, which confirmed the evolution of the romantic movement from right to left under the July Monarchy, symbolises the sentimental character of the republican ideal with its belief in the possibility of uniting diverse social classes in a moral consensus.

However, as in 1789–94 the dynamics of the revolutionary process rapidly exposed the antagonisms that lay beneath this superficial unanimity. Right from the outset it was apparent that the revolution had taken many of its beneficiaries by surprise. Neither Odilon Barrot's dynastic left, which had hoped to profit from minor franchise adjust-ments, nor indeed the moderate republicans around the newspaper *Le National,* had envisaged universal manhood suffrage, nor had they any taste for popular insurrection, and even the leader of the radical republicans, Ledru-Rollin, had feared that an uprising would result in disaster. Indeed, once the King had abdicated Thiers and Barrot had hoped to avert the establishment of a republic by floating the idea of a regency in favour of Louis-Philippe's grandson. However, the July Monarchy was too discredited for this to be an option, given the climate of opinion in Paris, and the small but active republican movement was able to present itself as the only viable alternative.

Republicanism itself was riddled with contradictions, and this was reflected in the composition of the provisional government. Most of the eleven ministers were liberals, wealthy *notables* who had already been deputies under Louis-Philippe, and though they favoured political freedom and an extension of the franchise, they were at best suspicious of notions of democracy and popular sovereignty. Neo-Jacobins like Carnot were more receptive to such ideas, and indeed to the revolutionary principle of aiding the struggles of the oppressed nationalities of Europe, but not all radicals were as open as Ledru-Rollin to proposals for social reform and to making common cause with the workers. The presence in the government of the socialist writer Louis Blanc and the worker Albert was a concession to the Paris popular movement but, given the balance of power in the new leadership, their influence was firmly circumscribed. The real divide in February, as Agulhon has argued,[1] lay between those who saw the Republic in pragmatic, institutional terms, and those who saw it as the incarnation of a political and social ideal.

These contradictions were soon brought to a head by the immense problems which the new government had to face. Against a background of industrial recession and agrarian crisis, an inexperienced and unprepared leadership had to appease a radical movement which was more active, better organised and more 'working-class' in composition than it had been in 1830, and at the same time win the confidence of a potentially hostile financial and industrial oligarchy. Furthermore, it needed to establish the national legitimacy of a regime that had been made largely in Paris, and this implied early elections, which were called for April. Thus, little time was left for the new Republic to win over to democratic principles a peasantry that was, in many parts of the countryside, politically inexperienced, socially conservative and still under the sway of reactionary local *notables*. Its task was made no easier by the ill-advised decision to increase the land tax by 40 per cent, a measure which sacrificed much of the goodwill the regime enjoyed in the more republican rural areas.

The results of the elections are not easy to assess, since virtually all candidates presented themselves as republicans irrespective of their true loyalties, a further element of confusion for an inexperienced rural electorate. Of the 900 deputies returned, it would seem, however, that only some 300 had been republicans before 1848, and most of the remainder were crypto-monarchists.[2] The majority of these were Orleanists, including many supporters of the former dynastic opposition, and events some twenty years later would prove that, unlike the die-hard legitimists, they could make the transition from constitutional monarchy to conservative Republic without too many qualms. What the elections certainly did, however, was dash the hopes of the radical clubs that the February Revolution would open the way to a new

République démocratique et sociale. If the provisional government had been at best ambivalent on social reform, what could be expected from a Constituent Assembly dominated by monarchists? The frustration of the Paris popular movement, where memories of the 1830 'betrayal' still lived on, made confrontation increasingly likely.

Symbolically, it was the traditional revolutionary theme of bringing 'fraternity and assistance' to oppressed peoples that first brought matters to a head. Most of Europe had, of course, experienced the contagion of revolution in early 1848, with uprisings in Vienna and Prague, in Milan and Venice, in Berlin, Frankfurt and Dresden. Magyars, Italians and Czechs asserted their national rights against Austrian domination, while in the independent Italian states, in the German Confederation, and at the heart of the Habsburg Empire itself demands were made for constitutional government, civil liberties and political rights. However, if Lamartine had once attacked Guizot for his timid, anglophile foreign policy, the government of which he himself was now part had no desire to invite foreign intervention by supporting revolutions elsewhere. In foreign affairs as in domestic policy, the revolutionary leaders of 1848 were intent on avoiding the violent conflagrations of the 1790s.

It is testimony to the altruism of republican nationalism that the demonstrations of 15 May in Paris were inspired not only by demands for food and work, but above all by sympathy for the Polish uprising against Russian rule and by demands for French military intervention in its favour. However, this day marked the beginning of a new phase and served as a pretext for a hardening of conservative attitudes in the Assembly. Leading radicals were arrested, political clubs disbanded, the Luxemburg commission wound up, and finally on 22 June it was announced that the national workshops would be closed. This latter decision detonated the popular uprising of the so-called 'June days', when the army under General Cavaignac brutally repressed a revolt of some 50,000 workers, of whom 1,500 were killed and a further 12,000 arrested.

THE ROAD TO BONAPARTISM

The events shattered the brief republican idyll of national unity. It seems entirely legitimate to see the June insurrection as the opening shots in a class war that progressively divided the French bourgeoisie from a slowly emerging class of urban, industrial workers, and which increasingly split the republican movement. It is, of course, true that the bulk of the June revolutionaries were not from the slim ranks of the factory proletariat, whose recruits were often politically inexperienced migrants from the countryside,[3] but from skilled artisan trades. Old corporate craft traditions shaped their attitudes as much as newer socialist doctrines, and their hostility was often directed as much against the threat of industrialism in general as capitalism in particular. It is also true that a *petite bourgeoisie* of small masters and shopkeepers, the victims of exploitation by landlords and merchant capitalists, played a part in an insurrection that cannot be called truly 'proletarian' in character.

However, the June days must be seen as a significant formative moment in the shaping of a genuine working-class consciousness in France. The movement threw up a spontaneous leadership which, for the first time, was not dominated by middle-class radicals, and indeed the radical republicans around Ledru-Rollin, despite their sympathy for many of the workers' demands, felt they could not identify themselves with an insurrection against an elected government. Equally significant for this sharpening of class identity was the reaction the uprising produced. In social terms, the broad ranks of the bourgeoisie and middle classes, with the exception of a minority of radical intellectuals and *petits bourgeois,* were horrified and alarmed by events, and found themselves on the same side as the old clerical and aristocratic elites. Political differences between legitimists, Orleanists and moderate republicans dissolved in defence of the social order. Though the radical republican tradition had not yet lost its credibility among urban workers, the process which would make many of them feel like social and political outcasts in their own community had already begun.

The defeat of the insurrection inevitably opened the way to reaction. Proposals for income tax and for subsidies to co-operatives were defeated by the conservative parliamentary majority, the 'right to work' was abolished and public relief schemes cut. The Cavaignac government filled Paris with troops, introduced press censorship and shut down radical political clubs in the capital. At the same time an intense anti-socialist propaganda campaign in the countryside sought to rally the peasant majority to the 'party of order', the coalition of conservative forces whose traditional dynastic, constitutional and religious antagonisms were set aside in the face of a shared enemy. As in the rest of Europe, counter-revolution appeared to be in the ascendancy.

Class rivalry had thus, not for the first time, undermined the revolutionary dream of democratic nationhood. If February 1848 had seen a challenge led by the disfranchised middle classes against the political hegemony of the Orleanist *grande bourgeoisie,* the events of June once again tied the former to the latter in a bourgeois alliance against the social threat posed by the working class. However, as under the Directory some fifty years earlier, this sanitisation of the Republic was no guarantee of its survival. French elites, while united in defence of property and the social order, were still divided over political strategy, and these divisions were brought to the surface by the presidential elections of December 1848.

The constitution of November 1848, reflecting the conservative preference for strong government, had established a presidency elected by manhood suffrage and with strong executive powers to balance those of the Assembly. The quest for suitable candidates revived the political divisions in the conservative bloc. Faced with the radical Ledru-Rollin, the royalist groups found the republican Cavaignac too 'liberal' for their taste, but for a number of reasons they were reluctant to field a candidate of their own. They therefore opted to support the candidacy of Louis Bonaparte, no doubt convinced that he could be manipulated.

On the face of it, Bonaparte's dramatic election victory confirmed the continuing ascendancy of the 'party of order' which had supported him, and which now received the lion's share of posts in his new government. Emboldened by their success, the parliamentary right pressed for new assembly elections in May 1849, which gave them outright victory with 50 per cent of the poll. The muted liberalism of the moderate republicans was now entirely submerged by the politics of the 'party of order', with religion increasingly invoked as the best guarantee of property and social stability. A French military expedition in mid-1849 helped to crush the Roman Republic and restore papal authority, while the Falloux law of 1850 extended Catholic influence in education. The intimidation of electors in May 1848 and the systematic purge of radicals and anti-clericals finally culminated in the law of May 1850 which disfranchised some 30 per cent of the electorate.

The chances of the regime evolving peacefully in this more conservative direction were, however, very limited. The unpopularity of the 'official' Republic had been confirmed by Cavaignac's decisive defeat in the presidential elections, and by the collapse of the moderate republican vote to only 11 per cent in the parliamentary elections five months later. To replace the Republic with a King was equally problematic, despite the parliamentary ascendancy now enjoyed by a coalition of various former royalists. Any attempt to restore the monarchy carried the risk not only of dynastic squabbles but of further revolution. Louis Bonaparte's landslide victory may arguably be seen as a vote for conservatism and order, but it was certainly not an endorsement of any kind of monarchist venture.

For the peasantry, which was the mainstay of the Bonapartist vote, the name of Napoleon had always implied the rejection of seigneurialism and legitimism. Louis Bonaparte studiously avoided the reactionary rhetoric of Catholicism and traditionalism, focusing instead on practical solutions to rural economic problems. At the same time he exploited peasant grievances towards the Republic with its 45 per cent land tax and towards the Orleanist financial oligarchy. In the towns too, his known preoccupation with social issues won him some support in the ranks of a demoralised working class, where Bonapartist and republican allegiances had often overlapped. In short, Louis Bonaparte's popular success implied a different kind of regime, however much the 'party of order' believed he was their creature.

The bourgeois elites were, however, to find the prospect of such an authoritarian regime increasingly attractive for other reasons. The victory of the 'party of order' was not the most striking aspect of the parliamentary elections of May 1849. Far more dramatic was the success enjoyed in rural areas by the radical alliance of *démocrates-socialistes* which won nearly 40 per cent of the vote! Less than a year after the defeat of the June insurrection in Paris, this may seem astonishing given the image cultivated by conservatives of an order-loving, red-hating countryside. In part it reflects the same forces that aided Bonaparte – agrarian crisis, the decline of traditional social allegiances, disillusionment with the 'official' Republic. But other studies have shown the genuine success of radical propaganda in adapting co-operative and associational ideas to old communal practices, in promoting practical solutions to everyday problems, in tapping peasant egalitarianism and in promoting attachment to newly-won political rights.[4] The alarm of the property-owning classes triggered a repression that was every bit as thorough as the one which followed the June days, but which now had to cope with a 'nationwide' rather than a largely Parisian problem. Despite this, the *démocrates-socialistes* continued to make progress in by-elections, and there was fear that they might even win the parliamentary elections of 1852!

The fear of social revolution had won the dominant *grande bourgeoisie* the support of the disillusioned middle classes and the acquiescence of the declining old elites. However, the conservative Republic, like the Directory before it, had failed to produce national reconciliation and

stability, while monarchism threatened to revive revolutionary conflict. In such a situation, when Bonaparte engineered his coup the
bourgeois elites saw much to recommend an authoritarian regime
which would be free to restore order and create a stable political
environment for the development of capitalist interests.

THE SECOND EMPIRE

As we suggested in Chapter 3, Marxist interpretations of the phenomenon of Bonapartism have focused above all on the reign of Louis
Napoleon rather than on that of his more illustrious predecessor, not
least because Marx himself gave special attention to the events of 1848–
52 in France. The general Marxist view that Bonapartism is produced
by a 'state of equilibrium' between the warring bourgeoisie and
proletariat,[5] is clearly more relevant to mid-nineteenth century than to
late-eighteenth century France, but it still smacks of an economic
determinism that requires substantial *political* qualification. In
particular, Marx's proposition that 'the bourgeois class had already
lost, and the working class not yet gained the ability to govern the
nation,'[6] seems grossly premature. In fact, the events of June 1848
marked the coming of age of the French bourgeoisie, whose various
ranks finally became conscious of their collective class interests, while
the French working class at the same date was only just embarking on
the process of self-recognition.

The political complexities of the situation which brought Louis
Bonaparte to power have been touched on in the previous section. As in
the closing years of the Directory some fifty years earlier, the way the
various protagonists perceived each other politically was every bit as
important as the real balance of social forces. French workers, with
their insurrectionary traditions and their new social demands, were still
tied to the struggle for political democracy, to a republican alliance
with the more progressive elements of the middle classes and the
peasantry. Hence for the bourgeoisie, the concept of a Republic still
carried with it a dangerous revolutionary egalitarianism which could
not easily be contained within stable institutions. Although a conservative Republic had successfully crushed the workers' revolt of June, this
was not enough to reassure its bourgeois clientele. The electoral
successes of the radical democratic alliance in and after May 1849 once
again raised the spectre of an idealistic republicanism which the
bourgeois elites did not yet feel capable of mastering and turning to
their own advantage.

This failure of the official Republic to stabilise bourgeois rule on a liberal-democratic basis had its roots above all in the unpredictability and relative political backwardness of French peasants, who represented well over half the working population. Parochialism, the weight of tradition, the regional diversity of political culture, sceptical attitudes towards the town and the state, all of these factors left many areas of the countryside outside the mainstream of national political life. Whether out of cynicism or political immaturity, peasants remained suspicious of ideology and their political behaviour often reflected that *esprit frondeur,* that spirit of opposition which the philosopher Alain later identified as the core of French radicalism.[7] The fluctuations of the peasant vote in the three major electoral consultations of the Second Republic are easier understood as a rejection of certain options than as a wholehearted endorsement of others.

This observation is crucial for understanding the rise of Louis Bonaparte to power. Peasant support in the elections of December 1848 reflected the magic of the name Napoleon for this the least politicised section of the electorate, but at the same time it reflected his success in turning to his own advantage the negative sentiments which other political traditions inspired. The same was true for other sections of the community, though among the social elites there was more calculation and less naïvety. The ambiguities of Bonaparte, 'all things to all men', invited everyone to see him as the least dangerous alternative to what they feared most.

No analysis of Louis Bonaparte's take-over can therefore neglect the domain of political strategy, where in 1849–51 he undoubtedly showed some skill. Despite the right's view of him as a manipulable buffoon, and Marx's dismissal of him as a nonentity, he played a subtle game, carefully distancing himself from the illiberal and pro-Catholic policies of the conservative bloc after his election as President and judiciously tailoring his rhetoric to the prejudices of whatever audience he addressed. Though he failed in July 1851 to win the parliamentary majority necessary to allow him to amend the Constitution and open the way to a second presidential term, this defeat in itself confirmed that he was not simply the creature of the 'party of order'. The success of his *coup d'état* in December of the same year proved his ability to appeal to the administrative and economic elites of the bourgeoisie over the heads of their political representatives.

However, despite the broad, if often negative, social appeal of Bonapartism, it was inevitable that the regime of Napoleon III would reflect the unequal distribution of wealth and power in capitalist class society. The coup itself foretold as much. Engineered by sympathisers in the army and upper bureaucracy, it was welcomed by business interests and accepted with varying degrees of enthusiasm and resignation by conservative politicians, save a handful of legitimists. It was radical leaders who were arrested, and the main opposition took the form of provincial revolt. This extraordinary movement, which in seventeen departments mobilised over 100,000 insurgents, was testimony to the recent successes of the *démocrates-socialistes,* and indicated that the image of a backward, passive countryside was losing its validity. The repression was fierce and widespread, effectively wiping out the left's political organisation but leaving a deep sense of bitterness. In Roger Magraw's words: 'The future "peasant emperor" had come to power by suppressing the largest rural rising in western Europe in the nineteenth century. Parts of rural France were never to forget or forgive.' [8]

Both the personnel and the policies of the regime were to confirm its close dependence on the elites that had already attained prominence under the Orleanist monarchy. As Jean Lhomme has indicated, the major financial and industrial dynasties retained their influence,[9] while the growing bureaucratic machine, despite efforts to recruit new men with solid Bonapartist sympathies, was largely staffed by established *notables.* In the political sphere many of the leading lights of the 'party of order' like Thiers, Guizot and Molé were swept aside, but their previously little-known successors like Baroche, Fould and Rouher were of substantially the same pedigree. In short, the *grande bourgeoisie,* its position reinforced by the defeat of the 'reds' and the taming of the middle classes, was well-placed to reassert its supremacy.

The period of the Second Empire was, for the most part, to serve business interests well. It undoubtedly represents the most dynamic period of growth and modernisation in nineteenth-century France, with a 50 per cent rise in industrial production and a 150 per cent increase in exports. The change was qualitative as well as quantitative, with the railway boom acting as the major catalyst. Quite apart from its considerable social effects, rail construction eased internal trade and had a major knock-on effect on the coal industry, heavy metallurgy and engineering. In these sectors there was rapid growth, an increasing concentration of capital and high investment, the latter aided by the 'credit revolution' which saw a dramatic expansion of industrial and deposit banking. The construction of canals and roads, land reclamation schemes, urban building projects like that of Haussmann in Paris, helped sustain a high level of industrial activity, and though the process was slowed by the slump of 1856–7 and declining business confidence from the mid-1860s, the period transformed some key industries and even led to considerable agricultural modernisation in some areas of the country.

The state itself played a considerable role in all this, financing public works, subsidising railway construction, encouraging mergers, promoting industrial exhibitions, fostering links between technocratic state bureaucrats and the more adventurous capitalist enterprises. Indeed, with the introduction of a free-trade policy with Britain in 1860, the regime revealed its willingness to challenge the protectionist preferences of some of the most powerful capitalist concerns in order to promote the overall competitiveness of the French economy. The Bonapartist state was forced to take such risks because it claimed to stand above parties and vested interests as an incarnation of the 'general will'. Where Napoleon I had made military glory and foreign conquest the main vehicle for the achievement of national consensus, his nephew offered the country a mission of economic modernisation which he hoped would promote general prosperity and win him the allegiance of all social classes.

THE LIMITS OF BONAPARTIST NATIONALISM

As in the case of the First Empire, the illusion of consensus rested on the construction of an authoritarian state which sought to minimise political activity and to reinforce executive authority at the expense of parliamentary control. True to the Bonapartist tradition of populism, the legitimating façade of universal manhood suffrage was retained, and in a climate of repression and resignation the plebiscite of 21 and 22 December, with its 92 per cent 'yes' vote, was used to justify Louis Napoleon's forcible seizure of power three weeks earlier. Unlike his uncle, Napoleon III also took the risk of retaining universal suffrage for the election every six years of a legislative assembly. However, this concession to principles of popular sovereignty was more apparent than real. Constituencies were gerrymandered and the electoral process closely supervised to the detriment of the opposition. The elected lower house met for only three months of the year, and could not initiate legislation. Ministers were responsible to the Emperor and could not sit in the Assembly. While the Senate was a largely decorative institution, real legislative control lay with the nominated bureaucrats of the *conseil d'état,* and at the local level the prefectoral corps ensured the tutelage of central government over municipal and departmental councils. Political clubs remained banned, the activities of the press were closely supervised, the army and the police apparatus were expanded, and all public officials were expected to act as agents of the regime.

As in 1799, the unity of the democratic nation, undermined by the class antagonisms of the revolutionary process, was converted into an artificial consensus imposed from above. The Bonapartist state sought to incarnate the 'general will' by projecting itself as a neutral agent of the national interest above political and social rivalries. The twin effects of economic prosperity and political repression were designed once again to 'make life easy for the ordinary householder who was content to let the great world of politics go its own way.' [10] However, in a society which was considerably more politicised and more socially divided than it had been under the First Empire, Louis Bonaparte was forced to work hard to win the co-operation of the elites and the acquiesence of the masses. Since the formation of a Bonapartist party would have undermined the apolitical pretensions on which the regime's legitimacy was based, a policy of compromise and the judicious appeasement of potential sources of opposition was an absolute necessity.

As far as the elites were concerned, the most divisive issues recalled those which had troubled the Orleanist political class – free trade and protectionism, religion and liberal political reform, the first two frequently linked to issues of foreign policy. The free trade deal with Britain exposed the traditional textile and metal industries to foreign competition, and stirred the deep anglophobia of republican nationalism, while renewed religious disputes fuelled rivalries over French intervention in Italy.

Catholicism, with its ramifications for educational policy, was undoubtedly the major source of antagonism amongst French elites in this period. In the wake of the 1850 Falloux law, which had extended Catholic secondary education and admitted religious teaching orders to state primary schools, Louis Napoleon allowed the Church a loose rein in the 1850s in the hope of using Catholicism to consolidate his regime. In the event the policy backfired by giving rise to an ultramontane clericalist revival, whose allegiance to Rome and to the reactionary doctrines of the papal *Syllabus of Errors* (1864) undermined loyalty to the state and even lent a new lease of life to legitimism. The consequent anti-clerical backlash, which led to the appointment in 1863 of Duruy, a partisan of secular schools, as Education Minister, led to intensified intra-elite conflict, and Duruy was relieved of his post in 1869 in an effort to retrieve Catholic support for the regime.

As the Empire began to falter, both liberal and conservative elites began to press for political reforms, and in 1869 press controls were relaxed and an ex-Republican, Emile Ollivier, was appointed Chief Minister. The constitutional reforms of the so-called 'liberal Empire', which allowed for parliamentary legislative initiative and a small measure of ministerial accountability, indicated the decline of the regime's autonomy in the face of an Orleanist and Catholic political revival. However, the 40 per cent vote for the opposition groups in the parliamentary elections of 1869 included votes for republicans and socialists as well as liberals and legitimists, reflecting a gradual falling off in mass support for the regime.

Bonapartist populism in the countryside rested above all on the calming effects of relative prosperity and a deliberate and often cynical cultivation of sectional and local peasant interests. Though the effects of religious disputes won the Empire enemies in the more conservative and Catholic regions, and while the legacy of *démocrate-socialiste* influence remained strong in Provence, Languedoc and the Limousin, the peasantry remained the passive bedrock of Bonapartism until the end, voting more solidly for the government majority in 1869 than any other social group.

Louis Napoleon's attempts to woo the urban workers and artisans were less successful, despite his reputation as a social reformer, the decline of unemployment in the 1850s, and the granting of the right to strike in 1864. The regime's promotion of powerful business interests was scarcely compatible with an evenhanded approach to labour disputes, and the general effect of industrial modernisation was to threaten the survival of artisans and craft workers, and to create an impoverished, insecure, badly-housed and diseased factory proletariat in France's growing urban centres. Although these new workers were often resigned and demoralised rather than militant, and although protest was often limited to specific economic demands, the 1860s saw a gradual reconstitution of the network of republican, and sometimes socialist opposition to the regime, in which, as before, the skilled worker and artisan was the key organising element. In 1869 the towns and bourgs consistently voted more heavily against the government than the surrounding countryside, and in Toulouse 80 per cent of the electorate voted for radical republicans.

The regime of Napoleon III rested dangerously on tactical compromises with the elites, on political repression, and on the capacity of the economic climate to lull the masses into passivity. At the heart of the system was an ideological vacuum and, in contrast to the First Empire, there was no charismatic personality to fill the void. Following his coup, Louis Bonaparte had announced *L'Empire, c'est la paix'*, but it was perhaps inevitable that the temptation of using foreign policy to cement national unity and to sustain the Napoleonic myth would prove too great. Traditional Bonapartist hostility to the Habsburgs and to the 1815 settlement, along with the Emperor's sentimental attachment to the cause of Italian nationalism, pointed to a policy that could attract liberal and republican sympathies. On the other hand, the need for British friendship and the threat of a powerful nascent Germany on France's eastern frontiers pointed to a very different strategy.

In the event the foreign policy of the Empire was contradictory, frequently rash, increasingly devoid of principle, and above all geared to domestic opinion. The Crimean expedition of 1856 with Britain against Russia was a success, but the intervention in Italy in 1859 on behalf of Piedmont against the Habsburgs was an embarrassment. Any pretence of aiding the cause of Italian unity was sabotaged by demands for the annexation of Nice and Savoy, and finally under Catholic pressure the army was used to defend the remaining Papal territories in Rome. Purely verbal support for the Polish rebellion of 1863 served to alienate Russia, and the Mexican expedition, designed to appease Catholic opinion by imposing a traditionalist monarchy on an unwilling Mexican nation, ended in military disaster. The final chapter came with the emergence of a new German nation following Prussia's defeat of Austria in 1866. With Britain and Russia alienated, and a weakened Austria refusing to be drawn into an alliance against Germany, Louis Napoleon's attempts to recover prestige drew an isolated France into a war against Prussia for which it was ill-equipped and ill-prepared.

THE PARIS COMMUNE

The question of whether the Second Empire would have fallen but for military defeat has been hotly debated by historians. It is certainly true that the government majority remained solid until the end, and it is at least arguable that the constitutional reforms of 1869 might have opened the way to something approaching a liberal-democratic regime, albeit under the auspices of an emperor whose dynasty was far from secure. However, as has already been suggested, 'liberalism' in this context did not imply a shift to the left but rather a concession to

Orleanist and Catholic *notables* who, alarmed by the resurgence of the republican and labour movements, were intent on regaining a direct political influence over government. The likelihood that such a development would have been acceptable to the wider political community seems remote, given the fate that had met regimes of this type in 1830 and 1848.

In the event, the military defeat of 1870 allowed such an eventuality to be by-passed. As soon as news reached Paris of the Emperor's surrender to the Prussians at Sedan, a Republic was proclaimed. The political circumstances were, however, very different from those which had inaugurated the Second Republic in 1848. The formal existence of universal manhood suffrage under Louis Bonaparte had deprived the republican movement of one of its main unifying themes, while the class struggles of 1848–52 had driven a wedge between the moderates of the 'official' Republic and the radicals, and had laid the foundations for an embryonic socialist and labour movement in the 1860s which was far more suspicious than ever before of an alliance with the progressive middle classes.

The need for a broad anti-Bonapartist front had allowed such an alliance gradually to take shape, and it was largely confirmed by the voting behaviour of workers in 1869. However, the republican platform offered few hopes of social reform, concentrating largely on the themes of anti-clericalism and secular education which had again achieved prominence thanks to the insidious progress of Catholic clericalism under the Second Empire. Though such issues had some appeal for workers, who saw the influence of priests and Catholic schools as an obstacle to their emancipation, they were hardly the basis for long-term political co-operation.

The main source of potential unity was the war itself, and the new Government of National Defence clearly hoped that the traditions of republican patriotism would weld a new sense of national solidarity. However, while the Minister of the Interior, Léon Gambetta, organised military resistance and struggled unsuccessfully to stem the Prussian advance, other more moderate ministers were more concerned by the potentially revolutionary situation in Paris, where the militant defiance of workers and *petits bourgeois* was stirred rather than reduced by the hardships of war. While officially prosecuting the war, the government was secretly seeking an end to the hostilities with a view to holding national elections which would reduce its dependence on the capital. Tensions increased as Paris was put under siege, and when news came of a further French surrender by a suspect Bonapartist general at Metz in October 1870, the government was forced to put down a socialist revolt in the city.

Things came decisively to a head in January 1871, when Adolphe Thiers successfully sealed an armistice, paving the way for elections, a new government and a peace treaty with Prussia. What followed the capitulation enraged the people of Paris who had suffered intense deprivation for their patriotic convictions. The peace treaty brought a partial, temporary Prussian occupation, heavy reparations and the loss of Alsace and Lorraine. When elections were held on 6 February, the royalists, who had been campaigning for peace, won heavy rural support and a sizeable parliamentary majority, while in Paris a massive majority for radicals and socialists confirmed the city's continuing support for the continuation of the war. Fearing a restoration of the monarchy, and further antagonised by govenment measures suspending payments to the Paris National Guard and lifting the moratorium on debts and rents in the capital, the Paris populace were driven to violent revolt in March when government troops tried to confiscate cannon purchased by public subscription. Municipal elections in the city gave 80 per cent support to the left, and the Paris Commune proclaimed its defiance of the government, now symbolically removed to the former royal palace of Versailles.

There has been much historical debate as to how far the Paris Commune was genuinely 'socialist', and Marx himself was later to revise his initial view of it as the precursor of the future workers' state. It was, of course, the mixed product of exceptional circumstances, but the harsher revisionist judgements tend to expect too much from a municipal government which survived less than three months and whose main preoccupation was inevitably that of defending itself against impending military assault. While it is true that the emphasis on anti-clerical issues like secular schooling and separation of Church and state reflected the presence of substantial *petit bourgeois* elements in the movement, some forty co-operatives were established in the capital and factories abandoned by their capitalist owners were taken over. Even more significant was the recruitment of working-class political cadres at every level, culminating in the elected Commune itself where nearly half the members were workers. Mass meetings made revolutionary demands, and the principles of direct democracy, with their emphasis on the popular control of all public officials, challenged the limited bourgeois concepts of representative government.

Inevitably in this context, the historical example of the *sans-culotte* movement of 1792–3 was often invoked. *Le Père Duchêne,* the radical people's newspaper of that earlier period, was revived, and the convergence of the themes of popular sovereignty and patriotic struggle were bound to stir folk-memories of the heroic phase of the Great Revolution. Students of the French revolutionary tradition find it tempting to trace these lines of continuity, and a similar temptation arises when the events are examined in relation to the 'national question'. In class terms, however, the two situations were qualitatively different, not least because the social bases of popular urban radicalism were now increasingly 'working-class' rather than simply 'plebeian'.

The demands of the *sans-culottes* had, of course, sharpened the antagonisms within the revolutionary movement and had led eventually to confrontation with the Jacobin state, which under the Great Terror purged and closed the popular sections in Paris. However, this conflict was not perceived primarily in terms of class. The *sans-culottes,* like the middle-class radicals, were inspired by the moral egalitarianism of the ideal of democratic nationhood. For them, the Revolution and then the Republic should have brought the reign of *virtue* and justice in which elected representatives would be the servants of the people. That this was not the case was due to the corrupting influences of counter-revolution, and the human failings of those in whom trust had been placed to defend certain unequivocal principles of liberty and equality. In short, there was an underlying faith in the capacity of generous ideas and values to transcend social divisions and forge a new democratic nation.

The French utopian socialists of the mid-nineteenth century were imbued with this same faith, and this implied a very different articulation of the national question from that later developed by Marxism. While Marxist doctrines of class struggle denied national loyalties, the utopian dream of social reconciliation on a moral basis retained the ideal of national consensus. At the same time, while Marxism preached internationalism, French socialists like Pecqueur and Blanc shared with the republican Michelet the image of France as the 'universal nation', whose aspirations merged with those of mankind and which was destined to lead humanity towards a higher civilisation.[11]

This complex heritage was manifested in the leadership of the Paris Commune, where radical republicans, insurrectionary socialists, federalists and internationalists reflected the diverse influences of Jacobinism, Blanquism, Proudhonism and Marxism.[12] Concrete historical circumstances were, however, a more decisive factor in shaping attitudes. Economic change had created the conditions for the emergence of working-class consciousness, and the political experience of the previous twenty-five years had accelerated the process. Class antagonism had been sharpened by the 'June days' and by the ensuing period of capitalist modernisation, and the republican alliance with the middle classes no longer came naturally. The events of September 1870–March 1871 had confirmed the growing gulf between even the more progressive middle-class republicans and an increasingly socialist Paris working class. The latter had shed the illusions of democratic national consensus, and the Commune marks the genesis of a distinctive 'class politics' on the left.

This was evident even on the theme of patriotic defence. Though committed to the continuation of the war, the Commune symbolically decreed and enacted the demolition of the Vendôme column erected by the Empire, denouncing it as

> a monument of barbarism, a symbol of brute force and false
> glory, an affirmation of militarism, a denial of international law,
> a permanent insult directed at the conquered by their conquerors,
> a perpetual attack upon one of the three great principles of the
> French Republic.[13]

This was the most eloquent statement yet of what distinguished the democratic movement from a Bonapartist tradition with which it had uneasily overlapped in the past. Underpinned by the Babouvist traditions of defensive war and citizens' militia, *communard* patriotism was anti-imperialist and anti-militarist, and indeed the collusion between the Versailles government and the Prussian invader rapidly transformed resistance to foreign occupation into a social and political challenge to bourgeois rule.

At the same time, in the various debates conducted inside the Commune on the means of extending the Revolution from Paris to the rest of France, the traditional centralising principles of the Jacobins and Blanquists were increasingly challenged by new federalist and municipalist ideas. The Commune called on the people of other major towns to rise up in support, and envisaged a network of autonomous socialist communes which would act as revolutionary poles for radicals in the countryside and which would pave the way for a new federated socialist Republic. Though this can be seen as a logical response to an unfavourable political situation in which the Versailles government held most of the cards, it also reflects a growing recognition of the practical realities of class politics, a rejection of the republican myth of national solidarity. Furthermore, the strategy appealed to the expanding practice of worker self-organisation in co-operatives, trade unions and friendly societies, itself a confirmation of declining dependence on middle-class leadership.

As Marx himself recognised, the Commune was doomed to fail because the working class was not sufficiently developed to provide political leadership for the other subordinate classes. Sister communes were established in a number of other towns, including Marseilles, Lyon, Toulouse and St Etienne, but although in the southern provinces the Versailles government was often genuinely unpopular, the deadweight of conservative rural France ultimately left Paris isolated. The reoccupation of the city by Thiers' troops in May was accompanied by ruthless repression, directed above all against workers and leaving 100,000 dead, jailed or exiled.

In the short term, the effects were to deprive the socialist and labour movement of its most energetic cadres, and to marginalise it politically for more than a decade. For a far longer period, however, at least until the turn of the century, the fate of the Paris commune created a legacy of bitterness which widened the gap between socialism and republicanism and indeed alienated the working class from the political 'nation'. While still conscious of its own 'national' revolutionary traditions, the workers' movement shed many of its illusions about the efficacy of class alliances *inside* the nation in favour of internationalist perspectives.

6

THE THIRD REPUBLIC AND THE NATION

> The fatherland is France in the past, France in the present, France
> in the future. I love it with all my heart, with an exclusive and
> jealous affection.
>
> (Ernest Lavisse)

Historians of French nationalism have always paid more attention to
the years *after* 1870 than to the earlier period. The works of Girardet,
Guillemin and Hoffmann,[1] which are conspicuous in a relatively under-
researched field, all choose the founding of the Third Republic as their
point of departure. Similarly, general histories of modern France do not
normally begin to use the term nationalism with any frequency until
they reach the 1890s, when sections of the French right explicitly
adopted the nomenclature of 'nationalist'.

This tells us a great deal about conventional interpretations of
nationalism, which for so many is irrevocably associated with chauvinism, imperialism and militarism, the attitudes which paved the way
for the bloodbath of 1914. Enough has already been said to indicate my
theoretical reservations on this point, and I will not reopen the question
here. I have, in any case, my own reasons for according more detailed
attention to this period than to any previous one. For between 1870 and
1914 the ideological and class character of nationalism undergoes a
profound transformation, which though foreshadowed earlier only
becomes clearly visible in these years.

THE BIRTH OF THE THIRD REPUBLIC

The circumstances surrounding the birth of the Third Republic were
hardly auspicious – military defeat and occupation, revolution in the
capital, a royalist parliamentary majority. And yet the regime was to

75

last for seventy years and to provide France with its longest period of constitutional stability. This anomaly was, however, more apparent than real, for three reasons.

First, the royalist victory at the polls in February 1871 was above all a vote for peace rather than an endorsement of monarchy. Indeed, once the republican Thiers had negotiated an armistice with the Prussians, the royalists could no longer make capital out of the image of a 'bellicose' Republic, and their political position was effectively undermined. Some of the more hard-headed Orleanists recognised that any immediate attempt to restore the monarchy would be dangerously provocative, and the possibility of doing so was further circumscribed by the continuing rivalry of the two royalist factions. Attempts at a dynastic compromise fell on the symbolic issue of the future royal flag,[2] but behind this lay deeper ideological and class antagonisms, reflected in different conceptions of monarchy itself. Where for legitimists monarchy was a moral imperative, for Orleanists it was above all a pragmatic institutional vehicle for the preservation of class rule.

The willingness of the Orleanists to play a waiting game drew them into a tacit alliance with the conservative republicans, who were themselves intent on preventing any further radicalisation of the Republic by building into the new constitution a variety of checks on the powers of the elected Assembly. This brings us to the second factor in the new regime's survival, namely its growing respectability. Thiers had not only ended the hostilities, he had also crushed the radical challenge of the Paris Commune. These two acts had done much to allay the traditional conservative fear that republics inevitably brought war, anarchy and social disorder. Though the royalists ousted Thiers in 1873 and elected the anti-republican McMahon as President, by the early 1880s many Orleanists, like Thiers himself before them, had become reconciled to the Republic.

The constitutional laws of 1873–5 had established a seven-year presidency with strong executive powers, and a part-nominated, part-indirectly elected Senate, both designed to limit the powers of a Chamber of Deputies based on universal manhood suffrage. However, a third and decisive development was not only to give the new regime popular legitimacy, but to transform the balance of powers implied by the constitution. In the legislative elections of 1876, the various republican groups won a sizeable majority in the Chamber which they were never again to lose. The twin effects of Thiers' reassuring conservatism and Gambetta's anti-clerical and anti-monarchist idealism won over broad ranks of the peasantry and middle classes, who increasingly saw the Republic as a better guarantee of order and stability than the disruptive and divisive prospect of royal restoration.

The monarchists, however, were unwilling to accept the principle of parliamentary sovereignty, which would jeopardise their hopes of eventually replacing a strong president by a King. President McMahon thus refused to nominate the leader of the new republican majority, Léon Gambetta, as head of government, opting instead for Jules Simon. The latter was soon forced to resign his post and, when the Chamber refused to endorse his replacement, the royalist Duc de Broglie, McMahon used his constitutional powers to dissolve the Assembly and call new elections in 1877. Against a background of constitutional crisis, with rumours of royalist and military plots, the President openly campaigned for a monarchist victory, only to be rebuffed when the new elections confirmed the republican majority. His eventual submission to the will of parliament marked the end of any realistic possibility of a restoration of the monarchy. The royalists lost control of the town halls when elections were introduced for the office of mayor, and this in turn republicanised the electoral colleges which chose the senators. The royalist defeat in the senatorial elections of 1879 deprived them of their last remaining representative bastion.

This sequence of events also had a decisive effect on the institutional evolution of the regime. Thereafter, no President of the Republic would ever again dare to use his constitutional powers of dissolution, and with rare exceptions the office was henceforth confined to purely formal and ceremonial functions. Executive authority passed in principle to the prime minister, or *Vice-Président du Conseil,* whose power was, however, firmly circumscribed by the constraints of parliamentary procedure and the shifting alliances of parliamentary politics. The main locus of sovereignty was the elected Chamber of Deputies, though the restraining influence of a conservative Senate, equipped with full legislative powers, indirectly elected, and heavily biased in favour of rural France, frequently made itself felt.

THE BOURGEOIS REPUBLIC

In terms of class, the political transition effected between 1871 and 1879 has been seen by Jean Lhomme as marking the end of the *grande bourgeoisie's* domination of the institutions of state.[3] The political groupings which most clearly represented its class interests, namely the Orleanists and the conservative republicans, had supposedly lost the battle to insulate elite authority against the intrusions of liberal democracy. It is certainly true that the establishment of a parliamentary regime based on universal manhood suffrage brought about a considerable renewal of political personnel, and allowed members of the provincial middle classes into ministerial and other influential positions. It is also true that electoral politics obliged deputies and governments to respond to a wider range of social interests than had been the case under monarchy or empire. However, Lhomme's conclusion requires some qualification.

First, the *grand bourgeoisie* retained considerable economic leverage under a regime which, unlike its relatively *dirigiste* predecessor, sought to mediate between vested interests rather than attempt to impose dynamic leadership. The long recession of 1865–96 did not favour the growth of new capitalist strata capable of challenging the position of the entrenched economic elites, and this persistence of France's dual economic structure meant that the capacity to invest and modernise was largely confined to firms that were already well-established. Secondly, although *grands bourgeois* were less prominent than before among both national and local political *notables,* they continued to dominate the *grandes écoles* and thus retained a powerful presence in the upper ranks of the state bureaucracy. This administrative influence was significant under a regime where political leadership was weak thanks to the instability of parliamentary majorities.

It is, of course, true that the Republic had to appease the aspirations of the broad middle classes and the peasantry in order to confirm its popular legitimacy. The gradual leftward shift of the regime's political centre of gravity away from the Thiers-style conservatives to the so-called 'opportunists' like Ferry, and eventually after the turn of the century to the Radical Party, reflected this democratic imperative. This process inevitably brought conflict, and the rhetoric of radical republicanism often inveighed not only against clerical and royalist reaction but also on behalf of the 'little man' against the power of capitalist 'monopolies'.

However, the real divisions in republican politics did not follow class lines. The renewed debate over protectionism and free trade set sector against sector, even firm against firm, rather than *grand* against *moyen* and *petit* bourgeois. In this respect it reflected the normal clash of sectional and individual interests in capitalist society, and it was resolved by piecemeal compromise. As Magraw points out, the Méline tariffs of 1892 were highly selective, and made France 'less monolithically protectionist than USA, Germany, Italy, Spain or Russia.'[4]

Similarly, the strictly political bones of contention like attitudes to the Church and indeed to the parliamentary Republic itself, cut across class barriers to follow cultural lines carved out by religious and regional divisions. Protestant and liberal free-thinking traditions were to be found in *grand bourgeois* circles, while in many areas clericalist and royalist loyalties lived on among the middle classes and the peasantry, and even among urban workers. The secularisation of education initiated by Jules Ferry in the early 1880s was itself a compromise, anti-clerical rather than anti-Catholic as such, and refusing the more radical call for the separation of Church and state. Similarly, the radical republican demand for the abolition of the Senate, regarded by them as a vestige of royalist influence, ceased to be a priority after the Boulanger Affair at the end of the 1880s.

To conclude, the new Republic should be seen as an expression of the collective interests of the French bourgeoisie rather than as the victory of the middle classes over large-scale capitalist interests. If the *grande bourgeoisie* lost some of its direct political leverage, it benefited from the newly-won legitimacy of a regime that was established on solid capitalist principles of private property and economic liberalism. The *nouvelles couches* invoked by Gambetta in his republican campaigns of 1876 and 1877 were not new 'classes' with economic interests that were antagonistic to the social order. They were the broad ranks of provincial businessmen, independent producers and tradesmen, tea-chers, civil servants, lawyers and property-owning peasants, who had hitherto been denied a political voice in the running of a capitalist society. This was the new 'political' nation, and it was the basis of a wide social consensus. As late as 1914, 43 per cent of the male working population were still engaged in agriculture, while in 1911 42 per cent of the total active population were classified as *patrons* living off their own means as opposed to those who lived off the sale of their labour in one form or another.

Economic liberalism has, of course, always been diluted in France by traditions of state intervention, and the Third Republic, though less dynamic in this regard than other regimes, was forced to arbitrate, above all on the issue of protectionism. In another crucial respect, however, *laissez faire* principles were allowed much fuller rein, namely in the social domain where, right up until 1914, France remained more backward than either Britain or Germany. Redistributive tax policies were avoided, labour relations were largely abandoned to the market mechanism, and problems of urban squalor and unemployment never received political priority.

It was above all in this neglect of the working class that the *bourgeois* nature of the republican consensus was underlined. For all but the most radical of republicans, the 'social question' simply did not exist. Universal suffrage, parliamentary democracy, secular education, freedom of association, and finally, in 1884, the legalisation of trade unions, had allegedly given to workers the tools of their own emancipation and the means of individual advancement. If Guizot had once proclaimed that personal economic success was the necessary qualification for the award of political rights, the Republic now insisted that political rights were a sufficient guarantee of formal social equality.

THE IDEOLOGY OF REPUBLICANISM

With the Third Republic, republicanism ceased to be a movement incarnating unfulfilled aspirations and became instead the official ideology of the state. After nearly a century of struggle, the principles of 1789 had allegedly at last been established on a firm constitutional basis. There were of course those on the radical wing of republicanism who believed that more remained to be done, and that the 'official' Republic did not yet measure up to the democratic ideals of the Great Revolution. However, the threat of clerical-royalist reaction, and later that of socialism, tended to drive these left republicans to the centre in defence of the regime. Gambetta soon abandoned the social reformism of the 1869 Belleville programme, claiming that the very existence of political democracy had resolved the 'social question'. While radicals in the 1870s and 1880s continued to call for co-operatives, welfare provision and state economic intervention, and campaigned for trade union rights and an amnesty for the *communards,* by the time a nationally organised Radical Party was formed in 1901 such social themes had largely been displaced by the rhetoric of anti-clericalism and 'defence of the Republic'.

There has been considerable historical debate as to whether the social concerns of early radicalism were based on genuine idealism or on an opportunistic attempt to win working-class support.[5] Such arguments are somewhat secondary, however, once it is recognised that in practice radicalism aligned itself with the underlying ethos of the capitalist order. Its ideology was individualist rather than collectivist, and its largely middle-class and peasant clientele was strongly attached to the principles of private property. Sincere or otherwise, its social reformism was inconsistent with its dominant political philosophy and with its electoral base. The consolidation of French capitalism and the establishment of liberal democracy had widened the social and ideological divide between radical republicanism and the socialist workers' movement.

The various shades of republicanism, from conservative to radical, were thus bound together by a bourgeois social consensus which largely confined intra-class conflict to discrete issues like education, Church–state relations, and foreign and colonial policy. Despite continuing harrassment from the reactionary right and the emergence of a more class-conscious socialist left, the Republic rested on a growing constituency of shared values and common preoccupations. Its efforts to secure its legitimacy reflect both this sense of social unanimity, and the determination to close the chapter of revolution and political upheaval. Gambetta, once seen by conservatives as a dangerous radical with socialist leanings, proclaimed that republicanism was the 'conservative party which assures the legal and peaceful working-out of the French Revolution.' [6] *Marianne,* that icon of the revolutionary republic and once 'part of the standard repertoire of opposition and contestation',[7] had by the 1880s shed her red liberty bonnet for a 'a halo of flowers and the motto *Concorde.*' [8]

In the words of Roger Magraw, 'the Republic was portrayed as the natural alliance of healthy, productive, useful capitalists with rising *nouvelles couches* – lawyers, doctors, teachers, peasants. Only the Republic could reconcile "sacred property rights" with the legitimate aspirations of the masses.' [9] The peasantry, which remained the key mass constituency, was crucial to the regime's legitimacy, and there were many reasons why it should be receptive to republican values. Republicanism, shed of its former radical associations, was able to exploit long-standing peasant grievances against surviving aristocratic and clerical influence in the countryside, free of accusations that it was the tool of 'red' Paris. Though royalist enclaves survived, especially in the west, and though socialism was making some progress in rural Languedoc, Limousin and Provence, peasants increasingly rallied to a socially conservative Republic which left their traditional individualism largely intact while offering them new channels of influence, representation and even personal advancement.

In his famous work *Peasants into Frenchmen,*[10] Eugen Weber has analysed what he saw as the *integration* of the peasantry into national political life under the Third Republic. Whatever the flaws in this thesis, there can be no doubt that the years 1870–1914 were a decisive formative period in the shaping of rural political attitudes. The integration argument does, of course, make light of the evidence of genuine rural class conflict, but it is clear that the development of clientele politics in a deputy-centred Republic drew many peasants into the mainstream of bourgeois political debate. Education, local politics and expanding public services widened peasant horizons and opened new career opportunities, while issues like agricultural protectionism and anti-clericalism forged new political alliances between the peasantry and the local business and professional community. The overall effect was to loosen dependence on traditional royalist and clerical elites, and to undermine patterns of rural deference and passivity.

Weber saw the key agencies of this 'modernisation' process as the extension of the railway network, military conscription, and free, compulsory, primary education. Mass schooling was inevitably seen by the republican state as a key vehicle of political legitimation, and above all as a means of combating the pernicious influence of the Church in this domain. Under the Second Empire and indeed during the early 'moral order' years (1871–6) of the Third Republic, an ultramontane clergy, reinforced by the reactionary doctrines emanating from the Vatican in the 1860s, had extended its influence in all sectors of education. The Ferry laws of the early 1880s brought higher education back under lay control, secularised both the teaching personnel and the syllabus in the state primary schools, and undermined Church influence in secondary education by banning certain Catholic teaching orders.

Anti-clericalism was the key mobilising theme of the Republic from the mid-1870s until the Separation of Church and state in 1905. In tactical terms it served a useful purpose for republican politicians who wanted to deflect attention from divisive social issues and cement unity by focusing on the threat posed by the anti-republican right. However, far from being just an opportunistic device, it was central to the whole ideology of bourgeois republicanism. Where the Church preached spirituality, humility and tradition, it proclaimed the values of rationalism and science, faith in human progress, the rights of the individual, the capacity of man to manage his own affairs. Something approaching a counter-religion was created. The newly-trained primary school teachers, posted to hostile clerical territory, were often compared to missionaries, while the expanding masonic lodges were the temples of free thought. Their ideas struck a deep chord in rural communities where the influence of clerical and aristocratic elites kept alive peasant fears of the return of 'feudalism'. Anti-clericalism often expressed peasant emancipation from a state of dependence, a new self-confidence nurtured by the practice of political rights.

REPUBLIC AND NATION

The new state schools were, of course, crucial to the inculcation of these republican principles and to the forging of national identity. The teaching of civic morality filled the gap left by religious instruction, and this involved no less than a reworking of French history in line with prevailing bourgeois values. The legitimacy of the regime depended in part on the claim that it was the final fulfilment of the revolutionary tradition of 1789, so official interpretations of the Great Revolution were tailored to this end. In particular the popular movement of 1793, so long an inspiration to socialists, was presented as a struggle to *defend* the achievements of 1789 rather than as an attempt to *transcend* those achievements. 'The Revolution is a bloc' insisted Clemenceau before the Chamber of Deputies in 1891, while the great historian Alphonse Aulard wrote that 'the Revolution consists of the Declaration of Rights, drawn up in 1789 and completed in 1793, and of attempts to put it into effect.' [11] The internal class antagonisms of the revolutionary movement were played down in the interests of a consensual bourgeois version of the Revolution.

Of course, in the famous primary school textbooks of Lavisse these subtleties were framed in cruder, more simplistic terms. The Revolution was provoked by the *méchants seigneurs,* and it brought 'liberty', 'equality', 'justice' and 'humanity'. Its internal struggles were translated in the manichean language of the good and the bad. More strikingly, however, as Suzanne Citron has pointed out, the Revolution arrives unannounced in a text which has made no mention of the Enlightenment, and which has hitherto invited pupils to admire Clovis, Charlemagne and Richelieu, 'the great men of "eternal France", Catholic and imperialist.' [12] *1789* is not presented as a decisive break with the past, but simply as a stage in France's evolving destiny. The continuity is supplied by the constant emphasis on *l'héroïsme guerrier* and *la grandeur de la France,* Lavisse's key leitmotiv, and the ideals of courage and sacrifice are for him the essence of the Revolution. It is significant that he never uses the word *nation,* vibrant with political significance, preferring that of *patrie,* the ethnic homeland stretching back to the time of the Gauls and the Franks.

This refashioning of national identity, with its emphasis on native patriotism and its reconnection with the pre-revolutionary era, hardly corresponds to the image cultivated by monarchists of a subversive, anti-clerical, republican education. The enterprise can be explained at two levels. First it may be seen as an attempt to widen social consensus beyond even the confines of republican politics, by emphasising ethnic loyalties and invoking the image of an 'eternal' France. Secondly, it represents a response to injured national pride following defeat in the Franco-Prussian war, a potentially explosive issue which threatened to undermine a Republic intent on peace and stability.

While the armistice with Prussia was essential to the early consolidation of the Republic, the humiliating terms of the post-war settlement were in the longer run to provide a new focus for opposition to the regime. Thiers had negotiated the Prussian release of French prisoners to help crush the Commune, had agreed to a heavy war indemnity, and worst of all had accepted the German annexation of Alsace-Lorraine. Republican politicians, including that erstwhile symbol of patriotic defence Léon Gambetta, were anxious throughout the 1870s to identify themselves with the cause of peace in order to avoid antagonising Bismarck. The official Republic's apparent neglect of what one author has referred to as the *mystique patriotique*,[13] which along with the *mystique sociale* had been a vital ingredient of radical republicanism, opened the way to a new form of nationalism which during the period of the Boulanger and Dreyfus affairs was to reshape the ideological cleavages in French society (see Chapter 7).

Faced with this potentially dangerous undercurrent of anti-German *revanchisme,* the moderate republican leaders had to steer a course between the need to establish the regime's patriotic credentials as the representative of the national interest on the one hand, and the risks of confrontation with its more powerful neighbour on the other. As Stanley Hoffman has perceptively indicated, the diplomatic choices open to the Third Republic revolved around four interrelated sets of alternatives, strategic, spatial, temporal and moral.[14] Should it adopt a traditional 'balance of power' strategy, or should it offer principled support for nationalist movements in the hope of weakening its major rivals? Should it remain fixated with the 'blue line of the Vosges' or should it look to colonial expansion as an alternative means of retrieving lost status? Should it actively prepare for an early war, or patiently build alliances and wait for a more favourable balance of forces? Finally, should the desire for power and revenge be an end in itself, or did the humanist values of republicanism decree that only a defensive war was legitimate?

The positions adopted by republican politicians on these issues in the last quarter of the nineteenth century frequently antagonised the converging ranks of popular *revanchistes* and conservative militarists, as we shall see in the next chapter. However, as Hoffmann points out, from the 1880s onwards there was more than one way of being a 'good patriot', and the image of a Republic led by pacifists and appeasers is largely a right-wing myth created by historians like the monarchist Bainville.[15] In reality the cult of *la patrie* was a central feature of state ideology and its symbolism was everywhere – from the black crêpe which veiled the statue of Strasbourg in the Place de la Concorde to the schoolroom where children chanted patriotic songs and learnt their history from Lavisse. While public education was not as overtly militaristic as hard-line *revanchistes* would have liked, there is no doubt that boys were taught to admire soldierly virtues, to accept their patriotic 'duties' and to look forward to the day when they would don the uniform. The popularity of youth organisations with strong military overtones was testimony to the successful inculcation of these official values.

For opponents on the right, of course, the patriotism of the Republic was an ideological smokescreen. Beneath the rhetoric of love of country they saw a policy of submission and resignation, and Jules Ferry's sponsorship of colonial expansion in Africa and Indo-China was regarded as a deliberate diversion from the obligation of *revanche*. Whatever the relative merits of the arguments over foreign policy, there is no doubt that the 'nationalism' of the republican leadership was geared above all to the requirements of internal politics. The regime sought legitimacy through self-identification with the *intérêt général,* and this involved nothing less than a redefinition of national identity in order to reflect the widest possible social consensus. The Republic and France must be indissolubly linked. Cultural uniformity must be achieved through the agency of a standardised educational and adminis-trative apparatus. And central to this common culture was an official patriotic discourse designed to offend as few people as possible.

Behind the symbolism of Marianne and the insignia of *liberté, egalité, fraternité,* the official appeal to national loyalty contained little that was specifically 'republican'! The regime claimed to have completed the work of the Revolution, and in its quest for consensus it sought to drain the concept of nation of divisive political connotations. The textbooks of Lavisse skate over the contradictions by personalising an eternal, abstract, 'France', sometimes equated with 'state' and sometimes with 'people', abused by evil leaders and rescued by exceptional heroes, moving inexorably through absolutism and revolution in fulfilment of her glorious destiny. The famous and widely-read *Le Tour de la France par deux enfants,*[16] published in 1871 under the pseudonym of G. Bruno and described by one historian as the 'little red book' of the Republic,[17] makes only one reference to the French Revolution, in a section on the life of Lavoisier!

Instead of the image of the democratic 'nation' forged in the fires of revolution, we find the bland 'depoliticised' notion of *la patrie,* rooted historically in the ethnic obscurity of Gauls and Franks and temperamentally in a tradition of heroism and sacrifice. Michelet's vision of France as the universal nation, the harbinger of civilisation, was thus appropriated for the conservative purpose of ideological integration. Catholic, imperial France and modern democratic France were united in the historic role of civilising a barbaric world.

This is, of course, much more than apolitical native patriotism, the natural affection for one's familiar spatial environment. The promotion of admiration for military virtues, the chauvinist juxtaposition of French culture and German barbarism, the racist presentation of France's 'civilising' mission in the new colonies, made these texts highly ideological in their content. As Suzanne Citron has noted:

> Lavisse's history of France offers the very opposite of a democratic education. The structure of the narrative is defined by 'France', an abstract deity, sometimes worshipped, sometimes blamed, but never inviting the qualities of lucidity, critical reflection, tolerance. She never encourages initiative or participation. She invokes the spirit of war and sacrifice, never that of intelligent and constructive creativity.[18]

The 'nationalism' of the official Republic thus has little in common with that of the democratic movement in the first half of the nineteenth century. Its primary purpose was that of bourgeois class consolidation, but until the turn of the century it sought long-term cultural integration and did not assume the guise of an aggressive, overtly political ideology. The passage of nationalism from left to right was not yet complete. To understand how that process was effected, attention must be paid to the ideological sea-change which occurred in the 1880s and 1890s on the extreme right of the political spectrum.

7

THE RIGHT AND THE
NATION 1870–1914

A nationalist who is conscious of his role accepts as a rule of thumb that a good citizen subordinates his feelings, his interests and his system of beliefs to the good of the Fatherland.

(Charles Maurras)

A nationalist is a Frenchman who has become aware of what has formed him. Nationalism is the acceptance of a determinism.

(Maurice Barrès)

The royalist right had secured a parliamentary majority in 1871 on the basis of a campaign for peace, and this was more than simple political opportunism. It was entirely consistent with the right's well-established hostility to a nationalist tradition which had hitherto been solidly identified with republicanism. By the turn of the century the picture had been utterly transformed, and nationalism was on the way to becoming the central unifying theme of conservative politics. This remarkable political and ideological realignment on the French right is the subject of this chapter.

ANTI-REPUBLICANISM

As we have already seen, the chances of a royal restoration diminished rapidly in the wake of dynastic squabbles and the growing respectability of a socially conservative Republic. Monarchist representation in the National Assembly fell from nearly 400 to only 150 with the republican election victory of 1876. The death of the Bourbon pretender, the childless Comte de Chambord, in 1883, marked the end of the legitimist line, and Bonapartism too was deprived of any credible figurehead when the death of Louis Napoléon in 1873 was followed by that of the prince imperial in 1879. This left the Orleanist Comte de

Paris as the only potential dynastic challenger to the regime, but he became an increasingly marginal political figure as Orleanists drifted into the conservative republican camp in the closing years of the nineteenth century.

However, the dwindling prospects of monarchism did not immediately break the hold of established anti-republican attitudes on the right. The legacy of previous political traditions, hostile to the principles of democratic control, was deeply entrenched in certain milieux. The upper echelons of the military establishment and of public administration were still dominated by royalists of various persuasions, and the financial and industrial *haute bourgeoisie* had developed in an era when republicanism was regarded as a dangerous and subversive force. Fashionable Paris society, and not least its intellectual life, was in the 1870s solidly identified with the anti-republican values of these military, financial and administrative elites, while in the provinces the Catholic Church, through the influence of its clergy and teaching orders, bolstered the position of the surviving royalist landowners and contrived to enlist the support of part of the peasantry and middle classes.

Deprived of a dynastic focus, the emphasis of anti-republicanism became more ideological, a critical counter-culture fighting a rearguard action in defence of crumbling values and hierarchies. The key elements of this opposition are already familiar – contempt for the 'abstract' ideas of 1789 in favour of a 'natural' social inequality, disdain for upstart republican politicians and for the whole ethos of political democracy. These elitist prejudices still found a popular echo in those parts of the country where deference, ignorance, or fear tied the masses to the traditional *notables*. However, the most powerful agent of popular hostility towards the regime was Catholicism. The years of so-called Moral Order (1871–6) saw a theocratic crusade that recalled the times of Charles X. In the words of Roger Magraw, 'with 51,000 secular clergy, 157,000 regulars and control of 40 per cent of school pupils, the church had reached the apogee of its nineteenth-century power.' [1] Against the rationalism and humanism of the republican ideal, the Church had recourse to a political mysticism which blamed military defeat on the collective guilt of a 'godless nation' and called for an atonement based on faith, humility and self-abnegation.

As in the past this clericalist anti-republicanism had no room for the invocation of 'nationhood', that doctrine of self-determination which epitomised human arrogance. With the state in the hands of the republicans and the prospect of royal restoration receding, the anti-republican right once again played the card of regionalist particularism and resistance to what it presented as the internal colonialism of the republican political establishment. At the same time, inspired by the 1864 Syllabus, the 1870 Declaration of Papal Infallibility and the Vatican's outlawing of the Republic in 1877, the clergy looked to Rome for its moral authority, and these ultramontane tendencies increasingly marginalised the more liberal and Gallican traditions in the French Church. In the wake of Italian unification, there was talk again in right-wing circles of a holy war to restore the Temporal Power of the Pope.

However, the consolidation of the Republic after 1879 progressively drove this aggressive, reactionary and obscurantist Catholicism back into its traditional regional bastions. The railways, military conscription, the development of electoral and clientelist politics, and above all mass secular schooling gradually reduced illiteracy and geographical isolation, diluted regionalist loyalties, weakened the local prestige of the clergy, implanted a more modern culture. The failure of the clericalist and anti-republican right to offer any response to contemporary economic problems beyond the anachronistic social paternalism of de Mun increasingly undermined its popular credibility. Dechristianisation went hand in hand with the loosening of the hold of clericalist politics over those who remained attached to the Catholic faith.

As Catholicism and royalism lost the capacity for political mobilisation which had once assured the old right a substantial mass base, so the ground was prepared for the ideological renewal of conservative politics. However, in order to understand the emergence of a new synthesis, attention must first be paid to developments elsewhere.

THE FIRST STAGE OF THE SYNTHESIS: THE POPULIST RIGHT

The emergence in the 1880s of an urban populist right was a complex process, not least because it drew on an ideological legacy and a social constituency that in the past had often been identified with the left. By way of an introduction it is therefore important to recognise that in some crucial respects the new Third Republic failed to satisfy the ideals of some sections of the democratic movement. Potential opposition focused on three main grievances – the regime's *parliamentary* character, its neglect of social issues, its failure to harness nationalist aspirations.

First it should be remembered that, for many of those on the radical

Jacobin wing, parliamentary institutions had profoundly reactionary connotations. They had been the vehicle, in both 1848 and 1870, for the return of anti-republican majorities which had proceeded to undermine the revolutionary aspirations of Paris. Indeed, parliamentarism was associated as much with the unrepresentative assemblies of the Restoration and July monarchies as with the brief 'democratic' interludes.

In many ways, the constitutional and political attributes of the emerging Republic were calculated to revive this latent anti-parliamentarism. The domination of parliament by a solidly bourgeois political class of moderate republicans, who restricted the field of debate to their own narrow preoccupations, recalled the traditional domination of the *pays légal* over the *pays réel*. The Jacobin proclivity for direct democracy found few echoes in a regime which limited the 'will of the people' to the ballot box and bolstered the power of rural *notables* through an unrepresentative Senate. The dullness of many republican politicians, the evidence of corruption, the shifting alliances of parliamentary politics, offended the Jacobin taste for the heroic, for *vertu*, for dynamic leadership.

Secondly, the regime did little to satisfy the romantic social egalitarianism of the Jacobin tradition. The so-called Opportunist Republic (1879–98) was profoundly bourgeois, both in terms of its political personnel and in terms of its underlying ethos. In line with the principles of capitalist liberal democracy, it restricted the legislative and executive intervention of the state to a limited public domain – political rights, civil liberties, public education – and largely abandoned the wider field of civil society to the free play of economic and social forces. Notwithstanding its legalisation of trade unions (1884) and its piecemeal economic protectionism, the Republic always ran the risk of alienating those social groups (notably the working class and the urban *petite bourgeoisie*) which lacked the means of defending their individual and collective interests.

Thirdly, for all its emphasis on national unity and the inculcation of patriotic values, the Republic was still regarded by some as the product of defeat, capitulation and humiliation. The early collaboration between Thiers and Bismarck, the pacific foreign policy of the 1870s, the deep sense of a loss of status and influence, inevitably left a legacy of bitterness, not least in radical Jacobin circles where the tradition of republican nationalism had sustained the patriotic resistance of 1870–1.

This combination of anti-parliamentarism, egalitarianism and nationalism was to undergo an ideological metamorphosis which produced a distinctly right-wing critique of the Republic. Crucial to our understanding of this process in class terms is the special situation of the urban *petite bourgeoisie,* which along with the urban working class had provided the main social base of radical republicanism since its birth in the *sans-culotte* movement. However, this class alliance had been progressively undermined by the maturation of capitalist relations of production and the revolutionary antagonisms of 1848 and 1871. As industrial workers developed a deeper sense of class identity and moved from republican to more specifically socialist perspectives, the urban class of small traders and manufacturers was increasingly isolated in its struggle for individual survival. The *petit bourgeois* of the 1880s, faced with the effects of economic recession and capitalist concentration, was anxious both to avoid assimilation into a despised proletariat and to seek protection against the power of the 'monopolies'. It was above all in this class that hostility to big business, fear of socialism and a growing alienation from an unsympathetic Republic provided the bases for right-wing populism.

Simple equations between social class and political affiliation are, of course, notoriously dangerous. Many *petits bourgeois,* like sections of the peasantry and middle classes, rallied to the parliamentary Republic with its promise to represent *les petites gens.* Others were reassured by the presence in the Chamber of radical deputies, who continued to lace their rhetoric with egalitarian and nationalist themes until the late 1880s. It was above all in Paris and other major towns that the political destabilisation of the *petite bourgeoisie* was most acute. It is evident also that the relative weakness of socialist and trade-union organisations after the crushing defeat of the Paris Commune exposed many industrial workers, especially those with the least political experience, to the politics of the new right.

In its first phase, right-wing populism is best exemplified by Paul Déroulède's *Ligue des patriotes,* founded in 1882 with the full endorsement of the Republic itself and counting Léon Gambetta as one of its first members. Its initial inspiration was preparation for *revanche* against Germany, and though its insistent militarism and call for the physical regeneration of the French race may in retrospect be seen as sinister in its implications, the movement did not initially appear to represent a threat to the regime. Indeed, the promotion of a cult of heroism which would unite the old France and the Revolution 'from Gaul to Valmy' [2] was, as we have seen, a feature of the patriotic 'republican' textbooks of Lavisse.

By 1885, however, Déroulède had moved to a position of hostility, increasingly convinced that the regime was incapable of undertaking the task of *revanche*. Jules Ferry's colonial policy was undoubtedly a contributory factor in this, but in more general terms Déroulède now saw the parliamentary Republic as weak, divisive, shallow and opportunist, incapable of uniting the nation and of providing the necessary moral leadership. Recalling the regime's origins in the anti-republican Versailles government and the constitutional compromise with the royalists in 1875, Déroulède's movement appealed to the legacy of anti-parliamentary populism, and specifically invoked the Jacobin tradition of direct democracy. In Sternhell's words, 'Déroulède's nationalism was the first to set the traditional Jacobin clientele against the Republic.' [3] The reality of what was being offered, of course, was an authoritarian plebiscitary Republic based on national unity and on the condemnation of socialism and all forms of 'sectarianism' as divisive. The willingness of sections of a formerly radical *petite bourgeoisie* to espouse what was essentially *neo-Bonapartism* is some measure of the growing class contradictions within the old revolutionary alliance.

As yet, however, the full mobilising potential of the new populism had not been realised, for Déroulède had no credible project to offer on the social question beyond a vague protectionism against foreign goods and foreign labour and a sentimental appeal to workers and employers to unite in the national interest. The theme which would give a new focus to social discontent, and at the same time add an extra dimension to an already chauvinistic and aggressive nationalism, was that of anti-semitism. Though absent from the discourse of Déroulède himself, hostility to Jewish finance and commerce was rife amongst his urban *petit bourgeois* clientele in the 1880s, and it extended into the working class and the socialist movement itself, especially the Blanquist tendency around figures like Rochefort.[4] Anti-semitism had occasionally surfaced before in the politics of the left, through the facile assimilation of Jews and capitalists. Now however, under the influence of propagandists like Drumont, it became a central integrating factor in a nationalist ideology that, while selectively anti-capitalist, was wholeheartedly anti-liberal and anti-democratic, and implicitly anti-socialist.

Drumont's *La France juive,* first published in 1886, multiplied the classic stereotypes of Jews as capitalists and usurers, as rootless intellectuals, as the friends of Germany, as racial and religious aliens, as a conspiratorial clique which had 'gained an occult control over the French government, the economy, the press and French society generally.' [5] Such prejudices added a new cutting edge to anti-parliamentary authoritarianism, to *revanchisme,* and to nationalism at large, and quickly proved their power of attraction for many of the social victims of economic recession, both *petits bourgeois* and workers.

Furthermore, anti-semitism provided a vital bridge between the new populist right and clericalist-royalist anti-republicanism. The Catholic paper *La Croix* had taken a violently anti-semitic turn in the 1880s, playing on the historic Christian antipathy for Jewry and at the same time attributing anti-clericalism, freemasonry, humanism and liberalism, all those forces that were deemed to have undermined the Catholic order, to the pernicious influence of the Jews and their Protestant allies. Increasingly the tone of these arguments merged with the more specifically racist anti-semitism of Drumont. As the old right lost faith in the possibility of a royalist restoration and in the mobilising power of traditional Catholicism, it began to recognise the potential of a nationalism that was no part of its heritage. Those who had campaigned for peace in 1871 now had fewer qualms about *revanche* against an anti-clerical Germany or indeed about the promotion of military virtues, given the widespread royalist sympathies in the upper ranks of the army.

The possibility thus arose of a convergence between the social and political outsiders of the republican consensus. The victims of capitalism from the declining landed aristocracy to the urban *petit bourgeois* and worker, Catholics, disaffected Jacobins and socialists, the remnants of Bonapartism, were all invited to lay their grievances at the door of the parliamentary Republic. The opportunity presented itself in the form of *Boulangism*.

THE SECOND STAGE: BOULANGISM

The elections of 1885 threatened to reverse the whole process of republican consolidation since 1876. The moderate 'opportunist' republicans lost their control of the Assembly and successive governments had to face a sizeable opposition on both left and right. The radicals demanded the abolition of the Senate, while the right called for the repeal of the laic laws. Both sides denounced the failure to respond to the social and economic problems of the recession, while Ferry's colonial policy aroused widespread concern. In 1887 the Wilson scandal, involving the President's son-in-law in the sale of honours and decorations from the Elysée palace, laid the Republic open to the charge of organised corruption, and in the same year the failure of the government to respond to the German arrest of a French customs official (the Schnaebelé affair) swelled the tide of *revanchisme*.

It was in this climate that the name of General Boulanger suddenly acquired political significance. He had come to prominence in 1886, when he was made Minister of War on the advice of Georges Clemenceau, leader of the radical group in the Chamber. The logic behind this appointment was Boulanger's reputation as a republican, and one of the tasks assigned to him was the 'republicanisation' of an army still staffed to a large extent by officers sympathetic to the monarchist cause. He took over his duties with great thoroughness, purging the army of many royalists, including the Orleanist Duc d'Aumale who had been responsible for Boulanger's own promotion to General! The success of his modernisation programme, his concern for the social welfare of his troops and his flamboyant personality soon won him a considerable popular following, which achieved even greater dimensions when he reacted to the Schnaebelé Affair by calling for a general mobilisation of the army.

By this time Boulanger was already in contact with Déroulède, who saw in him the providential strong man and whose *Ligue des patriotes* was to provide Boulanger with the nucleus of a political movement. The General's growing popularity had by now began to alarm even those who had sponsored his appointment, and when he proceeded to demand the revision of the constitution, the dissolution of the Chamber and the setting-up of an authoritarian presidential Republic, he was quickly relieved of Cabinet office and dispatched to the provinces. His subsequent dismissal from the army saw his emergence as an overtly political figure and, in the wake of the Wilson scandal, with the reputation of the regime at a low ebb, he won a series of by-elections in the Nord, Somme and Charente Inférieure. Through this device of multiple candidatures (once successfully practised by Louis Bonaparte), it would seem he hoped to achieve a sufficient national following to sustain either a *coup d'état* or a victory for his movement at the polls in 1889. When, in January of that year, he won an overwhelming by-election victory in Paris itself, the very stronghold of democratic republicanism, extensive street violence set the scene for the seizure of power that was expected by many of Boulanger's supporters. Wisely or otherwise, the General let the opportunity slip. The banning of the *Ligue des patriotes* and the return to single-member constituencies for the elections of 1889 meant there was to be no second chance.

Boulangism temporarily brought together widely different sources of hostility to the regime under the banner of authoritarian populism, nationalism and anti-parliamentarism, and this combination inevitably invites the analogy with Bonapartism. In terms of the history of ideas and the continuities of political culture, René Rémond is no doubt right to indicate the affinities,[6] and indeed the rump of the Bonapartist movement was among the first to rally to Boulanger. However, while Louis Napoleon had 'elicited the support of peasants who feared the "Reds" of Paris, soldiers impatient with Republican theorists, and merchants who hoped for stability and order,'[7] the social bases and historical circumstances of Boulangism were substantially different. The movement was above all urban rather than rural, *petit bourgeois* rather than peasant, and it was Catholic reactionaries rather than capitalists who opportunistically exploited it. It was financed by royalists like the legitimist Duchesse d'Uzès, and beyond the new populist right it attracted the sympathy of a minority of radicals, *revanchiste* and eager for the abolition of the Senate, and of some socialists, especially those still influenced by the Jacobin-Blanquist tradition of the *coup de main*. It undoubtedly also mobilised the socially disaffected and politically unaffiliated from a variety of backgrounds, though its mass support was more plebeian than proletarian. In the wake of the 1889 elections, the movement appeared to have left few traces. With Boulanger now in exile, his supporters gained only 38 of the right's 167 seats.

THE THIRD STAGE: FROM BOULANGER TO DREYFUS

For the various political formations that had flirted with Boulangism, the affair had been a salutary experience. The elections of 1889 restored the dominance of the opportunists at the expense of both the radicals and the right. The process of synthesis between the populist and the Catholic right was temporarily halted, while the left progressively abandoned *putschist* aspirations.

The royalists had severely compromised their image among their remaining supporters by publicly backing a 'republican adventurer'. This miscalculation no doubt played as great a part in finally eliminating the prospect of a restoration of the monarchy as did the Papal Encyclical of 1892, which advised Catholics to accept the Republic. The royalist tradition, which rested on the notion of hierarchy and order, had associated itself with the forces of demagogy and disorder. What remained of traditional royalist support in the provinces could not but be alarmed by this resurgence of Paris 'extremism' in a new and unfamiliar form. Suddenly, the conservative Republic appeared to be the best guarantee of peace and stability. The Vatican's endorsement of

95

the Republic paved the way for growing political collaboration between opportunists and Catholics in the early 1890s, cemented by a common fear of socialism, by a defusing of Church-state tensions, by shared colonial ambitions and by Méline's selective protectionism which partially reconciled landed and industrial interests. After the 1893 elections, this new bloc of opportunists and *ralliés* commanded a substantial parliamentary majority.

The radicals too were thoroughly alarmed at the company they had temporarily been led into by their *revanchist* and Jacobin wing. They lost their foothold in Paris to those who were prepared to carry the logic of populist nationalism far further than they dared. Thereafter, they abandoned their hopes for constitutional revision, and came to ignore the *mystique sociale* and the *mystique nationale* almost as thoroughly as did the conservative republicans. As the opportunists relaxed their anti-clericalism, so the radicals filled the breach and became the champions of provincial republicanism, implacably opposed to the 'reactionary' tendencies of Paris. The Boulanger, and later the Dreyfus Affair, were seen as confirmation that the Republic was in danger, and that it was worth defending, and the radicals profited from this new division of opinion.

As the socialist movement put down organisational roots and extended its parliamentary representation over the ensuing twenty years, it too contrived to forget its tenuous involvement in the Boulanger episode. A current of Jacobin nationalism undoubtedly persisted, and certain sections of socialist opinion remained implacably opposed to the parliamentary Republic. It is also true that in the 1890s socialist deputies found themselves voting with former Boulangists on issues of social reform. However, the impact of more rigorous doctrines like Marxism and revolutionary syndicalism increasingly lessened the risk of flirtation with the extreme right, and in the wake of the Dreyfus Affair, the majority around Jaurès was able to reintegrate the socialist movement into the republican tradition and to establish a distinctively 'parliamentary' socialism.

As for the former Boulangists themselves, now known as 'nationalists', the 1890s were to confirm their rightist orientation. Though Zeev Sternhell has insisted on their left-wing ancestry, he himself recognised that when Déroulède condemned poverty, exploitation and injustice, 'he blamed the parliamentary system rather than the social and economic structure.'[8] As for Maurice Barrès, an increasingly influential figure in nationalist circles, the fact that his support in Nancy was largely working-class, that his election slogan in 1898 was

Nationalism, Protectionism, Socialism, and that he proclaimed his attachment to a distinctly French 'patriotic' (as opposed to 'cosmopolitan, German' [9]) socialist tradition, should not be taken at face value. Behind the social populist façade, his ideas reflect the intellectual atmosphere of *fin de siècle* conservatism, which in fact called into question the whole edifice of rationalism and humanist optimism on which the ideologies of the left were constructed. His emphasis on the importance of race and milieu, his denial of the 'abstract' Declaration of the Rights of Man and the Citizen, his nationalist vitalism, provided a wider rationale for Drumont's anti-semitism which, in the wake of the Panama Scandal of 1892,[10] increasingly coloured the discourse of the new nationalism.

This attack on the Enlightenment heritage went beyond traditional Catholic anti-positivism, seeking its own scientific legitimacy. In an admirable summary, Roger Magraw has noted the convergence of Bergsonian anti-rationalism, doctrines of social Darwinism and biological determinism, Le Bon's study of mass psychology and the elitist political theories of Pareto.[11] The overall political effect was to promote the principles of order, discipline and hierarchy, and to proclaim the subordination of the individual to the national collectivity. In the process, the popular Jacobin heritage was shed in favour of an increasing identification with conservative national values, symbolised in the institutions of the Church and army.

The Boulanger episode had confirmed that there were still obstacles to a genuine synthesis between the old and the new right, and the period of the *ralliement* had apparently widened the gulf by drawing some Catholics into collaboration with the conservative republicans. The ideological evolution of the new right in the 1890s had narrowed the gap, but it is far from certain that this would have led to a further realignment on the right without the catalyst of the Dreyfus Affair, which not only undid the work of the *ralliement,* but in the words of one historian 'was destined to churn everything up like a ploughshare, to draw lines and furrows through political parties and even families.' [12]

The series of events that trace the course of the *affaire* from Dreyfus' arrest to his eventual reprieve, are sufficiently well-known not to require elaboration. The bare details of the injustice Dreyfus suffered would, in any case, give few clues to the symbolic importance it acquired. A Jewish officer on the general staff, he was convicted in 1894 of spying for Germany on evidence that later proved to be highly dubious. The campaign on his behalf only achieved public prominence in 1898, with Emile Zola's famous open letter, *J'accuse,* but from then until late 1899 the reverberations led to a substantial redefinition of the ideological and political divide.

For the right the issues raised by the affair temporarily broke the alliance of *ralliés* and opportunists, the latter splitting into an *anti-dreyfusard* majority around Méline, and a smaller group including Waldeck-Rousseau and Poincaré, which joined the radicals and most of the socialists in 'defence of the Republic'. More significantly, however, the anti-Dreyfus coalition brought together the populist right with its *petit-bourgeois* clientele, and the traditional Catholic right now augmented by most of the conservative republicans. In the process nationalism had completed its thirty-year journey from left to right, and it is now possible to offer some assessment of how it had changed in the process.

For the enemies of Dreyfus, his essential 'guilt' lay less in his having betrayed military secrets to Germany, than 'in having served to undermine the Army and the whole nation for five years.' [13] Indeed, whether Dreyfus was guilty or not of the crime for which he was sentenced was, for many of them, not the main concern. What mattered most was that he had become the focal point for a campaign which had split the country in two, and had challenged the moral authority of the army. The fact that Dreyfus was a Jew merely reinforced the right's contention that the *dreyfusards,* behind their high-sounding phrases about justice and human rights, were a subversive clique intent on destroying the social order and the unity of the nation.

The Dreyfus Affair reveals in striking fashion that the language and imagery of nationalism no longer involved the radical equation of 'nation' and 'people', the struggle for emancipation through popular self-determination. It was now identified with the conservative institutions of order and discipline – army, Church and state. It demanded a unity imposed from above, thereby reproducing the authoritarian formulae of Bonapartism, but adapting these to the historical circumstances of mature bourgeois capitalism. The very concept of free and equal citizenship, on which the republican national ideal was based, was replaced in the thought of Barrès, Drumont, Déroulède and Maurras, by the themes of race, ethnic tradition, 'rootedness', and *la vieille France.* Though the racist and vitalist themes of this brand of thought were too extreme for many conservatives, the implicit denial of the revolutionary origins of the 'nation' was, as we have already seen, echoed in the 'republican' patriotism of Lavisse with its invocation of an 'eternal' France.

Of course, within this new nationalism there were still significant contradictions – differing attitudes to the Republic, a residue of populist anti-capitalist rhetoric, and these were to surface again in the 1930s. As Sternhell puts it, 'there is a nationalism which is nationalist before it is rightist, and a bourgeois nationalism which is rightist before it is nationalist.' However, continuing his analysis of the nationalism of Déroulède, Barrès and Drumont, he offers this perceptive conclusion:

> Nevertheless, as its social consciousness points essentially to the integration of the proletariat within the national community, to the elimination of all forms of particularism, and to the defusing of the social question, nationalism must clash with Marxism and in this way become the ally of the right as a whole.[14]

A telling illustration of this conversion is the fact that in the early years of the twentieth century, most of the populist nationalists, who had so long insisted on their Jacobin, egalitarian credentials, now rallied to Charles Maurras' *Action française,* whose break with the entire revolutionary tradition was quite explicit. Of course, in as far as this new movement developed a fundamentalist critique of the Republic, calling for monarchy as the only form of government compatible with human nature, and invoking Catholicism as an essential agent of order and discipline, it undoubtedly helped to keep alive traditional anti-republican prejudices and to sustain old rivalries within the right-wing camp. However, the true appeal of Maurras' anachronistic political projects can be measured by the continuing decline of royalism as a political force before 1914. The real importance of *Action française,* which led one historian to describe it as 'the great didactic centre of the right . . . source and authority for a conservative mass otherwise devoid of doctrine,' [15] lay in its 'integral' nationalism. Maurras provided a systematic rationale for the primacy of 'national' interests, rooted in a deep anathema for all egalitarian and libertarian principles, and the overall effect was thus deeply conservative and 'integrationist'. For the *petits bourgeois* who had been won over to nationalism by Déroulède, Boulanger and Barrès, the influence of the ideas of *Action française* completed their incorporation into the right-wing camp.

It is, of course, a distortion of history to see ideology simply as a manipulative process whereby the dominant class bends popular values and attitudes to its own ends. The reality is infinitely more complex, as I have endeavoured to show. However, it is tempting to suggest that, just as republicanism reconciled the broad ranks of the peasantry and middle classes to the structures of bourgeois class society, so populist nationalism defused the frustrated social aspirations of a radical *petite bourgeoisie* in the interests of capitalist integration. It is certainly the case that in the Dreyfus Affair capitalism and its political defenders came to recognise the ideological utility of nationalism as a force for conservatism.

THE FINAL STAGE: 1899–1914

It is generally true that nationalism needs the external focus of a common enemy to realise its full integrative potential. The stimulus of *revanche* had been a vital element in the growth of populist right-wing nationalism in the 1880s, and the gradual emergence of a rigid system of rival military-diplomatic alliances around the turn of the century, with Germany in the enemy camp, further stabilised the image of an external threat. Furthermore, the fact that North Africa and Africa became the major arena of Franco-German tension after 1906 made past differences between colonialists and *revanchistes* on the right increasingly irrelevant.

However, the evolution of the international situation tells us little about the changing ideological character and social foundations of French nationalism in these years. The steady implantation of nationalist attitudes on the right continued, irrespective of the diplomatic temperature or indeed of the shifting perspectives of French foreign policy. Popular anglophobia following the Fashoda incident in 1898 made an anti-British stance a real possibility until 1901, and yet this was precisely the period of the Dreyfus Affair when nationalism established its hold on the right! Neither should it be forgotten that, despite a growing sense of the inevitability of war after 1910, the parties of the left won the election of 1914 largely on a campaign against the 1913 conscription law, and when war came it was greeted with resignation rather than with mass enthusiasm.

The real logic of the new nationalism was domestic. Its key function was that of an ideology of integration, designed to defuse conflict and to consolidate the established social order. To this end it emphasised the primacy of 'national' loyalties (i.e. loyalty to the state) over political and social affiliations that were deemed divisive or prejudicial to the 'national interest'. In this context, the external threat of Germany was far less significant as a mobilising force than the identification of a catalogue of subversive 'internal' aliens – Jews and Protestants, anticlericals and freemasons, socialist internationalists. Of course, the various factions of the right, from conservative republicans through the shades of Catholic opinion to the extreme 'integral' nationalists, did not share these prejudices in equal measure. However, what they did share was the insistence that loyalty to the 'nation' could only be measured in terms of loyalty to established institutions – be it the army, the Church, *raison d'état,* the official Republic or, as the bottom line, the capitalist system itself. Nationalism had completed its transition from a doctrine of emancipation to one of social conservatism.

Of course, in the aftermath of the Dreyfus Affair, with the radicals and their socialist allies now in the parliamentary ascendancy and an anti-clerical backlash paving the way for the separation of Church and state in 1905, issues which had traditionally divided Catholics and republicans were once again back on the agenda. The *anti-dreyfusard* coalition, which had united populists, royalists, Catholic *ralliés* and conservative republicans in a single nationalist bloc, was temporarily undermined. However, a new focus for nationalist realignment was already emerging, and after 1906 it was to become a major preoccupation, namely the perceived threat of socialism. The presence of the socialist Millerand as Minister of Labour in Waldeck-Rousseau's cabinet, and the parliamentary collaboration between socialists and radicals during the Combes ministry of 1902–5 had already raised the alarm. The establishment of a single unified Socialist Party in 1905, the steadily increasing number of socialist deputies (103 in 1914), the rising strike wave between 1906 and 1914, socialist and syndicalist debates on how to mobilise against 'imperialist' war, such developments were a growing source of bourgeois concern.

In this context it was the former *dreyfusard* alliance that was put under strain. As socialism mounted a challenge to the bourgeois republican consensus, so the main emphasis of nationalism shifted to mobilise opposition against a new, more dangerous 'enemy within' – strikers, anti-war propagandists, the agents of Marxist internationalism who 'took their orders' from the socialist and labour Internationals. The Radical Party, while maintaining its electoral collaboration with the socialists, was in fact being drawn inexorably rightwards by the new salience of the social question. Clemenceau and Briand's ruthless suppression of strikes after 1906 won the approval of conservatives and the support of most radicals save a minority of social reformers. At the same time, while Caillaux continued to reflect the pacifist instincts of the party's peasant clientele, many radicals were increasingly convinced of the inevitability of war after 1910 and came to recognise the value of a bourgeois nationalism which helped to isolate the 'unpatriotic left' of socialists and radical fellow-travellers. In Magraw's words, 'Radicalism became the law-and-order governing party,

101

espousing imperialism, smashing strikes, beginning to conciliate the army, needed for internal order and to meet the German threat to Morocco.' [16]

The period between the Dreyfus Affair and the First World War was an important transitional phase. As David Thomson put it, 'the thirty-five years between 1870 and 1905 were spent, in a sense, in liquidating the past – in thrashing out the old conflicts between Church and State, clerical and anti-clerical, Monarchy and Republic, militarism and parliamentarism.' [17] The essence of the process was that of bourgeois consolidation, the ironing out of divisive internal squabbles and the integration of other classes to provide the elements of mass legitimacy for bourgeois rule. From the closing years of the nineteenth century *nationalism* had become the key ideological means for the achievement of this end. By 1914 bourgeois nationalism had largely incorporated the formerly disruptive elements of the populist right and was on the way to winning over a Radical Party still partially imprisoned in its *mystique de gauche*. Though the contradictions within this consensus were to surface again in the 1930s, henceforth the key political divide in France was the one which separated the socialist and labour movement from the rest of the community.

8

THE LEFT AND THE NATION
1870–1914

There has been talk here of nations as something purely artificial or reactionary. But nations are something important in the evolution of humanity; they form a stage on the way to the great human nation.

(Jules Guesde)

As we suggested at the end of Chapter 5, the brutal repression of the Paris Commune represented a decisive turning-point in the relationship between the working class and the rest of the democratic movement, and between socialism and republicanism. The proclamation of a 'Republic' in September 1870, had invoked the symbolic unity of the oppressed 'nation', but this quickly collapsed in the wake of military defeat and the 'peace' vote at the elections of February 1871. Deserted by the liberal middle classes, and then by the radical *petite bourgeoisie* in the capital, the Paris working class was largely left to its own resources in the closing weeks of the Commune. While the rhetoric of patriotism lived on, the underlying logic of the traditional republican appeal to 'nationhood', to a broad class alliance of 'progressive' forces, had effectively disappeared. The working class had entered on a period of social and political isolation, faced with a growing capitalist consensus and a Republic which now represented the established order and which was determined to close the chapter of revolution.

From the outset, the underlying ethos of the Republic reflected a determination to expel the social question from the political agenda. Despite the efforts of radical and socialist deputies, the regime's record in the field of labour legislation before 1914 was appalling when compared with that of Britain or Germany for example. As Hoffmann has pointed out,[1] the Republic essentially repeated Guizot's formula of *enrichissez-vous* and offered workers little more than the hope of individual social advancement, a remote prospect indeed given the inherent elitism of the education system beyond the primary school level. The regime thereby accurately translated the bourgeois prejudices of the time, which saw the urban industrial workers as dangerous and unruly, as opposed to a peasantry which was glorified and wooed as the backbone of the nation, the guarantee of stability.

Such attitudes inevitably aggravated the objective class antagonisms, creating a psychological as well as a social divide. The worker of the 1870s and 1880s often felt excluded from the national community, unprotected against the effects of capitalist concentration and rationalisation, of deskilling in the traditional craft trades, of increasing urbanisation, and of the long economic depression. Some limited regulation of the use of female and child labour was introduced, but workers had to wait until 1906 before they received the legal right to a weekly rest day. Laws introducing rudimentary insurance against industrial accidents (1898) and retirement pensions (1910) were badly received and irregularly applied. The legalisation of trade unions in 1884 often remained a dead letter in the face of the intimidatory and paternalistic attitudes of a deeply hostile *patronat,* while the state placed police spies in union branches, used the army to repress strikes, and denied the right of public employees to unionise. Collective contracts on labour relations remained a rarity, and generally speaking, workers remained exposed to the whim of employers and the forces of the market.

The failure of the regime to fulfil the social promise of the republican ideal inevitably swelled the tide of working-class disillusionment and latent hostility. The sense of exclusion and impotence was aggravated by the minority status of the working class within a society that was industrialising relatively slowly. As late as 1906, the proportion of the working population engaged in industry (including employers) was only 30.6 per cent as against 42.7 per cent in agriculture. Numerical inferiority drove the working class still further into its ghetto, for the Republic had no need of its support to sustain the appearance of democratic legitimacy. Workers increasingly experienced the contradiction between the fiction of equal citizenship and the reality of social marginalisation.

SOCIALISM AND CLASS

This sense of marginalisation was not, however, easily translated into a sense of collective class identity, nor did socialist politics make much initial headway. The imprisonment and deportation of those *communards* who survived the bloodbath deprived the working class of political leadership for nearly a decade, and the amnesty of 1879 was followed by a further ten years of sectarian division and political impotence. Though the June days of 1848 and the Commune of 1871 are often cited as proof of the precocious maturity of the French working class as an independent political force, it should be remembered that the revolutionary movement in Paris was always more sophisticated than elsewhere in France. It is dangerous to measure the mood of a whole class by the attitudes and behaviour of militant minorities.

Furthermore, in sociological terms, we are dealing with a class still in the process of formation, still marked by its artisan origins, and held back in its development by the relatively slow pace of industrialisation in France. Despite the inroads of large-scale production, in 1900 some 60 per cent of industrial workers were still employed in units with less than ten employees. The coexistence of the artisan workshop and the factory, the skilled craftsman and the machine minder, produced a variety of distinctive life experiences, as did the widely different habitats of rural manufacture, the company town, the big city with its diversity of trades. To these social and geographical nuances must be added the ideological rivalries of hardened militants, and the political inexperience of the broader ranks constantly swelled by migration from the countryside.

This social diversity was mirrored in the political diversity of the socialist movement in the 1880s. Though the vulgarised Marxism of Jules Guesde's *Parti ouvrier français* made some headway among unskilled workers in heavy industry, revolutionary politics continued to feed on older domestic traditions. *Blanquisme* remained a persistent phenomenon, especially in Paris. The anarchism of the followers of Jean Allemane, though deeply class-conscious, owed as much to Proudhon as to Marx, and was tailored more to the psychology of the skilled artisan than to that of the factory proletariat. Others envisaged a more gradual social transformation within the political framework of the Republic, through the municipal socialism of Paul Brousse and the reformism of 'independent' socialists like Malon and Millerand.

These various political tendencies also attempted to impose their ideas on a nascent trade union movement, where ideological divisions crystallised on organisational lines between trade-based national federations and the local inter-union *Bourses du Travail*. The price of this sectarian in-fighting was high. Many workers were clearly repelled by esoteric doctrinal disputes and the absence of any coherent socialist project for change. Until 1893 socialism was barely represented in parliament, while only in 1895 were the first steps taken towards uniting the numerically weak trade unions.

Socialism would only begin to achieve a clearer identity once it began to address itself more systematically to the distinctive interests and aspirations of the working class. The obstacles to this lay in the very nature of the popular revolutionary tradition itself. In a society where the class divisions of mature capitalism had been slow to emerge, the radical democratic movement had long rested on an alliance of the *menu peuple* with disaffected elements of the middle classes. Despite the widening gulf between the interests of the propertyless proletariat and those of the *petite bourgeoisie* and the liberal middle class, these old solidarities proved hard to dislodge, and they coloured the perspectives of early French socialism itself. The *quarante-huitard* dream of a consensual social Republic achieved through moral persuasion still lived on, while insurrectionary *Blanquism* was essentially a derivation of Jacobinism, addressing itself to a vaguely-defined *peuple* rather than to the working class. Proudhon's mutualist and anarchist ideas were tailored to the culture of a nation of small producers. It was only under the influence of Marxism that these traditions gradually shed their *petit-bourgeois* characteristics, and developed a clearer class perspective on the nature of capitalism.

REPUBLICANISM AND BOULANGISM

The weakness and sectarianism of the socialist and labour movement in these early years inevitably left workers exposed to other political influences. Though clericalism and royalism had enclaves of proletarian support, working-class attitudes were shaped above all by the legacy of democratic republicanism. The democratic movement itself, however, had always had its internal nuances, reflecting its complex social composition. On the one hand there was a parliamentary and constitutional tradition, shaped by the aspirations of the liberal bourgeoisie, and on the other a more populist, insurrectionary tradition uniting workers and small property owners, essentially *petit-bourgeois* in character. The gulf between the two traditions widened as the new Republic took definitive shape. However, both were based on principles of class collaboration and, in their different ways, they both articulated nationalist ideals which denied the working class any autonomy as a political force.

The capacity of the parliamentary Third Republic to win working-class allegiance should not be underestimated. For generations, and despite frequent disillusionment, workers had placed their faith in the republican movement as a vehicle of emancipation. The final establishment of a formerly democratic and secular political regime brought with it the suffrage, freedom of the press, rights of assembly, trade-union recognition and access to education. These gains cannot be lightly dismissed, and the need to safeguard them against the continuing hostility of the traditionalist right led many workers to regard the Republic as worthy of their support. Neither was the theme of anti-clericalism seen simply as a bourgeois diversion, for it was deeply embedded in radical working-class culture. In those parts of the country where clericalist and royalist influence was strongest, semi-feudal notions of authority could colour life in the factory and workshop as well as on the land, and workers had as much of a stake as the peasantry in challenging the influence of reactionary *notables,* and in the liberation of schooling from church control.

Furthermore, until the turn of the century, the apparent commitment of radical deputies to the cause of social reform seemed to indicate that the Republic was still amenable to working-class demands for further action on their behalf. While the *solidarisme* of the radical Léon Bourgeois in the 1890s was transparently designed to pacify rather than to emancipate, and lacked the reforming zeal of Gambetta's 1869 Belleville programme, it was still capable of appealing to workers who had not been won over to socialist ideas.

These forces of integration helped perpetuate the republican myth of equal citizenship and the consensual vision of a classless 'nation' united against its internal and external foes. The children of workers, like those of other social classes, were exposed in the schools to the propaganda which equated Republic with *patrie,* and which sought to turn the schoolboy into 'a citizen fully aware of his duties, a soldier who loves his gun.' The *école laïque* acted, as one author has put it, 'as a conscious and explicit agency of transmission of nationalist ideas and values.' [2] In as far as it succeeded in instilling collective consciousness of membership of the 'nation', it inevitably militated against socialist efforts to establish a sense of 'class'.

The grim realities of social deprivation ensured that many workers remained outside this republican consensus, and such elements laid the foundations of the early socialist movement. However, there was a further obstacle to the development of genuine working-class consciousness, an infinitely more dangerous form of class collaboration which took shape in the Boulanger affair. The radical wing of the old democratic movement, with its anti-parliamentary and insurrectionary traditions, had endeavoured to unite the *menu peuple* of workers, artisans and small traders in what was essentially a *petit-bourgeois* alliance. The struggle for political emancipation had formerly made this social bloc an implicitly progressive force, vigilant in its mistrust of the bourgeois republican elite. However, political democracy had now been achieved, and the maturing class divisions of capitalism were emphasising the incompatibility of *petit-bourgeois* interests with those of the working class. Boulangism reflected the decisive rightwards shift of the more vulnerable sections of the radical *petite bourgeoisie,* who joined with clericalists and royalists in a concerted challenge to the Republic. The whole enterprise threatened to draw workers and socialists into association with the most reactionary elements of French society.

Boulangism was nonetheless able to revive the old populist coalition through a blend of social demagogy and, above all, aggressive nationalism. It played on the left's attachment to a nationalist ideal which had glorified France as the vanguard of the democratic struggle and as the champion of self-government throughout Europe. The theme of *revanche* for defeat and humiliation at the hands of a militaristic Prussia inevitably struck a chord with many former *communards,* for whom the Republic was tainted with the birthmark of defeatism and treachery. In their eyes, the bourgeois leaders of the regime had compromised with the forces of reaction and had collaborated with the enemy – their betrayal of the patriotic struggle went hand-in-hand with their suppression of the social revolution.

The Boulangist emphasis on the *bourgeois* character of the regime was, of course, a demagogic smokescreen. The real character of the movement was Bonapartist rather than Jacobin – a heterogeneous coalition of the disaffected which sought to reconcile the traditional social elites with the disparate victims of economic change. The target was the republican establishment rather than the capitalist system, and the idealist nationalism of the democratic movement was converted into *petit-bourgeois* chauvinism and authoritarianism.

Nonetheless, there is no doubt that Boulanger briefly enjoyed significant support from workers in his by-election campaign of 1888, and that this was instrumental in several of his victories, notably those in the *Nord* and in Paris. This working-class involvement was more than purely circumstantial, neither can it be attributed simply to political immaturity. It reflected the resilience of the populist traditions of the democratic movement, and indicated the extent to which the French working class had not yet developed a clear sense of its collective interests and a capacity for independent action. The image of the providential leader still exercised an appeal for many workers, and the socialist movement itself was not immune from this kind of adventurism. Sections of the Blanquist *Comité révolutionnaire central* also lent their support, as did Marx's son-in-law, Paul Lafargue. Guesde was reluctant to challenge Boulanger on the issue of nationalism, given the *revanchiste* enthusiasm he had generated, while the opposition of the *Broussistes* and other reformists was inspired more by the principle of *défense républicaine* than by considerations of class solidarity. Among leading socialists, only the anarchist *Allemanistes* made a determined proletarian commitment against Boulanger in the name of class, democracy and internationalism.

The impact of the Boulanger Affair on sections of the working class was never entirely eradicated. Some workers, especially those in frontier towns, were exposed by Boulangism to the continuing influence of the ideas of the nationalist right in the 1890s, as exemplified by the proletarian colouring of Barrès' electoral base in Nancy. Here the presence of some 30,000 immigrant workers added a chauvinist and racist dimension to the *revanchiste* themes, and this was far from being an isolated case. The sense of alienation and impotence experienced by sections of the working class inevitably exposed them to the demagogic identification of easy scapegoats, and this was particularly true of workers who had not yet fallen under the influence of the socialist and labour movements. As we have seen, anti-semitism had by this time become the key ideological focus for right-wing chauvinism, and working-class susceptibilities in this respect were exacerbated by certain ambiguities in French socialism itself.

The radical republican tradition since the time of the Great Revolution had never been entirely impervious to the easy equation between 'Jews' and 'capitalists'. Of course, the republican concept of equal citizenship implicitly involved the emancipation of French Jewry, and it is certainly true that anti-semitism was never systematically integrated into republican ideology. However, it remained a persistent undercurrent in the popular movement, occasionally breaking the surface, and early French socialism did not escape this influence. Both Blanqui and Proudhon identified Jews with usury and finance-capital, and it was the Blanquist Tridon who published the anti-semitic *Le Molochisme juif* in 1884. However, such attitudes were not confined to the Blanquists, and they even find some echoes in the writings of reformist socialists like Malon, not to mention Jean Jaurès himself.[3]

As Roger Magraw suggests,[4] many such cases reflected a careless use of language rather than genuine racism. The word Jew was often used, albeit irresponsibly, as a shorthand for certain aspects of capitalism rather than as a racial diversion, and socialists invariably distanced themselves from the biological anti-semitism of Drumont. However, it was not until the Dreyfus Affair that the dangers of this casual or opportunist pandering to racial stereotypes were brought home to many socialists.

SOCIALISM AND THE REPUBLICAN STATE

The period of the 1890s saw major advances in the popularisation of socialist ideas, the establishment of a more effective organisation and the first tentative steps towards the achievement of a more coherent identity. At the elections of 1893, forty socialists were elected to the Chamber of Deputies, while in 1895 the establishment of the *Confédération générale du travail* was the first attempt to unify the trade-union movement. In this process, the exorcism of the Boulanger Affair was a major preoccupation. After 1889, Vaillant led the majority of the *Blanquistes* away from the anti-parliamentary putschist tradition towards Marxist perspectives, leaving the minority around Rochefort[5] as the only 'socialist' residue of left Boulangism. As the right-wing character of populist nationalism became clear in the 1890s, socialist groups were unanimous in denouncing Caesarism and chauvinism as a dangerous blind alley for the working class.[6]

In the years that followed, the various socialist groups began to develop a core discourse under the impact of more systematic doctrines, notably Marxism and revolutionary syndicalism. Populist adventurism was eschewed in favour of a new emphasis on class solidarity, on the tasks of education, propaganda and organisation. Increasingly, hostility was directed against the capitalist system itself, rather than against the 'political class' of the bourgeois Republic. However, the question of what attitude to adopt toward this Republic and its institutions was still the principal bone of contention, and these strategic differences remained the major obstacle to organisational unity. Should socialists and trade unionists use these institutions as a framework for the progressive transformation of the capitalist system, or seek to build a revolutionary alternative? Should primacy be accorded to the industrial or to the political struggle? Should socialist parliamentarians seek electoral, parliamentary and even ministerial alliances, or should they preserve their freedom of action?

These questions of course raise the issue of working-class and socialist 'integration' into the republican consensus, and hence into the ideology of nationalism. As trade unions and socialist parties began to articulate demands for specific reforms and to use the institutions of the regime as a vehicle, would the working class develop a sense of 'belonging' to the political community, begin to internalise its values, develop loyalties towards it. This was the fear of the more revolutionary elements in the socialist and syndicalist movement at the time, and many historians have since argued that this was indeed the outcome.

The chain of cause and effect assumed by this argument is, however, in no sense inevitable. The fact that workers were increasingly involved in the political institutions of the nation state, as a terrain of struggle, does not necessarily imply their integration. The crucial consideration is the extent to which the working class retained a sense of its distinct collective interests and a capacity for independent action. This cannot, of course, be measured simply from the attitudes of socialist and labour activists, especially in France where actual membership of trade unions and parties was so low. The efforts of social historians have, however, laid the basis for some insights into the broader features of working-class culture.

Supporters of the integration thesis rightly emphasise the dangers of equating 'workers' at large with the socialist and labour movement itself. They point to the low level of unionisation in France and to the fact that in 1914, nearly twenty years after its birth, the CGT incorporated only half of all trade-union members. They also suggest that the legalisation of trade unions (1884) and the establishment of arbitration procedures (1892) had some success in promoting non-revolutionary, pragmatic unionism, pointing to the moderate reformism of important federations like the miners and textile workers, and the less skilled sections of heavy industry. Strikes were, they claim, largely economistic in nature, and did not challenge the priciples of capitalist enterprise. All of this leads them to conclude that the revolutionary syndicalists who controlled the CGT after 1906 were a thoroughly unrepresentative minority.

While such arguments are a welcome antidote to a historiography which has often measured working-class attitudes by CGT conference resolutions, they are profoundly one-sided. They ignore the evidence of growing militancy, with 100 strikes per year in the 1880s rising to over 1,000 in the 1900s. They fail to acknowledge that the repressive atmosphere imposed severe limitations on the scope and nature of industrial action, and on the capacity of unions to recruit. Above all, they commit the error of assuming that the views of the militant revolutionary-syndicalist minority can somehow be divorced from the working-class culture which produced them.

Revolutionary syndicalism fed on a fierce sense of craft independence, sustained by the survival of traditional trades and the continuing importance of skilled work even in heavy industry. Notwithstanding the diversity of the working class, these influences were pervasive, both in the workplace and in tightly-knit proletarian communities, where Pelloutier's *Bourses du Travail* were the authentic organised expression of working-class self-reliance. French trade unionism could be reformist in its sympathy for the co-operative movement, pragmatic in its industrial demands, revolutionary in its attachment to direct action and the weapon of the strike. Too much attention has been paid to the doctrinal divisions between 'reformists', *Guesdistes* and revolutionary syndicalists in the CGT leadership. At the rank-and-file level there was widespread impatience with these ideological rivalries, and the distinctions between reform and revolution were often seen as abstractions, having little to do with the concrete problems of organisation and struggle.

In many ways the famous CGT Amiens Charter of 1906 caught this wider mood. The refusal to affiliate to the newly-unified socialist party was an explicit rejection of the sectarianism of socialist politics in favour of the principle of class solidarity. Far from being apolitical, it expressed its faith in the capacity of the working class itself, through its own autonomous organisations, to mount the challenge to capitalism. While it would be wrong to suppose that these revolutionary perspectives enjoyed general support, there is no doubt that a deep sense of class antagonism extended well beyond the ranks of the CGT.

The 'integration' argument is more persuasive when applied to the sphere of party politics. Indeed, the organisational rift between socialism and trade unionism was strongly influenced by the revolutionary syndicalist fear that, given the bourgeois origins of many socialist leaders, parliamentarism and electoralism would trap them in opportunist compromise. Half of the socialist deputies elected in 1893 were unaffiliated socialist 'independents', who, together with the *Broussistes,* advanced a programme of pragmatic social reform, which won some support from the radicals and, more embarrassingly, from the former Boulangists. This strategy was viewed with disquiet by the followers of Guesde and Vaillant, and especially by the *Allemanistes* and the revolutionary syndicalists, who saw it as a betrayal of revolutionary class politics.

It is, of course, true that involvement in electoral and parliamentary politics exposed socialist deputies to the temptations of opportunism and ideological compromise, and given the minority status of the working class, the need to appeal to other social groups was a pressing consideration. However, in the context of the time this infiltration of the regime's political institutions cannot be seen purely as a capitulation to reformism. Marxism itself, in Germany and elsewhere, was at this time struggling to cope theoretically with the implications of universal suffrage and the possibility of the working class achieving power through the electoral process. Many French socialists believed that the development of capitalism would soon give the proletariat numerical superiority, allowing socialism to secure its objectives by legal means. At the *Porte-Dorée* banquet of 1896, where all socialist groups except the *Allemanistes* were represented, even the so-called moderates endorsed a common declaration which proclaimed the intention

> to abolish the capitalist system itself and to end the exploitation of one man by another, through the conquest of political power by the proletariat, the substitution of social ownership for capitalist property, and the international cooperation of the workers.[7]

The use of the regime's institutions was thus seen by many socialists as a class strategy rather than as a class compromise. A significant illustration of this was the growing recognition that local elections provided the territory for the conquest of town halls and experiments in municipal socialism. Originally a Broussist strategy, this was increasingly favoured by the Marxist followers of both Guesde and Vaillant, the latter describing the *commune* as 'an excellent laboratory of decentralised economic life . . . a fortress against bourgeois domination of central power.'[8]

It is dangerous, therefore, to assume so-called integration simply from the fact of socialist involvement in electoral and parliamentary politics. The real issue is how far socialism retained a sense of distinctive class identity, and a commitment to the transformation of the social and economic order. In this respect, of course, the Dreyfus Affair presents a thorny historical problem. Was it, as the Guesdist motion of 19 January, 1898, suggested, a purely bourgeois dispute in which the working class should not become embroiled? Or was it, as first Allemane, and then Jaurès, Vaillant and finally even Guesde himself acknowledged, a matter that raised issues that were central to the humanitarian values of the working class, and which offered socialists the opportunity to occupy the centre of the political stage?

Once again, it would seem that a question of strategy rather than one of class compromise was involved. Indeed, the Dreyfus Affair provided a sharper definition of the relationship between socialism and the whole revolutionary democratic tradition. It finally allowed socialists to break decisively with the chauvinist nationalism and anti-semitism of the populist right and of 'pseudo-socialists' like Rochefort. Furthermore, the Affair had exposed the fundamental contradiction between the ethos of the official Republic, with its insistence on *raison d'état,* and the universalist humanism of the as yet unfulfilled republican ideal. For the first time, the opportunity was there for socialists and workers to present themselves as the true vanguard of the radical egalitarian tradition, and to pose as the leaders of other oppressed social groups in the quest for human emancipation.

Another issue was more divisive, however, and did indeed raise the question of compromise with the Republic, namely the socialist Millerand's acceptance of the offer of a post in Waldeck-Rousseau's government of Republican Defence in June 1899. The presence in the same Cabinet of General Galliffet, who had held command during the repression of the Commune, made the issue particularly sensitive. This question of ministerial participation in a 'bourgeois' government was to bedevil all attempts to achieve greater socialist unity in the wake of the Dreyfus Affair, and it lay at the heart of the rift in May 1901 which saw the setting up of two rival parties – the *Parti socialiste de France* (Guesde and Vaillant) and the *Parti socialist français* (Jaurès's 'independents', the *Allemanistes* and the *Broussistes*).

Clearly, there were those whose socialism was gradually diluted by their attempts to win the electoral support of other progressive social groups and to build bridges with the rest of the republican left. The defection of men like Millerand, Briand and Viviani testifies to this trend. However, mainstream socialism constantly reasserted its attachment to its working-class base. Throughout the Millerand dispute, successive socialist congresses confirmed a growing convergence on the themes of anti-capitalist class struggle, and a strengthening commitment to internationalism. Indeed, growing disillusionment with the meagre results in terms of social reform of both Millerand's term of ministerial office, and the period of parliamentary collaboration with the radicals, had already begun to narrow the gap between the followers of Guesde and Jaurès before unification was imposed from outside, by the decision of the Second International at its Amsterdam congress of 1904.

In the light of this, it is important to understand the nature of the famous ideological synthesis engineered by Jaurès after 1905, which held the newly-unified *Section française de l'Internationale ouvrière* (SFIO) together until the Great War and has coloured French socialism ever since. It reflected Jaurès's humanist convictions and an equally sincere commitment to the Marxist method. It sought to integrate socialism not into the republican consensus but into a historical tradition of radical struggle. This was more than the invocation of a mobilising mythology. It recognised the positive value for working-class emancipation of political and trade-union rights, civil liberties, and indeed of anti-clericalism, which in his words had 'interrupted that old lullaby which comforted human misery.' [9] It saw socialism as the ultimate translation into the social and economic sphere of the egalitarian and libertarian ideal of the Great Revolution.

This blend of humanism and Marxism proved capable of extending its appeal beyond a minority working class to draw in support from the radical peasantry and middle classes. Of course, it remained open to the charge laid by more orthodox Marxists and revolutionary syndicalists that to fight on the institutional terrain of the bourgeoisie is to run the risk of being ensnared and emasculated. However, irrespective of this strategic debate, French socialism retained until the First World War resolutely anti-capitalist class perspectives, which fed on the proven incapacity of the capitalist system to deliver social reform, and the unprecedented combativity of the working class after 1906. Furthermore, the progressive defection of the Radical Party to the conservative camp on all issues which concerned the social and economic integrity of the capitalist order increasingly emphasised the class divide which separated socialism from the rest of the republican left.

NATIONALISM AND INTERNATIONALISM

It is hoped that the preceding discussion has laid some of the foundations for consideration of socialist and working-class perspectives on the *Nation*, and of how these affected responses to the growing threat of war from 1905 to 1914.

As Eric Cahm has pointed out,[10] most socialists in the 1880s and 1890s declared their commitment to proletarian internationalism, and gave little theoretical attention to the question of nationalism. While it is true that only the anarchists around Jean Allemane specifically rejected all obligations to *la patrie* as incompatible with international working-class solidarity, most other shades of socialist opinion effectively ignored the issue by taking France's status as a nation state for granted. They saw the nationality issue principally as a problem for the oppressed peoples of Eastern and Central Europe, whose struggles they supported. They showed little sympathy for the concept of an offensive war of *revanche,* though they were willing to justify the notion of a war of national defence based on a popular militia. The various foreign crises of the 1880s and 1890s allowed this patriotic undercurrent to surface but, as Cahm elegantly puts it, 'the revolutionary democratic nationalism of 1792 was not integrated with their socialist thinking, but remained as a substratum in their world-view, which they shared with the rest of the Republican Left.' [11]

In the absence of any serious French socialist contribution to the theoretical debate on the national question, it is however all too easy to adopt the orthodox view on the 'failure' of French socialist inter-nationalism in the years before the First World War. According to this, socialists were progressively 'integrated' into the republican consensus after 1893 by their involvement in the parliamentary process and the quest for piecemeal reform. Having a stake in the system, and wishing to defend it, they increasingly identified themselves with the nationalist values of traditional republicanism, thereby swelling the tide of right-wing chauvinism which was already shaping working-class attitudes. In this context, it was inevitable that socialist opposition to war would be ineffective and would melt away in 1914.

In the previous section we have already endeavoured to question the validity of this 'integration' thesis. However, the argument is simplistic in another respect, for it fails to explore the nuances of the word nationalism itself, to relate it to the realities of class politics in a particular historical situation. Popular identification with the *nation* does, of course, have distinctive, cultural features in different political communities, and it is true that the long historical association of the French left with the ideology of democratic nationalism makes France something of a special case. However, this should not be overstated. The proven willingness of French workers and socialists to defend their homeland against foreign invasion was hardly unique, and the danger of confusing apolitical native patriotism with an ill-defined nationalism is one that many commentators have failed to avoid.

A more realistic appreciation of the problem must start with some recognition of just how difficult it was to give the concept of proletarian internationalism tangible expression in the period under consideration. As in the case of other subordinate social classes, the geographical and cultural horizons of the proletariat were limited, and its only access to the wider world was through the socialist and labour movements itself. At this level, the launching of the Second International in Paris in 1889 provided a framework for the development of contacts, for the interchange of ideas and for attempts at co-operation and co-ordination, but while this experience undoubtedly influenced the perspectives of socialist and trade-union activists, it would be naïve to imagine that it could have any direct impact on the working class at large.

Any discussion of the degree to which socialists and workers in the 1890s were 'truly' internationalist must take account of these salient realities. Given the weakness of institutional links with foreign socialists, internationalism lacked substance and provided no clear reference points for political activity. As Jaurès said in June 1898:

> In the present state of the world and Europe, distinct and autonomous nations are a precondition for human freedom and human progress. As long as the international proletariat is not sufficiently organised to bring Europe into a state of unity, it could only be unified by a kind of monstrous Caesarism, a holy capitalist empire.[12]

The chief arena of class conflict remained the *nation state,* and the socialist struggle to wrest control from the bourgeoisie could not simply by-pass this 'home ground' in favour of some alleged 'higher plane' of organisational consciousness. To imagine it could is to confuse internationalism with cosmopolitan idealism.

Once it is recognised that the nation state remained, as Vailland put it, the 'necessary, natural milieu' of socialist action,[13] then it is patently absurd to measure 'nationalism' by the failure to live up to some impossible 'international' ideal. A more realistic criterion must be applied to the evolution of working-class attitudes if the decisive changes are to be properly appreciated. The break with Boulangism marked the beginning of a more determined and successful attempt by socialists to cultivate class solidarities, to combat the chauvinist, racist and militarist tendencies in right-wing nationalism, to reject imperialism in favour of the principle of the 'equality of nations', and indeed to share experiences and offer mutual support across national frontiers. In the context of the time, such positions must indeed be seen as genuine expressions of socialist internationalism, as a break with the *petit-bourgeois* nationalism of the old democratic movement, even if they could not immediately be translated into effective cross-national institutions or into a concrete sense of global struggle.

The essence of true 'nationalism' lies in class collaboration. To the extent that socialists succeeded in promoting a sense of working-class solidarity, they laid the foundations for the development of international consciousness. But given the problems we have described, it was inevitable that socialists would cultivate pride in their own domestic revolutionary traditions, and that they would be largely preoccupied with the territorial and institutional framework within which they operated. If this is nationalism, then the word has no value as an analytical tool.

This is not the whole story of course. Contradictions did indeed remain. The legacy of anti-semitism still surfaced occasionally in socialist discourse and, on the issue of colonialism, French socialism at large never developed a distinctive position, often appearing to subscribe to the consensual myth of the 'civilising mission', with its racist undertones. Furthermore, with the exception of Allemane and the revolutionary syndicalists, socialists remained sensitive to charges that they would be willing to sacrifice *la patrie* to their internationalism. Indeed, given the constant barrage of official jingoism and militarism in the years before the Great War, and the difficulties of achieving international socialist co-operation, it is scarcely surprising that some socialists and many workers fell prey to anti-German chauvinism. However, to divorce such reactions from their historical context, and to attribute them to the ideological legacy of 'revolutionary democratic nationalism', is at best a simplification.

SOCIALISM AND WAR

The fact remains that the involvement of socialists in the patriotic *Union sacrée* of 1914, and the absence of any initial working-class resistance to enlistment in the war effort, has been regarded by many historians as the acid test which proved that nation rather than class remained the primary loyalty of French workers. As we have already attempted to show, the juxtaposition of these two terms as irreconcilable opposites is itself simplistic and unrealistic. Short of giving the word a more precise definition, nationalism may be used indiscriminately to describe attachment to a variety of conflicting symbols, values and historical traditions, to a set of institutions, or indeed simply to a familiar spatial environment. Such nuances are at least worthy of investigation! As for the ties of class, the suggestion that these must, or indeed can, imply the abandonment of the national terrain in favour of a co-ordinated struggle against international capitalism simply ignores the realities of working-class politics.

Both Jaurès and Vaillant pointed to these dangers of assuming a direct antagonism between class and nation in speeches at the party congresses of Limoges (1906) and Nancy (1908). They stressed that, far from the workers having 'no country', they only acquired one through becoming a class. In Jaurès's words, 'as they group together for the struggle they become aware of their strength and become a class, they form the hope of one day controlling and appropriating this fatherland in the interests of all the workers.' [14] This perspective on the primacy of the national terrain was not generally regarded by socialists and trade unionists as incompatible with their efforts to build international working-class solidarity. Their internationalism was based, realistically given the context, on recognition of the cultural diversity of the international workers' movement, on mutual support rather than on the imposition of uniformity, on the principle of the 'equality of nations' rather than on cosmopolitan utopianism.

The issue of war, however, brought out the inherent tensions between national and international strategies for the advancement of socialism. The prospect of defending the fatherland implied defence not only of domestic socialist traditions and achievements but also of the whole apparatus of capitalist oppression. In short, it implied class collaboration, and it carried the risk of socialist values being submerged in a wave of chauvinism. It is not surprising, in this context, that efforts to avert war became a major preoccupation of socialist and trade-union congresses at both national and international level from the Morocco affair in 1905, through the escalating crises in North Africa and the Balkans, to the débâcle of 1914.

It is beyond the scope of this chapter to trace this process in detail. The picture which has emerged from recent studies of the work of the Second International and that of international trade-union conferences is that the French delegates worked frenetically to engage their German counterparts in serious discussions of how to organise joint action against war, with little success.[15] At the same time, both the SFIO and the CGT leaders attempted to promote an image of the powerful German socialist and labour movement as genuinely committed to the cause of peace, although they increasingly knew this not to be the case. The German movement, despite its strength and prestige, lived precariously under an authoritarian regime, and had more to lose from the charge of 'anti-patriotism' than did the French. Indeed, the Germans often regarded the French leaders, especially the revolutionary syndicalist union delegates, as unrepresentative utopians from a country where in fact the working class had fallen prey to *revanchiste* chauvinism.

It is certainly true that the socialist and labour movement was divided in its attitudes to war. Some on the reformist wing undoubtedly favoured class collaboration with the rest of the republican left in defence of *la patrie*. Indeed, even the 'revolutionary' *Guesdistes* were half-hearted in their internationalism, arguing that the struggle against war was a pointless diversion for the working class. Since war was endemic to capitalism itself, only the overthrow of capitalism could avert it. Whether this line was sincere, or simply a cover for the old populist *revanchisme* of earlier years, is open to debate. However, this scepticism about the possibility of successful international co-operation was inevitably aggravated by the German socialists' failure to respond to French overtures. Such pessimism could only reinforce the popular image of a bellicose Germany, and expose the working class to the tide of militarism and chauvinism being developed by the populist right and the conservative establishment. Given the legitimate mistrust of German intentions, the call for simultaneous general strikes or a joint refusal to mobilise for war seemed to imply a willingness to risk invasion and defeat for the sake of a fictitious internationalism.

In this context it was inevitable that even the most vigorous socialist campaigners for peace were driven towards the fall-back position, namely that a defensive war against an aggressive and authoritarian Germany would be justified to defend democracy and safeguard the future progress of the French working class. Gustave Hervé, initially a vocal exponent of revolutionary-syndicalist anti-militarism and anti-patriotism, eventually adopted an extreme anti-German chauvinist stance. Vaillant, who with Jaurès had led socialist efforts to avert war, revived in August 1914 the *communard* patriotism of his youth ('in the face of aggression, socialists will fulfil their duty for the fatherland, the Republic and the Revolution' [16]).

Jaurès himself, on the other hand, despite his belief that the preservation of democracy and of national sovereignty were essential to the emancipation of the working class, constantly reaffirmed his commitment to the avoidance of war. Indeed, he regarded war as destructive of all the values on which socialism rested, and he went so far as to insist that, if war came, workers should turn their guns on the government rather than on their proletarian brothers across the frontier. In his last speech in France, only six days before his assassination on 31 July, 1914, Jaurès warned that 'if the storm should break, we socialists would seek as soon as possible to remedy the crime that had been perpetrated by the country's leaders.' [17]

It should not be assumed that such sentiments were out of tune with the mood of the working class. Workers had, over two decades of struggle, indeed developed a class identity and a latent hostility to the bourgeois state, and they were far from unreceptive to the socialist and revolutionary syndicalist themes of anti-militarism and international solidarity. Despite the siren calls of right-wing nationalism, workers rallied in great numbers to the socialist campaign of 1913 against the three-year conscription law and in favour of a democratic, defensive citizens' militia. The issues of anti-conscription and a negotiated settlement in Alsace were at the forefront of the 1914 left election victory, where the socialists increased their vote by 300,000, advancing from 76 to 103 seats in the Chamber of Deputies.

It is, of course, impossible to weigh with any certainty the sentiments with which socialists and workers went to war in August 1914. According to Roger Magraw, the mood was one of 'dutiful resignation' and there were few indications of bellicose enthusiasm.[18] The failures of internationalism and the absence of any realistic alternative to the acceptance of war played a vital role in shaping attitudes, and it is misleading to insist solely on the supposed residue of 'nationalism' in French working-class culture. As the socialist Louis Dubreuilh put it, 'it takes two to refuse a fight.' [19] Jolyon Howorth concludes his excellent essay on the 'dialogue of the deaf' between French and German socialists from 1900–14 with the rhetorical question, 'What internationalism? '.[20] That is a question that cannot be answered unless we first tackle the question, 'what is nationalism? '. For some historians, regrettably, the answer appears to be, 'anything that happens in the nation! '.

9

PERSPECTIVES AND USES OF NATIONALISM 1918–40

> If we must have some kind of national-socialism in France, then so
> be it, however repugnant the idea may be to the French people.
>
> (*Le Bulletin quotidien,* 8 February 1934)

In the build-up to the Great War of 1914, there had never been any
doubt in France as to the identity of the foreign threat. *Revanchisme* had
made Germany the new 'hereditary enemy', and the emerging system
of international alliances provided the framework for an eventual
confrontation. The failure of working-class internationalism thus saw a
whole nation mobilised against a common enemy. Whereas in 1871 the
working-class *communards* had been isolated in their patriotic struggle,
the *Union sacrée* of 1914 implied class collaboration. The socialist
rationale for involvement in the conflict soon became indistinguishable
from that of other forces. Nuances of motive and perspective were
submerged beneath the military imperatives of collective effort in what
was the first truly 'industrial' war.

The two decades which followed the armistice in 1918, and which
paved the way for yet another world war, present an entirely different
picture. Widespread reluctance to face the prospect of another
bloodbath was further complicated by the absence of any consensus as
to where the true threat lay. The emergence of the Soviet Union, and
later of Nazi Germany, introduced ideological choices into the conduct
of French foreign policy, and the deep undercurrent of pacifism
engendered by the Great War posed further moral dilemmas. In this
context, the rich diversity of 'nationalist' discourse was transparently
revealed. It could be linked as much to the cause of peace as to that of
war. It reflected a multiplicity of political values and class interests. It
focused on different enemies both at home and abroad. In short, the
period is a fascinating laboratory for the dissection of nationalism both
as a theoretical concept and as a political reality.

WAR AND REVOLUTION

The Great War is commonly regarded as something of a watershed in France, marking 'the end of a certain economic and social order.' [1] The judgement is a perceptive one, as we shall see, but superficially it seems somewhat perverse. In terms of social and occupational structure, the characteristic features of the pre-war period remained largely intact. The industrial modernisation engendered by the war was limited in its scope and did not affect the fundamental dualism of the French economy. Though there was an acceleration of the rural exodus in the 1920s, agriculture was still overwhelmingly based on the small peasant farm[2] and continued to engage more than a third of the working population. The gradual expansion of industry and services did not induce general structural change, and the small unit of production and distribution remained the norm. According to the 1931 census, out of over a million registered industrial enterprises 75 per cent possessed no mechanical aids and 64 per cent employed no paid labour. More than half the industrial workforce was employed in concerns with fewer than twenty employees. As for commerce, the category of small traders and shopkeepers actually grew from 1,864,000 in 1906 to 2,343,000 in 1936!

The startling implication of the 1931 census figures is that 9 million people, around 43 per cent of the working population, derived their income, not from a wage, but from 'independent means' of some sort! This pattern of *petit-bourgeois* ownership had long been a stabilising factor in what Hoffmann has called the 'stalemate society' of the Third Republic.[3] It engendered a wide consensus in favour of capitalist property relations, and helped to marginalise a working class whose revolutionary traditions were a constant source of bourgeois anxiety. The regime thus sought to maintain this delicate social equilibrium by responding piecemeal to the demands of economically powerful or politically influential lobbies for tariff protection, subsidies and fiscal concessions. The defence of *droits acquis* tended to freeze the social structure and insulate it against the forces of economic change.

This process led to a very special relationship between state and civil society, which was characterised neither by the market-led economic liberalism of the British and American examples, nor by the dynamic interventionism of the Second Empire. Instead the state accepted the role of arbitrator rather than actor in the economic field, and became locked into a matrix of vested interests. It is in this respect, first of all, that the Great War represents a decisive turning point, for its economic consequences seriously undermined the capacity of the state to placate its disparate clientele. New external constraints limited its freedom of manoeuvre while at the same time internal pressures on its resources vastly increased.

The decision to finance the war, and the subsequent period of economic reconstruction, by foreign borrowing and the printing of money, turned France into a debtor nation with a substantial deficit both on her balance of payments and on her domestic budget. This integrated her more closely into international financial and trading circuits and exposed her to the vagaries of the world economy. At the same time, the economic responsibilities the state had assumed during the war itself, and social measures like the provision of war pensions, increased public expectations concerning the proper role of the state. The monetary and fiscal crises of the 1920s and the subsequent ravages of the world recession were increasingly regarded as the affair of government, and the pressure of vested interests threatened to paralyse the political system.

This growing crisis of the state was one element in the slow decay of the 'stalemate society', but the events of 1914–18 had also released other forces which were undermining the social fabric itself. While France's *petit-bourgeois* structures had apparently remained intact, there can be no doubt that the conflicts of the inter-war period were increasingly coloured by the class antagonisms of mature industrial capitalism. Socialism increasingly displaced liberal republicanism as the defining characteristic of the French left, and exercised an appeal well beyond the confines of the industrial working class. At the same time, opposition to socialism became the central preoccupation of the French right, and this polarisation on class lines cut through the *petit-bourgeois* foundations of the 'stalemate society'. In the 1930s the centre ground of politics was progressively undermined by intense social conflict and extra-parliamentary activity, and the republican consensus disintegrated.

Part of the explanation lies in the undoubted modernisation that had affected key sectors of the economy. Major technological developments had occurred in new fields like motorised transport, petrochemicals and electrical engineering, and in the industries most directly involved in the war effort a degree of mechanisation had been necessary to compensate for the shortage of labour skills and the use of a replacement female workforce. In qualitative terms, this had significant social effects. The increasing integration of large-scale industry with financial institutions (reaching its pinnacle in the Bank of France with its virtual veto power over government economic policy), the growth of cartels, the establishment of a national federation of employers,[4] such developments helped to promote the image of a politically powerful capitalist oligarchy, and did much to embitter class relations between the wars. At the same time, the social gulf between the capitalist and the wage-earner was widened by the introduction in the more advanced industries of mass production and assembly-line techniques, collective work processes that served to promote a deeper sense of proletarian class identity.

However, sociological explanations are inadequate to account for the change of climate. France's 6¼ million industrial workers still represented only about 30 per cent of the working population, and their political and industrial weight was further reduced by organisational weakness and ideological division. The intensity of the class animosities which evolved can only be understood at the political level, where the perceptions of the rival protagonists were shaped both by the Great War itself, and by the decisive impact of the Russian Revolution.

Few could have anticipated in 1914 the prolonged and barbaric war of attrition which left 1½ million Frenchmen dead and 3 million wounded. By 1917 pressure within the Socialist Party for a negotiated peace or revolutionary resistance was sufficient to oblige its ministers to withdraw from the coalition government. In the spring of the same year the widespread mutinies in the French Army during the disastrous 'Nivelle offensive' testified to the rising disillusionment of the troops themselves, and this growing war weariness was given a sharper political focus by the example of the Bolshevik Revolution and Russia's withdrawal from the war.

Any illusions that socialists and workers would be rewarded for rallying to the defence of liberal democracy were soon dashed. The aftermath of the armistice and the Versailles treaty was to confirm that the war had served only to consolidate bourgeois authority. At the elections of 1919, the socialists were isolated in the face of a *Bloc national* cemented by anti-Bolshevism and nationalist triumphalism. Though their membership had risen fourfold since 1917, and though they extended their pre-war vote from 1,400,000 to 1,700,000, they won only 68 seats as against 100 in 1914. On the trade-union front there was similar frustration. The CGT saw its membership increase from 400,000 in 1914 to nearly a million and a half in 1920, but the strike waves of 1919 and 1920 ended in defeat, and the only concrete working-class gain of these years was the eight-hour day law. Workers were quickly disabused of the belief that after the horrors of war a new age of social justice would dawn.

In this context, it is not surprising that the socialist delegates gathered at Tours for the special party congress of December 1920 should have voted by a large majority to accept Lenin's '21 conditions' for admission to the new communist Third International. The widespread condemnation of *le socialisme de guerre,* the desire to give 'internationalism' real substance, admiration for the achievements of the Russian Revolution, and recognition that under the right-wing *Bloc national* the parliamentary road to socialism was blocked, all of these considerations outweighed the arguments of the minority who pointed with alarm to the authoritarian implications of Lenin's terms. The organisational split between socialists and communists, followed a year later by a similar division in the CGT which produced the breakaway *Confédération générale du travail unitaire* (soon under communist control), was to lead to fifteen years of debilitating internecine strife, and has of course shaped the perspectives of French working-class politics ever since.

The impact of the Russian Revolution on conservative opinion was arguably even greater. If for the left it was a source of division, on the right it was to provide a new unifying theme and a dominant obsession, transcending older disputes. Anti-Bolshevism became synonymous with the fear of domestic social upheaval. The emergence of the first 'workers' state' threatened to destabilise the European capitalist order by providing a clear focus and inspiration for socialist activity across the continent, something the pre-war Second International had never managed to achieve. The wave of proletarian militancy between 1918 and 1920 in Germany, Italy, and even in France itself, lent some credibility to the Soviet project of world revolution, and the anxiety of the French right was eloquently expressed in the famous *Bloc national* election poster of 1919, which depicted the communist revolutionary as 'the man with the knife between his teeth'. In the following year the French government was to send a military expedition to aid the counter-revolutionaries in the Russian civil war.

Though the immediate threat of revolutionary contagion quickly subsided, anti-Bolshevism had become the linchpin of conservative ideology in France. The emergence of the French Communist Party in 1920, with its commitment to the Soviet Union and to revolutionary class politics, offered a clearer target than ever before to traditional bourgeois prejudices. Here was a party which was not only anti-capitalist, but which rejected 'republican legality' and owed its loyalties to a foreign power! For much of conservative opinion, despite the bitter polemics between the two parties of the left, the socialists were tarred with the same brush. They shared the same Marxist creed, and either they were 'wolves in sheep's clothing', or they would play Kerensky to some future Lenin. Some on the right, following the same logic, even regarded the timidly reformist Radical Party as the thin end of the Marxist wedge, thanks to its electoral collaboration with the socialists.

This intransigence inevitably had its repercussions on the left. The resistance of the mainstream parliamentary right to even the mildest proposals for fiscal and social reform,[5] and the increasing economic conservatism of the radicals, emphasised the class divide in party politics and hastened the process of polarisation. The economic crisis of the 1930s radicalised not only the working class but also the diverse victims of the recession in the *petite bourgeoisie* and peasantry. Anti-capitalism in its various reformist or revolutionary guises became the major focus of popular opposition to the established order as the old radical republican ideals lost their force and relevance. At the same time, new technocratic and corporatist ideas began to emerge on the right, offering authoritarian solutions that frequently resembled fascism.

At the centre of this process was the unresolved problem of the state. Unable to sustain the equilibrium of the *société bloquée,* its traditional role was now being called into question. In their very different ways, both the socialist left and the radical right were calling for a more dynamic, interventionist model. Inevitably, however, this crisis of the State was above all experienced as a crisis of the *Republic.* France's growing economic and social problems called for coherent and consistent policy responses, something the parliamentary regime, with its shifting party alliances and transient governments, was unable to supply. The consequent collapse of the old republican consensus amounted to nothing less than a disintegration of national identity.

NATIONALISM AND THE FRENCH RIGHT

The popular appeal of right-wing nationalism had always depended on the link it could make between an external threat and an 'enemy within'. The emergence of the Soviet Union, the Third International and the French Communist Party made the notion of a domestic 'fifth column' considerably more plausible than before the Great War, because now socialist internationalism could be presented as no more than an agency for the interests of a foreign state. In the mid-1930s the *rapprochement* between communists and socialists and the signing of the Franco-Soviet pact gave fresh impetus to this ideological perspective on the French right.

However, the problem for right-wing nationalism between the wars was that Russia could not always be convincingly identified as the main threat to French interests. If, for domestic purposes, the Soviet Union was the key ideological target, the fear of Germany remained the central preoccupation of French foreign policy throughout the 1920s. The *Bloc national* of 1919 was cemented, not just by anti-Bolshevism, but by germanophobia, and a determination to defend the Treaty of Versailles. Germany's failure to meet war reparation payments was the key focus of nationalist rhetoric from France's ill-fated military occupation of the Ruhr in 1923 to the Hoover moratorium of 1932.[6] Indeed, much of the imagery of right-wing nationalism drew on the experience of the war against Germany, with the myth of the 'spirit of the trenches' and the allegation that socialists and other 'pacifists' had stabbed the nation in the back by seeking a negotiated peace.

The difficulty of finding a clear external focus for the essentially *internal* purposes of right-wing nationalism was further complicated by France's weakened diplomatic status. The failure of the Ruhr expedition confirmed that she could only safeguard her interests by accepting a somewhat subordinate position within a system of collective security, and sections of the moderate parliamentary right were content to support Briand's policy of *reapprochement* with the Weimar Republic in the 1920s. A growing sense of impotence bred resentment as much towards her allies as towards the 'hereditary' enemy, blurring the picture still further. Britain was frequently the target for xenophobic sentiments, and the final *dénouement* of the war debts issue in 1932 led to anti-American rather than anti-German demonstrations in Paris.[7]

These contradictions were to come to a head in the subsequent decade, with the victory of Nazism in Germany and the re-emergence of the Soviet Union from its period of isolationism. The ideological division of Europe into rival communist, fascist and liberal democratic camps meant that foreign policy choices were no longer perceived in the traditional terms of national self-interest and the balance of power. If the very survival of the French nation state appeared increasingly to require mobilisation against resurgent German militarism, the internal logic of right-wing nationalism pointed to an anti-Bolshevist stance. The way that these contradictions were resolved in the period of appeasement, defeatism and collaboration is a telling commentary on the ideological motivation of right-wing nationalism.

VARIETIES OF NATIONALISM

However, it is impossible to proceed any further with the discussion of 'right-wing' nationalism without recognising that the term covers a number of distinctive political positions. The French right between the wars was in fact deeply fragmented. In the Chamber of Deputies there were about a dozen parliamentary groups to the right of the Radical Party, indicating the traditional individualism and low organisational level of conservative politics. Similarly, outside Parliament one of the distinctive features of the inter-war years was the proliferation of right-wing 'leagues', combative paramilitary forces which offered elements of the doctrine, organisation and populism which were otherwise rare in conservative politics. After the riots of 6 February, 1934 in particular,[8] they began to set the pace for the right at large. An increasing number of deputies were members of such groups, and leading political figures like the one-time moderate Tardieu, the ex-socialist Déat and the former communist Doriot moved to positions on the extreme right. Such trends inevitably raised the spectre of 'fascism', and for the left the main danger in this respect was Colonel de la Rocque's *Croix de feu*. Transformed from an ex-servicemen's association into a paramilitary political movement,[9] it became a full-blown party (*Parti social français*) when the Popular Front government banned the leagues in 1936, and was the only extra-parliamentary organisation to achieve a substantial mass base.

This political diversity was reflected at the ideological level and, more specifically, in the different articulations of the ideal of national unity. If the 'nationalism' of the right at large was geared to principles of order, authority and social integration, there was no agreement when it came to defining their specific political aspirations. Some looked to the past for their model, others were more concerned to defend the economic and social status quo, while a minority sought a radical redefinition of national identity in terms that borrowed heavily from the Italian and German examples. For this reason the terms *reactionary, conservative* and *fascist* seem appropriate for the purposes of classification.

Reactionary nationalism

The extreme right-wing nationalism of the pre-1914 period, despite its Jacobin and pseudo-socialist pretentions, had proved itself during the Dreyfus Affair to be the agent of the most conservative forces in French society. Its primary target was neither capitalism, nor indeed socialism *per se,* but the liberal-democratic institutions of the Third Republic. *Petit-bourgeois* populism was harnessed to the defence of a traditional order, exemplified by the institutions of Church and army and the notion of the superior interests of the state. The various strands of anti-democratic ideology – royalism, Bonapartism, and Boulangist anti-parliamentarism – converged in their hostility to the intrinsic values of the republican ideal. While the mainstream right feared socialism as a specific threat to bourgeois class interests, these fundamentalists viewed it simply as the hated democratic tradition in a new guise.

Despite the changing political and social realities of the inter-war years, these prejudices persisted in certain circles. Fundamentalist anti-republicanism had survived in the upper ranks of the army and the Church, in the more paternalistic sections of the *patronat* and in areas of the country where Catholic traditionalism was still entrenched. Similarly, the *putschist* legacy of Boulangism lingered on in some fractions of the urban *petite bourgeoisie* and working class, especially in Paris. Within the Chamber of Deputies, the extreme conservative wing was still marked by the values of the old anti-Dreyfusard coalition – Catholic, militarist, latently hostile to parliamentary democracy. As for the leagues of the early 1930s, despite their superficial resemblance to foreign fascist formations they were still the prisoners of this historical legacy. *Action française*, with its eccentric commitment to monarchy, was a product of the Dreyfus Affair, while the *Jeunesses patriotes,* though formed in 1924, was inspired by the example of Déroulède's *Ligue des patriotes,* first active in the Boulanger episode.

In these milieux, the notion that the Republic was corrupt, divisive and inherently incapable of defending the nation's honour remained a key factor of mobilisation, and it was classical issues like German war reparations and the Stavisky Affair of 1934 that raised the temperature.[10] Though the leagues and their sympathisers were far from indifferent to the more 'modern' populist themes of anti-Marxism and *petit-bourgeois* anti-capitalism, these were not the driving elements in their hierarchy of values. For them the enemies of the nation were still the anti-clericals and anti-militarists, the freemasons and liberal intellectuals, the entire 'political class' of *modérés,* radicals and socialists, the *pays légal* of the Republic.

The sectarian divisions within this reactionary community, between a minority of monarchists and those who favoured some form of plebiscitary dictatorship, served merely to confirm the anachronism of their politics. The common inspiration was nostalgia for the ordered hierarchy and stable values of a pre-democratic, pre-industrial age. The paramilitary parades, the street violence, the endemic anti-semitism of *Action française* and *Jeunesses patriotes* inevitably invite comparison with parallel developments abroad, but while the climate of the times offered them a new lease of life, essentially they were the products of an earlier era. The *reactionary* character of the leagues of the 1920s and 1930s is confirmed above all by their tactical perspectives. The simple authoritarian solutions they offered appealed to the patterns of social deference and political naïvety that had once sustained both monarchy and empire, but they were thoroughly out of tune with the new realities of mass politics and industrial society. Crude demagogy and the model of the *putsch* were no longer credible, and can in no way be assimilated to the radical form of mass mobilisation implied by fascism.

Conservative nationalism

Mainstream conservative opinion, as represented in the broad ranks of the moderate parliamentary right,[11] was no longer entrenched in outright ideological opposition to the Republic. Indeed, this sector of the Chamber included sincere and committed republicans in the Waldeck Rousseau mould, as well as those described by Chevallier as 'républicains de raison'.[12] Less Catholic and less militarist than those on the extreme right of the Chamber, these moderates were also more deeply integrated into the processes of the Third Republic by virtue of the key role they often played in the construction of a government majority. Their economic expertise frequently won them the tenancy of the Finance Ministry, where they defended the principles of social conservatism and financial orthodoxy.

However, the *ralliement* of the conservative bourgeois electorate to the Republic, hastened by the decline of the religious issue and the regime's successful prosecution of the war, was far from unconditional. It had already become apparent in the years before 1914 that this

131

bourgeois class was willing to sanction the repressive use of the state to defend its privileges against what it perceived as the growing threat of socialism. Its view of the regime was essentially an instrumental one, and this became increasingly clear in the embittered class climate of the inter-war period. In the 1920s strong government in the style of Raymond Poincaré[13] was sufficient to reassure these sections of opinion that the Republic was capable of defending the social order. As fears of the 'Marxist' threat increased, however, this faith in the regime was progressively undermined.

The pulse of conservatism was raised, not by anti-republican prejudice, but by the fear of social revolution. It was not the Stavisky scandal itself that mobilised conservative sympathy for the riots of 6 February, 1934, but the belief that in the aftermath of the affair a left-wing coup was being prepared.[14] The subsequent drift away from the republican consensus towards more authoritarian solutions closely mirrored growing conservative alarm at the rise of the Popular Front, the left election victory of May 1936 and the subsequent strike wave, the social reforms of the Matignon agreements.[15] It also reflected fears of Soviet international objectives, viewed as inseparable from these internal developments, and the issues of the Spanish civil war or the Franco-Soviet pact aroused as much anxiety as the forty-hour week. Conservative nationalism was therefore geared first and foremost to the defence of the social order against both the domestic and the international menace of 'Marxism'.

However, this defence of capitalism was further characterised by an unimaginative and short-sighted attachment to the status quo. André Tardieu's dream in the early 1930s of building a progressive conservative party on the British model[16] foundered on the unwillingness of moderate right opinion to make the necessary political and social sacrifices. Faith was placed essentially in the capacity of anti-Marxism to generate a spirit of national reconciliation, and in the parliamentary formula of *Union nationale,* which in the crisis years of 1926 and 1934 united radicals and the right behind the principles of strong government and national unity. As the political polarisation of the 1930s undermined these hopes, the new vogue was for constitutional reform, and even the radicals were fleetingly sympathetic to Doumergue's unsuccessful proposals for a strengthened Presidency in 1934.[17] After the Popular Front election victory of 1936, however, the temptation to abandon parliamentary principles in favour of vague authoritarian solutions was increasingly strong.

In this respect, the specifically conservative appeal of La Rocque's

Parti social français, with its sentimental invocation of social peace in a paternalist bourgeois state, must be emphasized. Indeed, though the left had equated the former *Croix de feu* with fascism, La Rocque's movement may more realistically be seen as a more combative extra-parliamentary expression of the rising fears of the conservative bourgeoisie. For sections of opinion that were traditionally more preoccupied with their 'interests' than with 'ideas', La Rocque offered a reassuring and complacent vision of the spontaneous dissipation of social conflict in a new moral order. Underpinned by the *ancien combattant* mystique of the fraternity of the trenches, this blend of social paternalism, political authoritarianism and economic liberalism corresponded closely to the bourgeois prejudices of the time, and this was reflected in the extraordinary success of the PSF in the late 1930s. A sober estimate puts its membership in 1938 at 750,000 which lends credibility to its claim that it would become the dominant force on the parliamentary right at the elections due in 1940.

Fascism

Authoritarianism, in these reactionary and conservative guises did not amount to fascism. It lacked both the populist anti-capitalist discourse which was essential to fascism's mass appeal, and the technocratic modernising ethos associated with both the Italian and the German regimes. It is true that in the early 1930s in France there were signs of the kind of political and ideological crisis which might have produced a radical synthesis of this type. Some of the 'neo-socialists' who split from the Socialist Party in 1933 adopted a national authoritarian brand of socialism, while a new generation of Catholic intellectuals who had broken with the archaic doctrines of Maurras began to develop corporatist doctrines of social regeneration.[18] Projects for technocratic government also emerged in the more dynamic modernising sections of the business community, around figures like Ernest Mercier and Jean Coutrot.[19]

However, it was only after the Popular Front victory of 1936 that a political vehicle for such ideas appeared, in the shape of the ex-communist Jacques Doriot's *Parti populaire français* (PPF). If fascism is seen as an essentially modern phenomenon, the product of the age of mass politics, a radical mass movement inspired above all by anti-Marxism, anti-liberal in its ethos but equally prepared to exploit populist forms of anti-capitalism, then the PPF was indeed the most authentically fascist of all French right-wing movements between the

133

wars. Hostility to Bolshevism was certainly its driving force, founded as it was by a former leading communist whose bitter break with Moscow had coloured his entire political outlook.[20] The defection to the PPF of much of Doriot's personal following in the Paris suburb of Saint-Dénis, his former fief as communist mayor and deputy, lent to the movement the plebeian flavour normally associated with fascism, and it also made a specific appeal to the *petit-bourgeois* membership of the earlier right-wing leagues. It drew together disaffected intellectuals from every political quarter, and looked to the creation of a fundamentally new kind of society rather than to the reconstitution of the past or the defence of the status quo.

The articulation of nation in the discourse of the PPF was therefore quite distinctive. Fascist doctrines are both ideologically eclectic and largely negative, the prefix *anti-* being the only consistent theme. In their attempt to forge a radical new synthesis from the debris of established ideologies, they reject the whole range of political values on which notions of community have traditionally been based. Instead, fascism therefore has recourse to crude statist and racist definitions of the 'nation'. The totalitarian ambitions of fascism made the concept of state central to collective identity, and the PPF was no exception to the rule. Alongside this was a crude atavistic image of the French race, almost *volkisch* in character, linking Joan of Arc with the Paris Commune as symbols of ethnic vitalism.

Nothing, of course, could be further from the political principles of self-determination and popular sovereignty which we have identified as the essence of nationhood. Fascism, to a greater extent than any other right-wing movement, raises the question of whether the use of the word nation as an ideology of social control properly deserves the title nationalism. As one author puts it, 'Doriot, in his passage to fascism was not primarily concerned about the destiny of the French nation. His nationalist dimension came to him as a result of his principal struggle which was a struggle against an international enemy.'[21] It should not be forgotten that the party was to enjoy its largest following after 1940 in occupied Paris. It is tempting to see the PPF as a precursor of invasion and collaboration, a prefiguration of the European fascist order, hiding behind the rhetoric of national regeneration.

THE PATH TO DEFEATISM

The different implications of these various right-wing perspectives for the realm of foreign policy were not yet apparent in the early 1930s.

Hitler's arrival in power in January 1933 was generally received with alarm and hostility on the right, where it was regarded as a reaffirmation of traditional German militarism and expansionism. Though *L'Ami du peuple,* the mouthpiece for *Solidarité française,* published an article entitled 'Avec l'Allemagne contre les Soviets' in November 1933, this attitude was in no sense typical, and through 1934 the main objective of the right at large remained that of building collective security against Germany. It is significant, however, that the main plank of this strategy was seen as Italy, and the *Stresa Front* of April 1935 was to remain one of the great illusions of right-wing foreign policy until the war. Britain was, of course, included in this alliance, but was generally regarded as a secondary partner. As for the Franco-Soviet pact of May 1935, the extreme right was hostile from the outset, while the mainstream parliamentary right never saw it as a military pact but merely as a device to ensure the Soviet Union did not move into the opposite camp.

This pursuit of Italian friendship undoubtedly reflected the admiration felt for Mussolini not only on the anti-republican right but in many sections of conservative opinion. For a while the policy, led by Pierre Laval, could be justified on purely pragmatic grounds. It was the Italian invasion of Ethiopia in October 1935 which offered the first evidence of growing tensions on the right between the real demands of international security and the pressure of ideological prejudices. Thereafter, as fascist and Nazi expansionism made ever-increasing claims, and as the current of anti-Marxism grew in response to both domestic and international developments, the former consensus on the right split into three identifiable tendencies.[22]

The first and least typical response was one which consistently recognised Germany as the main threat, and resolutely demanded the measures necessary to contain her. It favoured the Franco-Soviet pact, economic sanctions against Italy, and the unconditional pursuit of whatever alliances were necessary to block pan-Germanism. This position was rooted in an instinctive patriotism and in traditional hostility to Germany rather than in any specific ideological rationale. Those who, in different ways and at different times, came to defend this view, included deputies of the moderate right like Paul Reynaud and Ernest Pézet, and more conservative figures like Georges Mandel and, eventually, Louis Marin,[23] along with a number of newspaper editorialists. Indeed, it was the ultra-conservative journalist and deputy Henri de Kérillis who, speaking in the Chamber in defence of the Franco-Soviet pact in 1939, expressed this traditional patriotism more eloquently than any:

The regime of Soviet Russia, I assure you my dear colleagues of the Right, is as repugnant to me as to all of you. But when it is a question of appraising the permanent laws of the foreign policy of my country, I do not allow the *bourgeois* in me to speak louder than the patriot.[24]

The second and most widespread tendency, the one which most influenced right-wing government policy and therefore increasingly determined the course of events, is more complex to describe. While within it may be found considerable sympathy for Mussolini and unanimous hostility to the Soviet Union, it would be wrong to see it as favourably disposed to Nazism or indifferent to German expansion in Central and Eastern Europe. However, ideological prejudices certainly set the confines of its foreign policy, by ruling out any serious commitment to the Franco-Soviet pact. After the Popular Front victory of 1936, and as the left moved towards what the right called a 'bellicist' position, the pact was increasingly seen as a device by which the Soviet Union was seeking to embroil Europe in war and pave the way for revolution.

Security was thus to depend on the *Little Entente* (with Czechoslovakia, Yugoslavia and Romania), on the British alliance, and above all on friendship with Italy, and during the Ethiopian crisis the partisans of this strategy were at best lukewarm on the use of sanctions, for fear of alienating key allies. However, it is legitimate to ask whether on this basis they were really committed to security at all. They failed even to acknowledge that Hitler's invasion of the demilitarised Rhineland in March 1936 made the *Little Entente* inoperable, since France no longer had the means to attack the German heartland in defence of her Eastern allies. The subsequent capitulations by conservative governments on the *Anschluss* and the Sudeten crisis merely confirmed that most of the right had renounced France's responsibilities in Eastern Europe.

Neo-pacifism and the fear of German military might no doubt reinforced these tendencies to appeasement, but the growing conservative fear was that war meant social revolution. The temperature of anti-Marxist feeling, already raised by domestic events, reached fever pitch with the Spanish civil war, when even patriots like de Kérillis firmly supported Franco. Until the occupation of Prague in March 1939, at which point German intentions were obvious to all, the persistent theme was to exclude the Soviet Union from any system of alliances. So it was that, at the time of the Munich agreement in

September 1938, most of the French right preferred to support the so-called 'Four-Power Diplomacy' which required Mussolini to act as a mediator between Hitler and the democracies.

This stance in foreign affairs corresponded fairly closely to what we have described as conservative nationalism, and it reflects the bourgeois prejudice and selfish opportunism of both the parliamentary right and La Rocque's PSF. Not all of its erstwhile supporters maintained this ambiguous perspective after the invasion, but in many ways Vichy was its logical outcome.

Finally, to the right of this timid conservatism was a third position, where the current of anti-Marxism fused with a fundamental hostility to liberal democracy. What Charles Micaud has called the 'revolutionary right' [25] in fact incorporated the *reactionary* circles around *Action française* and the other former 'leagues',[26] and the more specifically *fascist* elements around Doriot's PPF and the neo-socialist Marcel Déat.[27] Broadly speaking it may be said that the former, historically anti-German, were more inclined to idealise Mussolini and eventually to pursue their political objectives under Vichy. The latter, on the other hand, found much to admire in the Nazi experiment and many of their leading figures ended up in Paris in more direct collaboration with the occupying power.

In terms of foreign policy in the 1930s, however, these positions merged in a general defeatist stance, where they were eventually joined by the moderate right deputy, Pierre-Etienne Flandin.[28] The position was expressed as early as October 1933 after Germany's withdrawal from the League of Nations, when a minority reacted favourably to the German proposals for direct talks. The explicit sympathy felt by the extreme right towards Mussolini led it to oppose any thought of sanctions in 1935, and to regard Italy as a natural ally. The attitude to Germany was more discreet, and though *rapprochement* was sometimes advocated, such proposals were tactfully witheld during the crisis points of the late 1930s. General in such circles, however, was the conviction that the Soviet Union was the main enemy, the hope that Germany's main territorial claims lay in the East, and considerable sympathy for the anti-communist and anti-liberal principles of the fascist regimes. This implied a willingness to abandon France's East European commitments, and a policy whereby France would only go to war if her own territorial integrity was directly threatened. Indeed, even after the Prague occupation of March 1939, the main theme on the extreme right was that Germany would lead a crusade against the Soviets and that France need not become embroiled. And while by then most conservative opinion saw Britain as the only possible ally, this tendency still looked to Italy, in the hope that the notorious 'Four-Power Diplomacy' might even be extended to negotiations over Poland.

The defeatist positions outlined above were, paradoxically, all defended in the language of nationalism. In their different ways, all the forces of the right claimed to incarnate some higher vision of France's true identity and interest, which the republican institutions of the day were unable to represent. Common to them all was a belief in order, hierarchy, authority, but the most powerful theme was the defence of capitalism against the prospect of domestic social revolution. The concept of nation was consistently invoked, but in the name of class interests that ran directly counter to the conditions for the nation's survival. Seldom have the 'ideological' facets of nationalism been so powerfully confirmed.

NATIONALISM AND THE LEFT

As we have already seen, the impact of the Great War on the parties of the left was decisive for the subsequent period. Denunciation of *le socialisme de guerre* and the reaffirmation of internationalist principles were crucial factors in the formation of the new Communist Party, which effectively subordinated itself to the interests of the Soviet-led international communist movement. The socialists, of course, were unwilling to make this sacrifice, but they too were anxious to live down their involvement in the wartime coalition. Their internationalism, moral rather than organisational, pacifist rather than revolutionary, was expressed above all in anti-militarism, in opposition to defence expenditure, in support for disarmament through the League of Nations and for reconciliation with a democratic Germany. As for the radicals, though the Jacobin nationalist tradition had reasserted itself during the war in the person of Clemenceau, in reality the party's increasingly rural and provincial electorate craved peace and stability, and Briand's policy of *rapprochement* with the Weimar Republic in the 1920s was entirely to their taste.

Nonetheless, the victory of Nazism in Germany demanded a substantial reappraisal of strategy by the entire European socialist and labour movement. The international climate of the 1930s would seem to have been tailor-made for a revival of the revolutionary patriotism of the French left, for the interests of *class* and *nation* coincided far more clearly than in the 'imperialist' war of 1914. The Popular Front movement, which united socialists and communists, and eventually the radicals too, in response to the right-wing riots of February 1934, was of course conceived as an anti-fascist alliance dedicated to the political and economic regeneration of French democracy. Its failure to achieve these ends, or to prepare the nation effectively for war, owed much to the bitter class divisions of the time, the enormity of the problems it faced, the intensity of the resistance it met. But at the same time, the Popular Front experiment fell under the weight of its own contradictions, emphasising the political and ideological diversity of the French left.

The radicals

It may seem anomalous that the Radical Party still thought of itself as a party of the left in the inter-war period. Well before 1914 its commitment to the capitalist economy and the timidity of its social programme had set it at odds with the socialists, and these contradictions became more acute in the 1920s and 1930s as economic and social issues became the main preoccupation of government. Indeed, the experience of these years reinforced the conservatism of the radicals in this domain. Their domination of the parliamentary middle ground made them an essential component of most governments, and this encouraged pragmatism, as did their growing awareness after 1924 that it was politically dangerous to antagonise powerful economic interests.[29] Their attempts to govern with socialist parliamentary support inevitably ended in failure, paving the way for joint ministries with the moderate right, a far more stable arrangement in political terms.

Despite growing evidence that parliamentary collaboration with the SFIO was not viable, the fact remains that in three of the five legislative elections between the wars the radicals chose to sign electoral pacts with the socialists.[30] The alliance had certainly proved advantageous to both parties at the polls, but electoral opportunism alone is not enough to explain the anomaly. Radicals continued to see themselves as the guardians of the republican tradition, and the scars of old political battles made reconciliation even with the most moderate elements on the right difficult, not just for the party itself but for large sections of its small-town and rural electorate. The alliance with the socialists rested on this *mystique de gauche,* but attempts to reawaken old republican solidarities on the themes of anti-clericalism and parliamentary sovereignty were now decidedly artificial. Such issues were no longer central to political debate, and on the more pressing social and economic problems of the day the radicals' underlying commitment to individualism and private ownership was utterly at odds with the collectivist and interventionist aspirations of socialism.

However, in the aftermath of the right-wing Paris riots of February 1934 the radicals were once again encouraged to ignore these contradictions and to throw in their lot not just with the socialists, but this time with the communists too, in the emerging Popular Front movement. Electoral calculations again played their part, but the activity of the right-wing leagues, and Doumergue's constitutional proposals for a strengthened executive, revived the party's *mystique de gauche* and reinstated the old radical theme of 'defence of the Republic'. Indeed, though they occasionally used the term 'fascist', the radicals tended to regard the growing authoritarianism of the right simply as *la réaction* in a new guise. This was a serious misreading of the situation for, as we have seen, the traditional anti-republicanism of the older leagues was not the key to these new developments. The social and political crisis engendered by economic recession and the inadequacies of the Republican State required a dynamic response, and this the radicals were unable to provide. They were in the Popular Front to 'conserve' rather than to 'transform', and their tendency 'to cling to the life-raft of the 1875 Constitution every time a new wind began to blow' [31] confirmed that their stock of ideas was exhausted.

Tragically, after the collapse of the Popular Front in 1938, it was again this ideologically bankrupt Radical Party which held the political stage in the last years of the Republic, divided and impotent in its response to world events and presiding over the death of an entire political tradition. While the anti-communism of most radicals was not sufficient to lead them to abandon liberal democracy, it had led many of their candidates in 1936 to defy the national electoral pact, and it certainly coloured their international perspectives. Hostility to the Soviet Union and a reluctance to face the prospect of war made their position virtually indistinguishable from that of the mainstream moderate right, and radical ministers like Daladier, Chautemps and Bonnet played a central role in the policy of appeasement.

In reality, however, the radicals were the victims rather than the architects of this process of decline. The republican consensus, which had been so central to national values and national identity, had been undermined by the gradual collapse of the 'stalemate society' and the political culture associated with it. The degeneration of the Radical Party into opportunism was an inevitable consequence. Those who clung to the party's liberal humanist traditions, like Edouard Herriot, had been overtaken by events, while the *rénovateurs* like Zay, Cot and Mendès France, who aspired to give the party a more modern 'social' commitment, were marginalised. It is significant that these names were to be found among the handful of radicals who refused to vote constitutional powers to Pétain after the military defeat of 1940.

The socialists

With the electoral victory of the Popular Front in May 1936, the Socialist Party assumed government office for the first time. Until then, socialists had always refused to accept ministerial posts on pain of expulsion from the party, and this had grave repercussions in the 1930s, thanks to the presence of a significant participationist wing among the socialist parliamentary group. The majority of the party rank-and-file were deeply hostile to any such arrangement, and indeed many thoroughly disapproved even of electoral collaboration with the radicals. Now, however, the socialists had displaced the radicals as the largest left group in the Chamber of Deputies. As senior partners in the coalition, they decided to accept their responsibilities, with their leader Léon Blum taking over as Prime Minister of a joint socialist-radical cabinet, and the communists offering parliamentary support.

It might appear that the Socialist Party was better placed than any other organisation to mobilise support for the struggle against fascism. Its ideological legacy allowed it to invoke both class and nation, to link socialism and democracy, and its leading position within the Popular Front made it the focus for a possible 'historic compromise'. Blum had made it clear a socialist transformation of the economy was not on the agenda. However, the combination of Keynesian economic interventionism with measures to promote social justice and defend democratic liberties were clearly designed to reconcile the left, to breathe new life into the flagging republican ideal and to promote a new sense of popular national unity.[32] Intense capitalist resistance contributed largely to the frustration of these hopes, but the internal problems of the left also played their part. Far from fulfilling this federative role within the alliance, the socialists were pulled apart by the centrifugal force of the radical and communist extremes.

As we have seen, the radicals joined the Popular Front to shore up the Third Republic. They had little sympathy for economic and social reforms, were deeply suspicious of the communists, and were thoroughly alarmed by the strikes of June 1936. Neither were they willing to translate anti-fascism into international terms by supporting military intervention in favour of the threatened republican government in Spain.[33] For very different reasons, the communists were equally lukewarm about the structural economic reforms proposed by the socialists, though their reluctance was often disguised by maximalist rhetoric designed to maintain their credibility with the working class. For them, the Popular Front was above all an instrument in the struggle against fascism at home and abroad, not least to ensure the survival of the Soviet Union, and other issues were subordinated to this end. Their most vigorous campaigns were those conducted in support of the Franco-Soviet pact and for French intervention in the Spanish Civil War.

The collapse of the Popular Front on these internal contradictions accentuated the ideological divergences within the Socialist Party itself. Isolated from their former coalition partners by March 1938, socialists were deeply divided in their response to the international crises that preceded the outbreak of war. While fascism was repellent to all sections of the party, the prospect of resisting it by military means was another matter. Differing attitudes to communism and liberal democracy, and the powerful legacy of pacifism and anti-militarism, interacted to produce four discernible foreign policy positions within the SFIO.[34]

The most consistent proponent of intransigent pacifism was the party secretary, Paul Faure, whose leftist image and popularity with the rank-and-file derived largely from his opposition to the *Union sacrée* of 1914. His sincere hatred of war combined with a deep anti-communism, which led him to claim that the 'totalitarian' powers of Nazi Germany and the Soviet Union were equally repugnant, and that the latter was intent on dragging France into a European conflict she had no hope of winning. His unlimited faith in negotiation, his unwillingness to envisage war for any other purpose than the defence of national territory, made his position virtually indistinguishable from that of Marcel Déat and the most defeatist elements on the extreme right.

The true 'left' of the party, however, was represented by Jean Zyromski's *Bataille socialiste* and Marceau Pivert's *Gauche révolutionnaire.* As with the *Fauristes,* Pivert's tendency was strongest outside Parliament among party activists, and it was inspired by both Trotskyism and revolutionary syndicalism. Here the argument was that war could only be averted by revolution, and that military alliances between the bourgeois democracies and Stalinist Russia constituted a counter-revolutionary bloc every bit as hostile to working-class interests as fascism itself. Zyromski's more influential group adopted a completely contrary position, close to that of the Communist Party. The struggle against fascism was seen as essential to the interests of the international working-class movement, and thus Zyromski was committed to the Franco-Soviet pact as a basis for military resistance to Nazi Germany. Whatever his differences with the communists, he considered the Soviet Union's survival to be essential to the revolutionary cause, and he also explicitly believed that war itself might create the conditions for socialism in France.

Finally, in contrast with these relatively clear-cut positions, the majority behind Léon Blum, which included many of the leading figures in the party, found it harder to resolve the conflicting pressures. Blum's own moral dilemma, as leader of the Popular Front government, exemplifies the tensions involved. Though his ministry took some initial steps towards rearmament, he remained a pacifist idealist, convinced that peace was a pre-condition for socialism and that the power of human reason could still avert disaster. These convictions no doubt weighed in his eventual refusal to intervene in Spain,[35] and not until the *Anschluss* of 1938 does he appear to have accepted that the fascist powers were bent on war. Thereafter, he and his supporters advocated the building of security on both the British and the Soviet alliances, but by then they were in opposition, mere spectators of the events. Reformist socialism had failed to reinvigorate the Republic, and in the aftermath of defeat on 10 July, 1940, a majority of the socialist deputies and senators voted constitutional powers to Pétain and abandoned the regime.

The Communists

From its foundation in 1920 to its dramatic change of tack in 1934, the French Communist Party eschewed all alliances and engaged in bitter polemics against its former socialist colleagues, in line with the strategy of the Third International. It paid a heavy price for its isolation, in terms of both membership and votes, and quickly lost the numerical superiority it had enjoyed at the Tours Congress. However, in 1934 it rejoined the mainstream of French political life by playing a leading role in the construction of the Popular Front alliance.

The precise mechanics of this process are still the subject of historical debate, for it is clear that the right-wing riots of 6 February 1934 gave the situation in France a special dynamic of its own. However, there can be no doubt that what confirmed the Communist Party in its new course was a shift in Soviet foreign policy, and a consequent switch in the strategy of the international communist movement. The victory of Nazism in Germany posed a direct threat to Soviet interests, and Hitler's success had partly been made possible by the divisions of the German left and the communists' hostility to the Weimar Republic. The new Soviet policy therefore sought international alliances with the liberal democracies against the fascist powers, and communist co-operation with other sympathetic parties to resist the rise of fascist movements elsewhere, hence the concept of Popular Fronts.

It is ironical indeed that the only French party that argued consistently and unanimously for resistance to fascist aggression, from the summer of 1934 to August 1939, was one which had long been regarded by so many of its opponents as an 'enemy of the nation'. By espousing the cause of democracy and patriotism, there is no doubt that the Communist Party enormously increased its credibility as a political force, and it was rewarded by the doubling of its vote to 15 per cent at the 1936 elections. Its discourse changed dramatically. The workers, far from having 'no fatherland', were now proclaimed as the heirs of 1789, the guardians of the Republic, and at the mass demonstration on Bastille Day 1935 the communists outdid the radicals in their enthusiasm for the tricolour flag and the *Marseillaise*.[36]

The capacity of the PCF to act as a catalyst for the regeneration of French democracy was, however, limited by its strategic perspectives. It refused to enter the Popular Front government, and opposed any economic measures that would threaten the principle of private property. Jacques Duclos wrote in *L'Humanité*, the party newspaper, on 27 June, 1936, that the government had no mandate for economic and social reform beyond the old programme of the Radical Party! Indeed, the Communist Party's preoccupation with building the widest possible anti-fascist alliance led its leader, Maurice Thorez, in October 1936 to call on Catholics and even *Croix de feu* to assist in the building of a *Front français*. The nationalism espoused by the PCF, imitating the language of *Le Petit Lavisse*, was soon drained of specific political connotations. As early as 11 July 1936, the editorialist Vaillant-Couturier could write in *L'Humanité*:

> Our party did not fall from the sky. We have deep roots in the soil of France. The names of our leading militants have a strong, honest, native tang . . . Our party is a moment in the history of eternal France.

Above all, however, this dramatic change smacked of opportunism, and the patriotic rhetoric was unlikely to convince those on both left and right who regarded the communists simply as the tool of Moscow. Their suspicions were confirmed by the signing of the notorious non-aggression pact between Stalin and Hitler in August 1939, which at a stroke invalidated the popular anti-fascist movement which had been set in motion five years earlier. Though many communists were appalled by it, few openly condemned it, and the consequent disillusionment and demobilisation of the most active anti-fascists in the working class undoubtedly swelled the tide of defeatism.

France thus entered the war socially and ideologically divided, divested of any sense of collective national purpose. The republican ideal, once central to the national value system, had been undermined by a growing crisis of the state which discredited the regime and its institutions. Behind the complexities of this experience lie some possible conclusions concerning the nationalism of both left and right.

The inter-war period tragically confirmed that right-wing 'nationalism' was above all an instrument of internal social discipline and control rather than an ideology geared to the preservation of sovereignty against foreign aggression. For the left, on the other hand, the period proved once again that democratic republican 'nationalism' had lost its strictly internal function as a progressive unifying ideal. The social forces that had once constituted *le peuple* had been divided by class antagonisms, and the political contradictions of the Popular Front were a further confirmation of the fact. External circumstances demanded a 'nationalist' response from the left, but its inability to offer any prospect of social and political emancipation tied it to the defence of a bourgeois regime which had lost popular credibility.

10

NATIONALISM FROM LIBERATION TO DE GAULLE

The struggle for peace is the patriotic battle of the French people
against the American imperialists and their servants who want to
submit the French nation to an enslavery and a fascist dictatorship
which will be still more barbaric than that of the Hitlerian
dictatorship.

(François Billoux, former communist minister, 1950)

In 1940, France was invaded by Germany for the third time in seventy
years. As in 1870, war brought swift and humiliating military defeat,
foreign occupation and intense civil conflict. As in 1914, the ensuing
period inflicted immense human and physical devastation which
scarred an entire generation. However, the years from 1940 to 1944
offered France neither the consolation of continuing sovereignty in
defeat, nor the solace of a victory achieved through her own collective
efforts. Defeat and occupation at the hands of Nazi Germany
emphasized a growing sense of national decadence and impotence,
while liberation confirmed her weakened status in a changed world.

The armistice signed by Pétain on 22 June 1940, divided France into
an occupied zone (the north and the Atlantic coast) and an unoccupied
zone, where the French government took up residence in the town of
Vichy. The new regime's jurisdiction in the occupied territory was
always largely fictitious, and its impotence was further underlined in
November 1942, when the Germans invaded the southern zone to
secure the Mediterranean seaboard against Allied invasion from North
Africa. In the interim, however, the illusion of a sovereign state was
sustained in the unoccupied territories, where an attempt was made to
reshape the French social and political order under the banner of *La
Révolution nationale* (an ironic title indeed, for an enterprise conducted
under the watchful eye of an invader!).

Revenge on the Third Republic and the Popular Front was swift. There was to be no legislature, no multi-party system, no free trade unions, and civil liberties were increasingly circumscribed. The Head of State addressed his 'subjects' under the heading 'We, Philippe Pétain' and the revolutionary *Liberté, Egalité, Fraternité* was symbolically replaced with the slogan *Travail, Famille, Patrie*. It is doubtful whether this dramatic break with the country's democratic traditions could ever have achieved a degree of popular legitimacy but for the *force majeure* of defeat and armed occupation, but there can be no doubt that the vast majority of French people initially acquiesced in the new regime, if only as a refuge against the possible alternative of full German military rule.

There is widespread agreement that the Vichy regime cannot properly be dubbed fascist, although the willingness of Laval, among others, to placate and even anticipate growing German pressure eventually saw the development of a repressive police apparatus, anti-semitic laws and other trappings of Nazism. The main pro-fascists like Doriot and Déat were active in occupied Paris, but the ideology of Vichy drew on different sources. As the new triptych indicated, the emphasis was to be on solid traditional virtues, sustained by Catholicism and attempts to extol the timeless values of the land and of peasant culture. This reactionary tone reflected the influence in Vichy circles of members of the former leagues of the 1930s, but it was equally and more decisively reassuring to the broad ranks of France's conservative bourgeoisie, which welcomed the notion of a strong government of national reconciliation dedicated to the elimination of class antagonisms.

However, despite the comfortable conservatism of Vichy ideology, the regime was paradoxically to be the harbinger of more modern developments. The determination to break with the republican past meant that few parliamentary figures of the pre-war right were recruited into influential positions. The preference was for civil servants, experts and professionals, perhaps an inevitable development in a regime which was free of legislative control, but the trend was boosted by increasing German demands on the French economy to fuel the Nazi war effort. This necessitated a degree of planning, and institutions like the sectoral *Comités d'organisation* and the co-ordinating *Délégation générale à l'équipement national,* staffed by the more technocratic elements from the administrative and business communities, were to provide some of the structures and personalities of the Fourth Republic's planning processes.

However, the influence of Vichy on the politics of the post-liberation period was less overt than that of the growing resistance movement. The initial mood of shock and resignation was marked only by a few isolated gestures of defiance, and De Gaulle's legendary *Appel du 18 juin* on London radio, whatever its later symbolic importance, initially fell on deaf ears, when indeed it was heard at all. Subsequent developments, however, provided a more propitious climate, and the first and arguably the most important of these was Hitler's invasion of Russia in June 1941. This gave the green light to communists to enter the Resistance, where they became the most numerous and certainly the best organised force. The changing tide of war in favour of the Allies from late 1942 was another major factor, for two reasons. First, the material possibility of the liberation and victory stirred latent hostility into action, and in the later phases no doubt led to some more opportunistic conversions. Secondly, as the German war effort became increasingly stretched, a series of measures brought more French people into direct contact with the realities of the occupation. The invasion of the unoccupied zone in November 1942, the introduction of the compulsory labour draft to Germany in February 1943, the increasing brutality of both the German and the Vichy police services, all helped to swell the ranks of the resistance.

De Gaulle's initial preoccupations were not with the internal resistance struggle. He was above all concerned to win the recognition of Britain and the United States first as a legitimate interlocutor for French interests and later as a credible future leader of liberated France. To this end he sought first to construct the embryo of a 'government in exile', and secondly to secure the allegiance of the sizeable contingent of the French Army based in North Africa. He recognised, however, that his legitimacy as a leader after the liberation would depend on the loyalty, or at least the acquiescence, of the resistance movements, and his efforts in this direction, through the agency of Jean Moulin among others, eventually won him the support of the *Conseil national de la Résistance*. This body, first conceived in 1942 by the socialists, represented a wide range of resistance opinion and was geared above all to the preparation of a political programme for the post-liberation era.

NATIONALISM AND LIBERATION

As a clandestine movement, the Resistance never of course achieved disciplined, unified organisation. In the words of one historian, 'it was as fragmented and diffuse as the "Mafia" or the "Enlightenment".' [1] This makes it difficult to assess either its influence or its political character. While those actively engaged in armed struggle, sabotage, intelligence gathering and propaganda probably amounted to no more than 1 per cent of the adult population, the readership of underground literature may have reached 2 million.[2] As for resistance politics, while the Vichy regime attracted the hostility above all of the left, in the occupied north opposition to the invader mobilised a wider range of political tendencies.

However, though the resistance movement included its quota of conservative patriots, its political centre of gravity was inevitably on the left. The campaign to liberate the national territory went hand in hand with the struggle against fascism, and given the pro-Vichy or outright collaborationist positions adopted by so many figures on the right and by much of the business community, the oppressor was often conceived as much in social as in national terms. Indeed, much of the blame for the humiliation of 1940 was laid retrospectively on the social conservatism, industrial Malthusianism and narrow self-interest of the capitalist establishment. The need for a fundamental break with the past was widely recognised and the experience of resistance radicalised sections of the community that had not previously been open to left-wing ideas. This trend was reinforced by the break-up of pre-war party political structures, and the reconstitution of political life on a clandestine and often non-partisan basis at grass-roots level. The trade-union legacy brought together socialist, Catholic and communist workers in resistance networks like *Libération-Nord, Libération-Sud* and *Franc-Tireur,* while even the communist-led *Front national* sought the widest possible affiliation, subordinating sectarian principle to the task in hand.

Given the circumstances, nationalism was inevitably the unifying ideological theme in the enterprise of liberation. Indeed, the word assumed something of its original sense in this popular struggle for the recovery of national sovereignty. For the first time, the opportunity was presented for a largely working class movement to take the lead, and identify its own social and political aspirations with those of the 'nation' at large. In 1870-1 the patriotism of the *communards* had isolated them from the rest of the community. At the time of the Popular Front, the internal ideological and social contradictions of the alliance had sabotaged the ideal of national regeneration through social emancipation. Now, however, the conditions seemed ripe for a genuine convergence between the interests of socialism and the principle of national sovereignty. The strength of this collective purpose brought resistance leaders together in the widely representative *Conseil national de la Résistance,* where plans were laid for the post-liberation era. Its famous Charter of March 1944 juxtaposed the demand for retribution against traitors and collaborators with the promise to establish 'a true economic and social democracy, entailing the eviction of the great economic and financial feudalities.' [3]

However, the possibility that nationalist liberation struggle might lay the foundations for a break with capitalism and the establishment of an independent socialist democracy proved to be an illusion. Despite the moral authority and political sympathy it enjoyed in 1944, the resistance movement had failed to produce an alternative leadership to that of De Gaulle. The various non-communist groups that Jean Moulin had succeeded in uniting in the *Mouvements unis de la Résistance* in 1943 had been won over to the General, followed by the *Conseil national* itself a year later. As for the communists, their main priority had been the expulsion of the invader, and in an echo of their 1936 position, they played a minor role in the preparation of the Resistance Charter. Though widely suspected by both De Gaulle and the Allies of insurrectionary ambitions at the time of the liberation, the party apparatus seems to have had no such plans, no doubt conscious that, given the delicate international circumstances, attempted revolution in France was unlikely to receive Soviet approval or support.

Though the armed resistance provided significant support for the Allied invasions, and liberated some towns in the south single-handed, its role was inevitably secondary, and this left the key to France's political future in the hands of De Gaulle and the Allies. Of course, De Gaulle needed the legitimacy of resistance approval, and this implied at least some recognition of the Resistance Charter. However, he let it be known after the liberation of Paris that the *Conseil national* would not form the basis of his new administration. Instead he chose his interlocutors from among the resurgent political parties, while at the same time offering two-thirds of the posts in the provisional government to his Algiers entourage rather than to those who had been involved in the internal struggle.

The fact that the resistance was represented on a party political basis through the PCF, the SFIO and the new progressive Catholic MRP was a considerable disappointment to sections of the rank-and-file, who had hoped that the solidarities of the war years might be translated into a single *Grand Parti de la Résistance* committed to democratic socialism. It is ironic too, given his later position, that De Gaulle pandered to these re-emerging party structures and partisan loyalties. However, the strategy reflected his desire to seek a wider legitimacy than that provided by the internal resistance movement, and to secure a swift return to institutional legality. His insistence that Vichy was an illegal interlude and that the Republic had never died, his decision to disarm the *maquisards* and to integrate many of them into the army for the remaining months of the war, the relative moderation of the judicial 'purge' of collaborators after the initial resistance reprisals, all of these were designed to control the revolutionary impetus of liberation and to effect a wider reconciliation of French opinion.

The discussion of De Gaulle's own special brand of nationalism will be reserved for later. Suffice it to say that, though it was at odds with the democratic nationalist traditions of the left, it had little in common with the conservative bourgeois nationalism of the collaborationist right, for which he had nothing but contempt.[4] His main preoccupation was with the recovery of France's international status as a sovereign power, and his recognition that this depended on state-led economic modernisation made him sympathetic to some of the proposals in the Resistance Charter. On the other hand, he was for the selfsame reason determined to restore order and to maximise national unity, and this implied safeguarding capitalism and holding some of the more revolutionary impulses in the resistance programme in check.

In this enterprise, he was aided by the attitude of the Communist Party, which had concluded that revolution was not on the cards and which remained sceptical about the possibility of a legal transformation of capitalism. It therefore decided to consolidate on its newly-won popularity, and urged workers to throw their energy into rebuilding the national economy in the so-called *bataille de la production*. In a disturbing echo of former times, this left the socialists as the main initiators of social reform, flanked (and electorally outdistanced) by the Communist Party and the new MRP (*Mouvement républicain populaire*), which was progressively pulled to the right after 1945 by its increasingly conservative, Catholic electorate (*Machine pour ramasser les Pétainistes*).

However, a major programme of structural reform was indeed effected, much of it under De Gaulle's provisional regime (until his resignation in January 1946), and all of it before full parliamentary institutions were re-established in July 1946. On the face of it, of course, the measures represented a dramatic break with the past – widespread nationalisation in the fields of energy, transport, banking, and insurance,[5] the establishment of an extensive public health and social welfare system, the first steps towards the planning of the economy. As we shall see, these changes provided a vital impetus for France's subsequent economic and social modernisation. However, those who had hoped that they would mark the beginning of a break with capitalism itself were to be disappointed. Most of industry remained in private hands, worker participation measures were to prove insubstantial,[6] and the new state sector was run on traditional *dirigiste* rather than socialist lines. Indeed, many of the new technocrats who were recruited to manage and plan the new mixed economy had learnt their trade under Vichy.

ECONOMIC GROWTH AND SOCIAL CHANGE

The thirty years that followed the liberation of France undoubtedly represented the most rapid and radical period of social and economic change in French history. After the initial phase of reconstruction, the years from 1954 until the first oil crisis of 1973 saw the economy grow at a rate of 5 per cent per annum, accompanied by major increases in productivity and investment, the establishment of a modern infrastructure, a significant shift and expansion in foreign trade, and a tripling of industrial production between 1946 and 1966. Initially, the emphasis was on the rebuilding and modernisation of France's basic industries, but later the country was to feel the full effects of the consumer-led boom of the post-war era with its promotion of new industries and services based on rapidly-advancing technology.

Much of France's unprecedented success in keeping pace with these broader changes in the international capitalist environment reflected the opening up of the French economy to wider influences. The impact of the post-war economic settlement through institutions like the Bretton Woods monetary system and the General Agreement on Trade and Tariffs (GATT), and moves towards a European common market were vital in this respect. At the same time, however, the break with Malthusian and protectionist attitudes and with the traditional over-reliance on colonial trade,[7] owed much to a new forward-looking and expansionist business ethos, and here the role of the state was crucial in the initial phases. On the one hand the creation of a substantial social welfare system helped to boost domestic demand, as did the demographic boom of the 1940s and 1950s, itself favoured by generous maternity and family allowance payments. On the other hand, investment and modernisation in the nationalised industries acted as a motor for the economy at large, while the new economic planning processes brought together the most dynamic elements in public administration and private enterprise and forged a new mood of optimism and a new commitment to growth.

Inevitably, the increasing integration of the French economy with those of other advanced industrialised countries was to have significant repercussions for attitudes to nation and national identity. Pride in economic recovery was tempered by the knowledge that France was a subordinate partner in an international capitalist bloc dominated by the United States. In reality, this new balance of economic power had already been evident during the inter-war period, but it had been disguised by American diplomatic isolationism and France's attempts to insulate herself from outside economic influences. Now, however, the United States had become more assertive, both economically and diplomatically, and France, like other West European powers, aspired to the American model of consumerism and technological change. As we shall see later, this was to have profound implications for the articulation of French nationalism.

Economic modernisation was to have equally important consequences for the notion of class and class consciousness. France's social and occupational structure was transformed in these years, as the agricultural sector rapidly shed labour in favour of expanding industries and services, and as the urban population grew from just over 50 per cent of the total after the war to 70 per cent in 1968. The most spectacular feature of this process was of course the rural exodus, which saw the farming community shrink from 36 per cent of the working population in 1946 to only 16 per cent in 1968. Initially this served to swell the ranks of the industrial working class, as economic growth and the generalisation of mass assembly-line production in France's basic industries boosted the demand for semi-skilled factory labour. This continued the trend of the 1920s, and though the industrial sector never enjoyed numerical supremacy in France (outweighed by agriculture until the 1950s, and by services thereafter), the first twenty years after the war gave the manual working class a greater social weight than ever before or since.

At the same time, economic developments transformed the structure of the French middle classes. Growing concentration of enterprises in both industry and commerce gradually squeezed out small and medium-sized businesses in favour of large-scale operations, which needed to recruit an increasing number of trained managerial, technical and clerical personnel. These trends were further accelerated by the rapid expansion of both public and private services in the tertiary sector. The category of *cadres* doubled in importance to over 15 per cent of the working population between 1954 and 1968, and this reflected a broader phenomenon of *salarisation*. While in 1954 over one-third of the active population were still deriving their income from sources other than a wage, fourteen years later the proportion had fallen to less than a quarter.

These dramatic shifts in both social structures and social attitudes sounded the death knell of the *société bloquée* with its *petit-bourgeois* patterns of ownership, its conservative preoccupation with balance and stability, and its inherent suspicion of change. We will return later to the deeper implications of all this for the concept of class. For the moment, however, it must be recognised that this sociological and cultural transformation did not have an immediate effect on the structures of the political system and on party political allegiances. At this level, the Fourth Republic proved unable to break with habits and prejudices inherited from the past.

THE FOURTH REPUBLIC

The party politics of the immediate post-war period was dominated by the three parties with the best resistance credentials, communists, socialists and MRP. The Radical Party suffered from its association with the discredited Third Republic, while the old formations of the pre-war parliamentary right, reformed in 1949 as the *Centre national des indépendants,* were too deeply associated with Vichy and collaboration to attract much support in the post-liberation climate. The long-delayed institution of female suffrage did not, contrary to traditional left-wing fears, boost the weight of the conservative Catholic vote, and in the three legislative elections of 1945–6 the socialists, communists and MRP together commanded three-quarters of the electorate. Their collaboration was to provide the basis of government under De Gaulle and his successors until the exclusion of the communist ministers in May 1947.

The most pressing preoccupation of the first period was the drawing up of a new constitution, and to this end a constituent assembly was elected in October 1945. The proportional electoral system ensured that the communists' fractional advantage in votes over the MRP was translated into seats, and this gave the PCF and the third-placed socialists an overall parliamentary majority. Their known preference for a unicameral parliament with strict control over the executive convinced De Gaulle that the *régime des partis* would be re-established, and that the time was not yet ripe for his own constitutional proposals –

a strong President elected by universal suffrage and an upper house with significant countervailing powers. He quickly sought the pretext for resignation in January 1946. This raised the possibility of a communist-led coalition with the socialists, but the latter were unwilling to take the risk, and they succeeded in persuading the MRP to join the alliance as a counter-weight under the premiership of the socialist Félix Gouin.

Although the MRP were more sympathetic to De Gaulle's proposals, it was the package favoured by their allies that was eventually put to referendum in May 1946, only to be rejected by 53 per cent of the voters. The subsequent elections to a second constituent assembly confirmed the shift of opinion, the MRP overtaking the communists as the largest party, and the socialists continuing their disappointing decline. The revised constitutional text was thus a compromise, but the principle of a sovereign assembly was essentially maintained, and the presidency was confined to its traditional non-political role. An upper house was established, but its functions were purely consultative, while the Prime Minister's new right to dissolve the National Assembly was hedged about with conditions that rendered it ineffective in practice. Though the text was approved in the referendum of October 1946, its endorsement was hardly enthusiastic, with 31.1 per cent of the electorate opposing it and a further 31.2 per cent failing to vote.

The first legislative elections of the new Republic took place the following month, restoring the communist advantage in votes and seats and reducing the socialists to only 18 per cent of the turnout, in comparison with 24.6 per cent a year earlier. The gradual resurgence of the Radical Party (11.4 per cent) and the conservative *indépendants* (15.4 per cent) ensured that only a tripartite alliance of the PCF, SFIO and MRP could command a parliamentary majority, but the tensions already revealed by the constitutional debate were soon compounded by other issues that made governmental collaboration between the three parties increasingly problematic.

Mutual suspicion, centering on doubts about the Communist Party's true intentions and on mistrust of the MRP's Catholicism, poisoned the climate from the start, but these latent antagonisms were soon given something to feed on. Worsening relations between the United States and the Soviet Union in 1946 prefigured the onset of the cold war, which would drive a wedge between the communists and the rest of the political community. The loosening of France's hold over her colonies during the war was reflected in the emergence of nationalist movements in Madagascar, Indo-China and the Maghreb, early warnings of another divisive problem that was eventually to bring the Republic down. Finally, the soaring price rises of 1946–7, and the deflationary response of the socialist ministers concerned, led to widespread labour unrest, which eventually culminated in the violent strike movement of the autumn of 1947. Afraid of losing the initiative to the Trotskyist left, the CGT and the PCF were forced to respond, and the communist refusal to vote confidence in the government's economic policy in May 1947 gave the socialist premier, Paul Ramadier, the pretext to dismiss the PCF ministers, thus ending the period of *tripartisme.*

The subsequent entrenchment of the Communist Party in near-permanent opposition was mirrored on the right by De Gaulle's decision in the spring of 1947 to launch a new political movement, the *Rassemblement du peuple français* (RPF), founded jointly on virulent anti-communism and constitutional hostility to the Fourth Republic. In the words of one historian, 'in the space of a few months the Republic which claimed descent from the resistance became estranged from its two principal sources of legitimacy: communism and Gaullism.' [8]

Though the RPF did not have the opportunity to contest a general election until June 1951, forty deputies immediately declared their allegiance and formed a Gaullist parliamentary inter-group. With the addition of the communists, there were thus some 200 deputies who refused to participate in any government majority, and this situation persisted thanks to the election of over a hundred Gaullists in 1951, and of fifty Poujadists in 1956. The parties of the centre were thus driven together to defend the Republic against the two extremes, which between them regularly represented over 40 per cent of the popular vote. The various combinations of socialists, MRP, radicals and *indépendants* which were necessary to secure a parliamentary majority condemned the regime to a series of weak and ineffective ministries, whose average lifespan of six and a half months compares unfavourably even with the 109 governments of the seventy-year Third Republic.

What Maurice Larkin has described as the three divisive 'Cs' of French politics – constitution, class and Catholicism – combined with yet another, colonialism, to fracture the political landscape. If the constitutional question separated the centre from the extremes, the other issues undermined any possibility of consensus between the parties of government. Despite the rightwards drift of the MRP and the increasing moderation of the socialists, their social and economic policies were still too interventionist for the taste of the radicals and the *indépendants,* while the revival of the religious debate over the issue of subsidies to Catholic schools lined up the old Popular Front alliance against the MRP and the combined forces of the right. On the question of decolonisation, the divisions lay within the parties as much as between them, as we shall see. In this context any coalition, be it centre-left (SFIO, radicals, MRP), centre-right (radicals, MRP, *indépendants*) or a combination of the two, was put at risk as soon as the focus of political attention shifted to a new problem.

The inherent instability of the party political system was further aggravated by the volatility of the right-wing electorate. The MRP, too progressive for many of its Catholic supporters, lost much of its support in 1951 to the re-emerging *indépendants* and above all to the Gaullist RPF. However, when De Gaulle wound up his party in 1953, large sections of its electorate transferred to the new Poujadist movement in 1956, which itself disappeared only two years later. Indeed, the character of Poujadism, as much a pressure-group for small business interests as a genuine political party, highlights a further attribute of parliamentary life which the Fourth Republic shared with the Third. In the absence of coherent, programmatic government, party loyalties were often subordinated to the defence of influential vested interests, and the powerful colonial lobby was just one example of a parliamentary coalition which cut across formal political divisions within the Assembly.

This progressive dissipation of the liberation consensus should not be blamed just on the self-indulgence of the 'political class', let alone on a failure of constitution building. The political fragmentation of the Fourth Republic was not simply the product of ideological 'anachronisms'. It was also provoked by the enormous and unprecedented problems the regime had to face, especially abroad, and indeed by the destabilising effect of rapid social and economic change. The modernisation of the political system required as its preliminary the adaptation of party politics to new sociological and cultural realities. Pierre Mendès France was well aware of this when, in 1954, he sought in vain to encourage a more disciplined and realistic code of parliamentary behaviour.[9] If, after 1958, De Gaulle succeeded where Mendès France had failed, this was due not to the intrinsic merits of his constitutional formula, but to the psychological shock of the Algerian crisis which acted as a catalyst for a major realignment of political forces.

NATIONALISM IN A CHANGED WORLD

The character of nationalism in Europe since 1945 has been profoundly conditioned by the bloc structures of the post-war settlement. The division of the continent into zones of influence for the American and Soviet monoliths has set firm limits to the sovereignty of the nation state. In the case of France, her liberation at the hands of the western Allies placed her in the capitalist camp, and her geo-political situation decreed that she should remain there. France's influence in the international agreements of the post-liberation period depended largely on the goodwill of the United States and Britain, and De Gaulle's cultivation of Soviet friendship in no way reflected a policy of genuine neutrality or equidistance between the two emerging superpowers. Soviet support was a useful counterweight in negotiations with Roosevelt and Churchill over the future of Germany, but there was never any doubt where France's ideological and economic allegiances would lie if the choice had to be made.

Indeed, France's chronic economic plight had already drawn her into the American ambit even before relations between the United States and the Soviet Union took a decided turn for the worse. The negotiation of the Washington loan in May 1946 paved the way for her acceptance of Marshall Aid in the following year, and as the cold war gathered pace France was increasingly integrated into the institutional edifice of the capitalist bloc – the Bretton Woods monetary system, the GATT trade agreements, the International Monetary Fund, and finally in the realm of defence, the setting up of NATO in 1949, which placed her under the American nuclear umbrella. This growing economic and military dependence on supra-national institutions had significant repercussions for the articulation of national interests. Whereas before the war nationalism was above all a factor of internal class antagonisms, now these antagonisms were projected onto the international plane. Anti-communism no longer necessarily produced a nationalist discourse as in the 1930s, for now it required French allegiance to an international bloc under American leadership, and the subordination of state sovereignty to the 'defence of the free world'. Nationalism was thus increasingly shaped by external factors, for whatever its domestic class base, it necessarily implied a challenge to this hegemonic relationship.

However, in France's weakened state the only realistic way of mounting such a challenge appeared to lie in a supra-nationalism of another sort, namely the construction of a more united Europe. French participation in this enterprise – from the founding of the Organisation for European Economic Cooperation in 1948 and the Council of Europe in 1949 to the European Coal and Steel Community in 1951 – had many motives, as we shall see. Genuine idealism played its part, and there were also those who believed Europe might emerge as an independent 'third force' in the world, thereby releasing France from the constraints of the polarised bloc system. In reality, however, the panoply of European institutions became a key pillar of the post-war settlement. Co-operative economic reconstruction and political reconciliation in Western Europe were central to American interests. Increased prosperity would stabilise capitalism against 'communist subversion', while Franco-German *rapprochement* would pave the way for the rebuilding of the West German state as the front-line of the Atlantic alliance.

Both Atlanticism and Europeanism thus tended to tone down the nationalist emphasis of liberation discourse, and this was particularly true of the political forces that provided the bases for government under the Fourth Republic. In the case of the resurgent radicals and right-wing *indépendants,* their solidarity with the Western bloc was never in doubt given their deep attachment to the principles of liberal capitalism. As for the MRP, it had some claim to originality by virtue of its initial social reformism and its early advocacy of European integration, but even in its more progressive phase it was deeply anti-communist, and there was never any question of it pursuing its European ambitions outside the framework of the Atlantic alliance.

A more interesting and ambiguous case is that of the SFIO, which had rediscovered its democratic-socialist inspiration in the resistance, and which thus might have been expected 'to favour, at the very least, a policy of neutrality between the communist East and the capitalist West.' [10] On the contrary, however, it evinced an early sympathy for the camp of the Anglo-Saxon democracies, and Léon Blum himself led the negotiations which secured the Washington loan in May 1946. This no doubt reflected the growing realisation that France could not achieve economic recovery single-handed, but the choice of the western camp also confirmed that for the majority of socialists democracy, albeit under capitalism, was preferable to totalitarian communism. The choice was made easier by the example of the pre-war American New Deal and the achievements of the post-war British labour government, which encouraged the belief that the Atlantic bloc would not be irredeemably capitalist in character.

The SFIO was also one of the earliest proponents of the concept of a 'United States of Europe'. The rationale for this drew on the liberal idealist strain in the party's ideology. International peace had often been conceived as a pre-condition for socialism, and added to this was the new conviction that nationalism carried within itself the germ of fascism and war. For many socialists, reconciliation with Germany thus became a moral imperative. At the same time, the position was given a more socialist gloss by the argument that the nation state was no longer capable of insulating radical domestic policies against external capitalist pressures. Only a 'United *Socialist* States of Europe' could safeguard the process of social reform against international capitalism and the logic of the bloc system.

This socialist case for Atlanticism and Europeanism was, of course, cruelly exposed by the realities of the cold war. It soon became apparent that loyalty to the 'free world' implied the endorsement of capitalism, while the European ideal, far from promoting a third democratic socialist force in world politics, became a key factor of integration within the western bloc. This inevitably led to factionalism within the SFIO, and indeed to expulsions and defections, but for the mainstream of the party the contradiction between these international commitments and socialist principles simply remained unresolved. Guy Mollet was elected party secretary in 1946 as the guardian of the SFIO's Marxist doctrinal purity against the 'revisionism' of Mayer and Blum, and yet he was to fall victim to all the cold war prejudices of the time. Author of the famous quip that the Communist Party 'is not on the left, but in the East', he was, as prime minister in 1956, to condemn the Americans' failure to see the Algerian war as part of the international struggle against communism. As for the socialists' closest trade union allies, the *Force ouvrière* which had broken with the communist-led CGT in December 1947, the organisation was funded by the American unions and, allegedly, by the CIA.

It was in the ranks of those opposed to the regime that the most consistent expression of nationalism was to be found. On the left, the Communist Party was well placed to exploit fears that the Republic was sacrificing national independence on the altar of international capitalism. The party's resistance record enhanced its patriotic credentials and allowed it to recall to good effect the sacrifices the working class had made for the nation at large both during the occupation and in the post-liberation *bataille de la production*. Its allegiance to the Soviet Union was less of a liability in the context of the post-war settlement, for it could legitimately claim that whereas the Soviet Union had no territorial designs on France, the development of the Atlantic alliance and of European integration was deeply prejudicial to French national sovereignty. Once again, as in the resistance struggle, nationalism and anti-capitalism appeared to converge.

It is significant, however, that the PCF's critique of Atlanticism and European supra-nationalism focused less on the economic implications (a new stage in the internationalisation of capital) than on the military ones (an aggressive anti-Soviet alliance). This was understandable in the cold war climate, given the party's continuing commitment to the Soviet Union, but this emphasis also lent further weight to the nationalist bias in communist ideology, on the grounds that European integration implied the rearmament of the new West German state. The claim that resurgent German militarism and neo-Nazism was part of the American plan for military aggression against the Soviet Union was the central plank of communist opposition to Franco-German *rapprochement,* and this argument drew as much on xenophobic sentiments derived from the occupation as on any serious socialist rationale. Indeed, when these matters came to a head with the proposal in 1950 for a European Army incorporating German divisions (the European Defence Community), the nationalist emphasis of communist propaganda became increasingly hard to distinguish from the parallel case put by the Gaullists.

The logic of Gaullist nationalism was, of course, very different. The primacy it accorded to the recovery of national status implied on the one hand maximum cohesion within the community, hence its impatience with the political divisions wrought both by parliamentary sectarianism and indeed by class, and on the other hand maximum independence from the two world power blocs. For both reasons it was inherently anti-communist, for the PCF was identified both as a socially disruptive force and as a direct representative of one of the superpowers. On the other hand, the main threat to French sovereignty lay in the process of integration within the western bloc, and here the rhetoric of Gaullists and communists often converged. As we have seen, in its opposition to Atlanticism and Europeanism the PCF increasingly played down the elements of socialist analysis which alone distinguished its position from that of Gaullism. The two main currents of the resistance legacy thus met on the terrain of nationalism, feeding on resentment at the loss of national independence, and on the xenophobia this generated towards the dominant Anglo-Saxon bloc within the alliance and above all towards a resurgent Germany.

The question of the European Defence Community, which was not finally resolved until the National Assembly buried the project in August 1954, had the effect of reviving such nationalist sentiments on a far wider front. Initially a French initiative pioneered by the MRP, it won favour with the United States as a means of reconciling French opinion to the rearmament of Germany, by placing German divisions under collective European control. However, perceptions of the Soviet 'threat' changed with the end of the Korean war, the death of Stalin and a thaw in super power relations, and in this context sympathy for German rearmament in whatever form declined. French opposition to the EDC gathered pace, focusing on hostility to American hegemony and to the revival of Germany, drawing support not only from the Gaullists and the communists, but also from some radicals and many sections of the SFIO, which was split virtually in half by the affair. Indeed, the opponents of the scheme saw the line-up of forces, anachronistically and no doubt unfairly, almost as a continuation of the resistance versus Vichy, with on the one side the defenders of national independence, and on the other anti-communism and 'collaboration' with *revanchiste* Germany.

NATIONALISM AND DECOLONISATION

On the other major issue that awakened nationalist feeling in the 1950s, political divisions were much harder to categorise. The problem of decolonisation, posed by the development of independence struggles in France's empire, did more than any other issue to undermine the credibility of the Fourth Republic. The war against the national liberation movement in Indo-China began in 1946 and dragged on for eight years, until the French defeat at Dien Bien Phu in May 1954 paved the way for Mendès France to negotiate the Geneva armistice in July of the same year. By that time serious trouble was also brewing in the Maghreb, especially in Tunisia and Morocco, and though these countries, like France's territories in Black Africa, were eventually to achieve independence relatively peacefully, the nationalist rebellion in Algeria in November 1954 drew France into another war lasting nearly eight years, which was to carry the Fourth Republic with it.

The Indo-Chinese conflict, damaging and debilitating though it was, did not have the same political impact on public opinion as that later exercised by the Algerian war. It was a distant struggle conducted by professional soldiers, and though powerful colonial interests were involved, there was no sizeable settler community to complicate matters. Furthermore, the conflict was progressively 'internationalised' by American, Russian and Chinese involvement, and it was soon obvious that in this proxy confrontation between the super powers France's colonial sovereignty was of secondary concern. Domestic support for the war fed on anti-communism rather than on any realistic hope of maintaining French rule, and in the end negotiation was seen not as abdication but as a welcome escape from an impossible situation, and a recognition that France could not be expected to bear the brunt of the defence of the 'free world' thousands of miles from home.

However, French defeat in Indo-China confirmed a growing sense of national impotence, especially in the ranks of the armed forces, where the desire to restore the reputation of the army undoubtedly stiffened the resolve to seek a successful military conclusion in Algeria. The political sensitivity of this new problem was further aggravated by other factors. Algeria was France's oldest colony, and was commonly perceived as an integral part of metropolitan France, linked to the homeland by ties of 'kith and kin' through the presence of a million-strong settler community, many of whom were of French extraction. Furthermore, France's use of conscript soldiers in Algeria ensured that the war would have a far more direct impact on public opinion than the earlier conflict in Indo-China. Finally, France's growing international isolation on the issue inevitably fuelled the resentment of those who were determined to cling on to France's last vestiges of empire. The United States' refusal to back the abortive Anglo-French Suez expedition in November 1956 had already signalled its impatience with the colonial pretensions of the old imperial powers, and the unwillingness of the Americans to see the Algerian war as relevant to the containment of world communism rubbed salt into the wound of frustrated nationalism.

Imperialist ideology, though never as central to the articulation of national identity as it was in Britain, had nonetheless been gradually integrated into the value system of the French right. By the 1930s a third of France's export trade was with the empire, and the colonial lobby had become a significant component of the capitalist establishment. The empire had compensated militarily for France's demographic weakness, provided a wider stage for the army and the Catholic Church, and sustained the racist prejudices of great power chauvinism. Now, with France struggling to restore her status, 'the imperial mystique was carried to a level rarely equalled in the history of French colonialism.' [11] And as Rioux records, the resistance had produced a widespread consensus over the colonies: 'the extension to the overseas territories of the Republican liberties recovered by the population of metropolitan France would, it was claimed, assure the future of a rejuvenated Empire.' [12]

Thus, it was a government led by the socialist Guy Mollet which was responsible in 1956 both for the Suez expedition (itself partially motivated by Nasser's support for the Algerian *Front de libération nationale*) and for an intensification of war and repression in Algeria. Though this in part reflected the narrowing options of an embattled regime, it also revealed the deep ambiguities in socialist attitudes to colonialism. The SFIO had inherited the old republican ideal of France's *mission civilisatrice*, whose colonial expression was the principle of *assimilation*, the raising of the indigenous population to a cultural level which would entitle it to the rights associated with French citizenship. If most socialists were unwilling to apply the traditional republican concept of national self-determination to colonial peoples, this no doubt reflected the Euro-centrism of their ideology, but it also indicated at best an underlying paternalism and condescension in their attitudes to the 'under-developed' world.[13] If the party was divided over the choice of liberal or repressive measures in Algeria, the notion of independence was anathema to the vast majority.

It might have been expected that the position of the Communist Party would be free of such ambivalence, given the commitment of the international communist movement since its inception to anti-imperialist struggle in colonial territories. However, though in the climate of the time its opposition to the war and its advocacy of a peaceful solution were not without courage, it hesitated to throw its full support behind the Algerian FLN. This caution no doubt reflected the desire to avoid political isolation on the issue, but it also indicated some unresolved ideological problems. On the one hand there was a reluctance to support a liberation movement that was not communist-led, and this confirmed that the party was unable to come to terms with the strictly nationalist dimension of anti-colonial liberation struggle. On the other hand, the PCF's own 'nationalism', in its campaign against French subordination to American imperialism, had created some dangerous ambiguities, which threatened to rebound on the party when the issue of French sovereignty was raised in this very different context. Indeed, in January 1948, a communist assessment of the Marshall Aid plan had claimed that part of the strategy of American capitalism was to make the old European countries 'yield up the colonial empires whose riches American imperialism covets.' [14]

The most principled opposition to the war thus came from outside the main political parties of the left, among students and intellectuals, ex-communists and dissident socialists, progressive Catholics from *Action catholique* and the CFTC trade-union confederation (*Confédération française des travailleurs chrétiens*),[15] and the modernising elements associated with Mendès France. Though few of these were to engage in active support for the FLN, this convergence around the theme of anti-colonialism in the 1950s was to be the nucleus for the emergence of the 'new left' in the subsequent decade.

Of course, in the absence of consistent support from the mainstream left, this opposition was marginalised by government repression and propaganda, but by September 1957 a change of public mood was discernible. Large sections of the population were simply indifferent or resigned, but opinion polls revealed a growing readiness to envisage negotiations.[16] However, such signals were themselves calculated to alarm the Algerian settler population, and indeed the army which was now enjoying some success in its campaign against the FLN, and in this context the civil authority of Paris was gradually undermined. Dogged by the perennial problem of constructing piecemeal parliamentary majorities, the politicians of the Fourth Republic increasingly lost control of the Algerian situation as events on the ground gathered pace.

CONCLUSION

The 'nationalisms' of the Fourth Republic had a strangely shallow and ephemeral character, lacking in ideological substance and coherence. They appear to have been provoked above all by external factors, by perceptions of France's changed status within the international community, rather than by the internal dynamics of class which was so central to nationalist ideology in earlier times. The right-wing emphasis on national unity as a stabilising, integrative force had of course been exposed and discredited by the experience of Vichy and collaboration. However, it was further undermined by the new realities of the post-war settlement, for the supra-national principles of Atlanticism and Europeanism now appeared to offer a surer guarantee against communism and social upheaval than that provided by the weakened structures of the nation state. In this context, the nationalism invoked by the struggle to preserve France's empire had an anachronistic air, denoting the failure of bourgeois interests to adapt to the new circumstances of international capitalism.

The nationalism of the PCF also appeared somewhat anomalous once it became clear, at the time of the liberation, that the workers' movement was not strong enough to 'incarnate' the nation and lead it in a socialist direction. Given the party's wider ideological perspectives, it might then have been expected to seek an accommodation with other anti-capitalist and anti-imperialist forces on both the domestic and the international front. Instead, it increasingly chose to adopt a traditional nationalist rhetoric, often tinged with xenophobia. It was of course natural and understandable that the party made maximum capital out of its patriotic resistance credentials, and it is true that its growing isolation during the cold war, as the SFIO rapidly moved to the right, obliged it to seek allies elsewhere. However, the fact remains that the party's nationalist discourse was often barely distinguishable from that of the Gaullists or the Poujadists, and on a number of occasions the PCF offered active encouragement and support to these movements.[17]

The function of the PCF's nationalism was to revive the traditional coalition of workers with the small property owners of the urban and rural *petite bourgeoisie*. However, while under the 'stalemate society' of the pre-war era this social bloc had provided the basis for progressive reform even in the field of social legislation, the new circumstances of the post-war period had transformed the character of such an alliance. Rapid industrialisation and modernisation now threatened these *petit-bourgeois* and peasant strata not just with economic impoverishment but with social extinction, and their response, classically expressed in Poujadism, often involved the reassertion of the defensive, anti-modernist values of the old populist right. The willingness of the Communist Party to play on the anti-Americanism, the anti-republicanism and the introspective nationalism implicit in such attitudes, echoed the miscalculations of the *Blanquistes* at the time of the Boulanger Affair.

However, as might be expected, the PCF provided a 'socialist' economic rationale for this stance, which has arguably contributed to the problems of ideological adaptation within the party ever since. In the words of Michael Newman, its policy was predicated on 'unconditional defence of the small against the large, existing methods against modernisation, and all employment against any unemployment, on the assumption that any modernisation increased exploitation and strengthened monopoly capitalism against labour.' [18] The nationalism implied by the class alliance of workers with threatened *petit-bourgeois* and peasant interests thus involved the party in the defence of the most backward-looking and the least economically viable sections of the community. Indeed, these increasingly marginalised strata were a key social constituency for all the various forms of nationalism under the Fourth Republic, including Gaullism and most certainly Poujadism.

On the other hand, the dynamic modernising forces in French society, which were promoting a more cosmopolitan and optimistic view of the outside world, were unable to give coherent political expression to their growing social ascendancy. The divisions of parliamentary politics, though partially compensated for by the autonomous action of the state administrative elites, prevented the emergence of the consensus necessary for a fundamental commitment to economic growth, social change and a review of France's international role. In this respect, political modernisation was the *sine qua non* of further development. However, this could not be accomplished unless the nationalist case, that France was a declining power engaged in abdicating her sovereignty and status, was taken on board. The achievement of De Gaulle after 1958 was to resolve these contradictions, and to develop a nationalist discourse that was geared to an ethos of modernisation.

11

THE SWANSONG OF THE NATION STATE?

The re-emergence of the Nation, with its hands free, evidently modifies the rules of the international game which, ever since Yalta, seemed destined to be limited to two partners.

(Charles de Gaulle, 1965)

The Algerian crisis, which paralysed government in the last year of the Fourth Republic's life, reached its climax on 13 May 1958, when representatives of the settler population took control in Algiers with the acquiescence of the army. In the weeks that followed, De Gaulle lived up to his own recorded definition of *l'homme de caractère* in history who, by seizing the initiative at a decisive moment, may turn the course of events in the direction he desires.[1] While there is no doubt that his supporters in Algiers were active on his behalf, he himself retained the serenity of an elder statesman in retirement, fully aware that as the regime's most respected critic, he was the most likely recourse, as a rampart against civil war or a military take-over in Paris. Timing his interventions to perfection, and refusing to reveal his hand, he first announced on 15 May that he was 'ready to assume the powers of the Republic', and then allowed the tension to mount as rumours circulated that paratroopers from Algeria were to be dropped on Paris. At the same time he privately sounded out key political figures, before declaring on 27 May that he had initiated the standard process for the formation of a government. Irregular though this statement was, for the Pflimlin government was still in office, it had the weight of a self-fulfilling prophecy, and on 1 June De Gaulle appeared before the Assembly to seek investiture as the last Prime Minister of the Fourth Republic.

The Assembly's endorsement, not only of De Gaulle's government, but also of his request for full powers for six months and of his proposal to submit a new constitution to referendum, recalled the fate of the

168

Third Republic some eighteen years earlier, which similarly voted for its own extinction. Indeed, the demoralisation and impotence of the political class in the face of the Algerian problem gave De Gaulle valuable room for manoeuvre, and it was four years before any significant domestic challenge to his authority materialised. His June government included the Socialist Mollet, Pflimlin of the MRP, the radical Berthoin, the *indépendants* Pinay and Jacquinot, and only a handful of Gaullists, symbolising the principle of national unity and reconciliation, and the sole opposition came from the communists, half the socialists, and the supporters of Mendès France.

However, even more decisive in the long term than the acquiescence of the politicians was the widespread sympathy De Gaulle commanded at the level of public opinion. This was strikingly confirmed in the referendum of 28 September 1958 when the text of the new constitution was approved by 79 per cent of voters, with only the communists campaigning against it. The following month the first legislative elections of the new regime were held, and were marked by the spectacular success of the *Union pour la nouvelle République* (UNR), the new movement that De Gaulle's supporters had hurriedly constructed to campaign on his behalf. Its performance owed much to the disappearance of the Poujadists and above all to the restoration of the two-ballot majority voting system last used under the Third Republic. Though all the other parties save the communists maintained their levels of support, and though the UNR won only 17.6 per cent of the votes cast in the first round, the Gaullists benefited greatly from the practice of alliances at the second ballot, and ended up with 189 of the 532 seats in the Assembly. Since they could count on the support of the 132 conservative deputies of the old *Centre national des indépendants et paysans* (CNIP), a stable and durable government majority appeared to have been secured, and with the MRP, radicals and socialists reduced to parliamentary impotence, De Gaulle had freed himself from dependence on at least some of *les partis du passé.*

The new constitution had provided for a strengthened presidency, and De Gaulle's election to this office by a widened electoral college of 80,000[2] was a foregone conclusion. However, the political authority he enjoyed owed less at this stage to the new constitutional provisions, which will be discussed later, than to the powers invested in him to deal with the Algerian emergency. The primacy of this issue for the next four years, and the widespread conviction that he alone held the key, served to consolidate his authority and that of the office he occupied. Indeed, once he embarked on the course of self-determination and eventual independence in Algeria, he was able effectively to widen the bases of his support in metropolitan France. The growing public desire for an end to the war brought him sympathy in unexpected quarters, and this more than compensated for the disillusionment of many conservative supporters of *Algérie française*. Though a handful of Gaullist deputies defected on the issue, notably Jacques Soustelle, the vast majority remained loyal to the General whatever their feelings, not least the Prime Minister Michel Debré, whose sympathies for a continuing colonial presence were well known.

The main opposition to De Gaulle thus inevitably came from the settler population in Algeria, who believed he had betrayed the trust they had placed in him in May 1958, and from sections of the army, whose continuing military success against the FLN blinded them to the fact that such wars of liberation can only be resolved politically. The promise of self-determination for Algeria in October 1959 triggered the so-called *révolte des barricades* in Algiers the following January, from which the army held aloof, but the successful referendum on self-determination in January 1961 led to a far more serious rebellion three months later, implicating four retired generals and ten regiments. De Gaulle, who invoked emergency powers under Article 16 of the constitution to deal with the situation, undoubtedly increased his legitimacy by his determination to defend 'republican legality', and the refusal of many conscripts in Algeria to obey officers sympathetic to the attempted *putsch* brought the crisis swiftly to an end. The path was thus effectively cleared for a settlement through negotiations with the FLN, and the Evian agreements giving Algeria full independence were approved by referendum in France in April 1962.

POLITICAL REALIGNMENT AND MODERNISATION

The constitution of the Fifth Republic introduced some fundamental changes in the balance of institutional power. The Senate was restored to its full legislative role, thus creating a genuine bicameral Parliament. The capacity of government to control the parliamentary agenda, to curtail parliamentary debate, and to evade parliamentary defeat was considerably reinforced. Parliament also lost its sovereignty over its own affairs thanks to a new constitutional definition of the legislative domain, and the restriction of parliamentary sessions to prescribed dates. Furthermore, ministerial office was deemed incompatible with a parliamentary mandate, so deputies and senators who were invited to join the government were required to give up their seats. This attempt to promote a greater sense of ministerial responsibility also encouraged the practice of appointing ministers from outside the assemblies, further diluting the parliamentary character of the regime.

Pride of place in the constitutional text was nonetheless given to the new role envisaged for the President of the Republic. In addition to the traditional dignified functions exercised by previous Heads of State, Presidents of the Fifth Republic were given the right to assume emergency powers in times of crisis, and to dissolve the National Assembly before the end of its five-year term on their sole initiative. The President was also empowered to appoint his prime minister, and since the latter assumed office from that moment, rather than after investiture in the National Assembly as under the previous regime, it was clear that the Prime Minister was responsible not only to Parliament but also to the President.

The issue of where executive power actually lies was left imprecise, though there is nothing in the text that prevents the Prime Minister from exercising his traditional functions as Head of Government. Indeed, the regime remained potentially a parliamentary one, for no government could expect to enact its programme or to avoid defeat and resignation on a question of confidence unless it enjoyed at least the acquiescence of a majority in the National Assembly. The evolution of the Fifth Republic towards stable majority government under presidential supervision is thus the product not of the constitution itself, but of the wider historical circumstances which favoured its approval and application. The Algerian crisis had created a consensus in favour of constitutional reform. The continuation of that crisis in the early years of the new regime helped to consolidate the role of the presidency. And finally, a substantial realignment of political forces laid the foundations for a solid parliamentary majority loyal to the President, which in turn allowed him to extend his functions at the expense of his prime minister.

This realignment was already evident in embryo at the 1958 elections, but there was no guarantee that its effects would be permanent. Once the Algerian problem was resolved, there was every chance that the return to political normality would allow the old party divisions to re-emerge, jeopardising not only De Gaulle's own position but the entire presidential orientation of the regime. De Gaulle's determination that this would not be the case led him in 1962 to propose a major constitutional amendment, namely that henceforth the President of the Republic should be elected by direct universal suffrage on the same two-ballot system used for legislative elections. Other considerations also weighed in his decision, including the need to assure his succession following the attempts on his life by the pro-*Algérie française* terrorist group *Organisation armée secrète*. However, the overriding concern was to institutionalise the new power of the presidency, by giving it the democratic legitimacy which alone could compensate for the charismatic authority he himself enjoyed.

This issue was likely to involve a confrontation with the old political establishment, for the procedures for a revision of the constitution required that any such proposals be first approved by both houses of Parliament before being submitted to referendum. Given that the Gaullists had as yet made few inroads in the Senate,[3] and that in the National Assembly there was still a strong attachment to parliamentary traditions, even among the conservative *indépendants* who had been the Gaullists' closest allies, the success of the project was far from assured. De Gaulle therefore decided to flaunt legality and seek the endorsement of his proposal by referendum alone. This led to a successful vote of censure against the government, which was therefore obliged to resign, but De Gaulle decided to persevere, dissolving the Assembly and allowing the referendum to go ahead. Popular approval for his proposal on 28 October 1962 was less than convincing, with 62 per cent voting in favour on a 77 per cent turnout, but the results of the legislative elections in the following month were a striking confirmation that a major realignment in French party politics had indeed taken place.

The Gaullists, together with their new allies the *Républicains indépendants* (the group of conservative *indépendants* under Giscard d'Estaing which had supported De Gaulle in the referendum campaign), won an unprecedented 37.7 per cent of the vote at the first ballot, and eventually commanded a parliamentary majority with a combined total of 268 of the 490 seats in the Assembly. The major victims of this landslide were the various parties that had collaborated against De Gaulle's referendum in the so-called *cartel des nons*. The opposition *indépendants* were forced to regroup with the remnants of the MRP in the *Centre démocrate,* which won less than 17 per cent of the vote and only 55 seats. The radicals (7.8 per cent of the vote and 39 seats) and the socialists (12.5 per cent, 66) suffered a similar collapse. The communists, on the other hand, recovered from their disastrous 18.9 per cent in 1958 to 21.8 per cent, a level they were to maintain for nearly twenty years. While their 44 seats in the Assembly reflected their continuing electoral isolation in all but those few constituencies where local deals were struck with socialists, their character as a genuine mass organisation with strong influence in the trade unions made them the gaullists' major political rivals. The process of 'bipolarisation' was beginning to assert itself, justifying André Malraux's famous judgement that in the space between the gaullists and the communists there was 'nothing'.

The emergence of stable majority government, which allowed Georges Pompidou to occupy the post of prime minister free of parliamentary embarrassment for six years from March 1962 until June 1968, and the legitimation of the presidential role through universal suffrage, transformed the bases of party politics. Gaullist dominance excluded all other parties from a role in government, and this necessitated a major realignment of the forces of opposition, for only by combining their weight could they hope to challenge the parliamentary ascendancy of the UNR and its allies. The urgency of the problem was exacerbated by the nature of the presidential electoral system, where at the second ballot only the two best-placed candidates could stand. However, the new situation was no longer amenable to the shallow opportunistic coalition-building of the Fourth Republic. Electoral choice was increasingly geared to the exercise of power, and the opposition parties were therefore obliged to seek a new kind of electoral credibility, involving not only the presentation of a coherent government programme but also the provision of a leader capable of assuming the presidency.

The process was to take an exceedingly long time, and only after twenty-three years of the regime's life was the right's hold on the Fifth Republic to be broken. The problem, of course, was the political heterogeneity of the forces of opposition, from the *Centre démocrate* to the Communist Party, and as so often in the past it was the SFIO which, despite its continuing organisational decline in the 1960s, occupied the pivotal position. While the party's moderate anticommunist wing favoured an alliance with the radicals and the MRP elements in the *Centre démocrate,* this was never a viable course. The old bogey of Church-state relations haunted dealings between the socialists and the Christian-democrats, and a centrist alliance excluding the communists would have insufficient electoral weight to challenge the Gaullists. The question of collaboration with the communists, who were beginning to emerge from their 'ghetto' in the more relaxed international climate of the mid-1960s, thus inevitably posed itself, and the answer was provided in 1965, when presidential elections were held on the new principle of universal suffrage. François Mitterrand, the leader of the *Convention des institutions républicaines,* succeeded in winning the support of the radicals, the socialists and the communists as the single candidate of the left, and unexpectedly forced De Gaulle into a second ballot, where he achieved the respectable score of 45.5 per cent.

This was conclusive proof that only an alliance which included the communists had any hope of challenging for power, and it was confirmed at the legislative elections of 1967, where electoral pacts between the PCF and the non-communist left so reduced the Gaullists' parliamentary dominance that they were forced to draw on the support of the dwindling centre opposition. However, this electoral marriage of convenience on the left was a far cry from the genuine convergence on items of policy which might create the conditions for victory. A first step in this direction was made in 1965, when Mitterrand succeeded in uniting the SFIO, the radicals and other elements of the non-communist left in the *Fédération de la gauche démocrate et socialiste* (FGDS), which agreed on single candidacies at the first ballot of the 1967 elections. Furthermore, in the course of 1967–8 the FGDS was to negotiate a limited common platform with the PCF. The process was to be interrupted and delayed by the events of May 1968, and not until 1972 was a revived and expanded *Parti socialiste* to negotiate a common political programme with the Communist Party. However, long and painful as the process was to be, a fundamental political realignment was taking place, which would present the electorate with the clear programmatic political choices the Fourth Republic had failed to provide.

THE GAULLIST SYNTHESIS

The process of realignment considered above was set in motion by the success of De Gaulle, and the party that supported him, in building an unprecented consensus, which provided the basis for Gaullist majority government for sixteen years until the death of President Pompidou in 1974. Though initially, as the opinion polls confirm,[4] the theme of constitutional reform and strong government was a central element in De Gaulle's popularity, in the longer term this was only part of a much more comprehensive ideological synthesis, whose organising theme was that of nationalism.

De Gaulle's own special vision of France, recorded in the famous lines from his war memoirs,[5] allowed him to construct a consensual version of nationalism which trancended many of the divisions the concept had always inspired in the past. His major preoccupation was France's role in the international community, and the internal implications of nationalist ideology were subordinated to this end. The presidentialisation of the regime and the use of the state to promote the most dynamic and prestigious sectors of French industry were geared to the pursuit of national independence and grandeur rather than to the defence of specific class interests. Similarly political and economic modernisation was seen as a means of liberating France from sterile sectarian debates, and of fostering the sense of national unity that was essential to the recovery of her international status. Even the Gaullist concept of *l'association capital-travail,* with its cultivation of profit-sharing and worker-representation in the firm, was conceived less in terms of capitalist consolidation than as an instrument of social peace and national solidarity.

However, if De Gaulle and his closest supporters were, like the followers of Déroulède seventy years earlier, 'nationalist before they were rightist', [6] objectively they served to consolidate the capitalist order by seeking to integrate the proletariat and other dissident elements within the national community. Indeed, this conservative bias was implicit in De Gaulle's own conception of 'France' which, perhaps reflecting the influence of Déroulède and *Le Petit Lavisse* in his childhood, was that of the eternal 'nation' stretching back to the Gauls and transcending 'all its political forms and institutions.' [7] As such it owed nothing to the revolutionary concept of republican citizenship, and indeed France stood above and beyond the French, whose 'propensity to divisions and disputes' [8] De Gaulle frequently castigated. The nation was thus not identified with the people, but with some abstract higher interest, whose interpreters could only be the enlightened guardians of the state.

However, what separated De Gaulle decisively from Déroulède, and the whole backward-looking, *petit-bourgeois* nationalist tradition of the populist right, was his commitment to economic and political modernisation, and his willingness to use the power of the state, sometimes quite ruthlessly, to that end. In this respect, Gaullism undoubtedly displayed some of the features of Bonapartism, though the comparison is clearly anachronistic in economic and social-class terms given that France had now reached the stage of an advanced capitalist society. However, the parallels are tempting, for Gaullism, like Bonapartism, was a politically and socially ambiguous movement when it first came to power, and indeed the RPF under the Fourth Republic had drawn much of its support from the most conservative elements of the economic community. De Gaulle's decision to abandon *Algérie française* was symbolic in this respect, for by turning his back on the archaic colonial legacy he was also renouncing a traditional France that still clung to the economic and social structures of the past.

There was, of course, an element of pragmatism in De Gaulle's Algerian policy, and the question of whether and when he had a change of heart is still hotly debated. Clearly he recognised that the decolonisation process was irreversible, just as by espousing the cause of economic modernisation he simply lent his weight to what were already the dominant forces in French society. However, this pragmatism cannot be understood outside the framework of his ambitions for France's role in the world at large. Algeria was a drain on her resources, a source of international opprobrium, a distraction from more urgent diplomatic priorities. Similarly, a modern and successful economy was the *sine qua non* of status in the contemporary capitalist world.

It was above all in the realm of foreign policy that De Gaulle was able to develop a nationalist discourse which often transcended the barriers between right and left. Decolonisation was a case in point. The left was broadly sympathetic to the dismantling of empire, and generally appreciative of De Gaulle's subsequent support for the cause of national self-determination in the Third World against the inroads of neo-imperialism. On the other hand, the right was partially reassured by the assiduous cultivation of economic and cultural ties with France's former colonies, which guaranteed a continuing sphere of influence. However, France's success in repairing the damage done to her image in the Third World by the Algerian war owed much to De Gaulle's own policy of national independence, which helped to distance France from the rest of the Atlantic bloc in the eyes of the non-aligned countries.

The linchpin of this strategy was De Gaulle's decision to implement France's military nuclear capability. As in so many other fields, he drew here on the legacy of the Fourth Republic, when the key research and development work had been done, but following the American rejection of his demand in 1958 for a French share in the direction of NATO, he determined that French nuclear weapons would be placed exclusively under national control. Having refused to sign the Test Ban Treaty of 1963, he subsequently withdrew France from the integrated military command of NATO, and finally in 1966 obtained the withdrawal of American forces from France and the removal of NATO headquarters from Paris. The powerful symbolism of this act was reinforced by other demonstrations of French independence from American influence – condemnation of American military intervention in Vietnam, support for the Arab cause in the Six Day War, resistance to the encroachment of American multinationals and to the dominance of the dollar. At the same time France went further than any other western government in cultivating links with the Soviet Union, and was the first western power to recognise communist China in 1965.

Similarly, De Gaulle was to develop a distinctive national position on another legacy of the Fourth Republic, namely the European Economic Community, which had been established by the Treaty of Rome in March 1957. While he clearly recognised the advantages that might be derived from the exposure of the French economy to competitive forces and wider market opportunities, he was determined to resist the strengthening of supra-national Community institutions, which he saw as a threat to French national sovereignty, hence his successful insistence on provision for a national veto (January 1966). His preference was for a *Europe des patries* based on the co-operation of sovereign states, and founded ideally on a special relationship with Germany which might pave the way for a Europe that was genuinely independent of the superpowers. This vision of a 'European Europe', implicitly under French moral leadership, (and ideally one day to encompass the continent 'from the Atlantic to the Urals'), was instrumental in his refusal on two occasions to approve British admission to the EEC (January 1963 and November 1967), for Britain's presence would have greatly reinforced the Atlanticist tendencies within the Community.

This vigorous pursuit of national independence was not, of course, without its opponents, especially among the committed Atlanticists and Europeanists on the moderate right and on the social-democratic left. However, its popular impact on a nation eager to recover its self-respect and identity was undeniable, and this cut the ground from under the feet of De Gaulle's political critics. Issues like the EDC, Suez and Algeria had left a strong current of hostility towards the United States and Britain even in sections of right-wing opinion, and those conservatives who disagreed could comfort themselves with the thought that France was still a member of the Atlantic Alliance and the EEC, and that her missiles pointed East. As for the electorate of the left, and especially that of the Communist Party, the Gaullist refusal of American hegemony in the name of national sovereignty could not fail to evoke a sympathetic response. The PCF was clearly embarrassed to find De Gaulle had stolen some of its clothes, but it had itself contributed to the outcome by its own opportunistic cultivation of nationalism at the expense of socialist analysis in the 1950s.

The legacy of Gaullism has, of course, been considerable. The institutions of the Fifth Republic remain intact and the political realignment initiated by the rise of the Gaullist Party has had lasting effects. Furthermore, the discourse, if not the practice, of national sovereignty and independence has become the new orthodoxy in the field of foreign policy. However, twenty years have passed since De Gaulle disappeared from the political scene, and since then the validity of the nation state as a political framework has been called into question. In the case of France, the events of May 1968 challenged the state's internal structures, while the further evolution of the international environment has thrown doubt on the capacity even of a strong middle-ranking power like France to secure a measure of economic, military and diplomatic independence.

Many would argue, of course, that De Gaulle's own nationalism was no more than bluff or self-delusion, a rhetorical device which drew a veil over the realities of France's deep integration within the western capitalist bloc and the relative weakness of her industrial and military resources. France remained part of the Atlantic Alliance and within the sphere of American economic imperialism, and sceptics doubted whether France's 'independent' nuclear weapons really made her any less reliant on the American nuclear umbrella. Similarly, De Gaulle's strong support for the United States during the Cuban missile affair in 1962 indicated that in times of acute international crisis there would be no doubt where his ultimate sympathies lay. However, as we shall see, developments over the last twenty years have not only exacerbated these underlying external constraints. They have also tended to undermine the internal ideological foundations of nationalism.

NATIONALISM AND THE RIGHT SINCE DE GAULLE

This book has dealt with broad historical trends, and clearly any attempt to identify these in the period covered by the last twenty years is bound to be hazardous and speculative. It involves an attempt to abstract what is essential for our theme from a welter of events that have not yet been properly digested by the historian, so this section has no pretensions to offer an adequate coverage of recent French history. We seek merely to focus on changes which may prove to have a lasting significance for the evolution of nationalism and the principle of nationhood.

In this respect a key theme would appear to be that of a growing 'crisis of the state', which has tended to undermine two of the assumptions implicit in the Gaullist consensus of the 1960s. The first of these was the illusion that the French state had the capacity to exercise a degree of autonomy in world affairs, and the second, closely related to the first, was the belief that the state could be used to promote the competitiveness of French industry. Central to the decline of both these Gaullist articles of faith has been the gradual integration of the French economy into a complex international capitalist system, within which it occupies a subordinate position in relation to both the United States and other more dynamic industrial economies.

While in the 1950s, in a relatively protected economic environment, the state had been a key agency for economic growth and industrial reconstruction, the situation changed once France lost her captive colonial markets and entered the EEC. Thereafter, increasing exposure to foreign commerce meant that international market forces became the major catalyst for modernisation, with state industrial policy reduced to a secondary, supportive role within this overall process. However, the boom years disguised the fact that, as France's exchanges with other advanced capitalist countries increased, so the competitiveness of many of her key industries was being reduced. Her trade balance with other industrialised countries was unfavourable in many crucial sectors, and the penetration of her domestic markets by imported manufactures was accompanied by a rapid inflow of foreign capital into her industries.

These trends were already at work under De Gaulle, but they accelerated under President Pompidou (1969–74) and became positively damaging under Giscard d'Estaing (1974–81) when the oil crisis of 1973 brought the long post-war boom to an end and seriously undermined France's trading position. The strictly capitalist logic of this situation implied acceptance of the growing internationalisation of the economy, harmonisation of economic policies with those of other leading capitalist states and, given the increasing drain on state resources under the recession, reliance largely on market forces to restore the competivity of French industry. However, the popularity of De Gaulle's grandiose *dirigiste* industrial policies made it politically difficult for either of his successors to abandon them. The strategy of designating and promoting certain large enterprises as 'national champions' was maintained and, under Giscard, the state was also obliged to support endangered firms in the old declining sectors. This appeared anomalous at the time, for Giscard, the first non-Gaullist President of the Fifth Republic, came from a political tradition associated with economic liberalism, and initially there had been much talk of the need to sacrifice 'lame duck' enterprises. However, though Giscard's second Prime Minister, Raymond Barre (1976–81), sought through a variety of measures at the macro-economic level to allow market forces freer rein, there was no disengagement of the state in the field of industrial policy.

However, over the last ten years the French right has experienced the attraction of the neo-liberal doctrines that have become the vogue throughout the advanced capitalist world. Monetarist theory and the so-called 'crisis of big government' has led to the advocacy of deregulation, privatisation, the enterprise culture and the rolling back of the state, and the right-wing government of Jacques Chirac (1986–8) of course made substantial moves in this direction. Though limits have been set to this process by France's *dirigiste* and technocratic traditions, and by the sensitivity of public opinion, the new liberalism has undoubtedly effected a major sea change in French attitudes. In this respect it is striking that the political pace was set by Chirac's neo-Gaullist *Rassemblement pour la République* (RPR), which has abandoned the interventionist Gaullist legacy. Even more striking, of course, is the new economic liberalism of the socialist left, to which we will return later.

This growing willingness to allow market forces to shape the economy involved an acceptance of its internationalisation and of its integration within the world capitalist system. This had clear implications for the perception of France's overall diplomatic status within the western alliance, and a change was already evident when Pompidou replaced De Gaulle after the latter's resignation in 1969. Though the popularity of the independent line in foreign policy ensured that Pompidou would maintain privileged links with Eastern Europe and oppose supra-national initiatives in the EEC, there was an undoubted thaw in relations with the United States and, above all, a change of heart on British admission to the EEC, which was finally negotiated in 1972. In the words of one commentator, 'Pompidou accepted realities such as US predominance, but looked to European co-operation for greater influence than was available to France alone.' [9]

Giscard's position was politically more delicate. Precisely because he came from a more Atlanticist, pro-European tradition on the French right, he was anxious to preserve the appearance of an independent line. His ill-judged meeting with Brezhnev in 1980 after the Soviet invasion of Afghanistan was one example, but the main scope for national self-assertion lay in the Third World – recognition of the Palestine Liberation Organisation, the cultivation of strong cultural and commercial ties with African countries including military intervention in Chad and Zaire, continued links with the Arab oil-producing states where French economic interests outweighed his own personal sympathy for Israel.

However, economic interests equally implied a readiness to co-operate with both the United States and the rest of the EEC. Between 1973 and 1976 a new international monetary system was effectively established involving 'a degree of Franco-American co-operation inconceivable in the time of De Gaulle.' [10] Within the EEC Giscard sought close ties with Germany, made concessions to supra-nationalism by accepting the establishment of a European Council and direct elections to the European Parliament, and actively encouraged progress towards monetary union. As for the realm of defence, while Giscard refused to rejoin NATO's command structures, there was a growing harmonisation of strategic thinking between France and NATO, and this *rapprochement* was strengthened in the late 1970s with the collapse of *détente* between the superpowers.

The trend of right-wing thinking has thus been towards a substantial dilution of the Gaullist nationalist tradition, even though much of the rhetoric remains intact. Today, of course, it is difficult to extract the distinctive attributes of the right's foreign policy from the broad consensus which now appears to exist on such issues. However, the fact that the neo-Gaullists now accept with equanimity the prospect of further steps towards the single European market in 1992 is some measure of how far things have changed, as indeed is their broad acceptance of American defence initiatives in the last ten years. The notion that France has a world role to play is of course unchallenged in conservative circles, but today this is overlaid with a more pragmatic recognition that within the advanced capitalist camp France's vocation is one of competitive partnership rather than 'independence'.

Some would argue that De Gaulle, himself a pragmatist, was fully aware that a middle-ranking power like France could only achieve influence through judicious co-operation with others, and that his pretensions to national independence were simply designed to give France the confidence to play this less ambitious role more effectively. Certainly, behind the changes of rhetoric, there has been an underlying continuity in French foreign policy ever since the onset of the 1950s cold war – implicit, though not always acknowledged, acceptance of American leadership and the attempt to develop a European counter-weight within the western alliance. However, as Stanley Hoffman has pointed out, while in the past France has attempted to 'use' Europe for these purposes, the future of such a policy now appears to depend on a degree of supra-nationalism which would make even the illusion of national sovereignty increasingly hard to sustain.[11]

These shifts in foreign policy have their parallels on the domestic front. The Gaullist quest for consensus involved the presentation of the state as the legitimate interlocutor for the collective interests of the 'nation', but this has largely been abandoned in favour of a neo-liberal view of the state as the guarantor of a free-market economy. In the process the discourse of nationalism has inevitably given way to that of individualism. At the same time, the impact of the enterprise culture and high-technology consumerism on those social groups that have access to them is making their tastes and values increasingly cos-mopolitan, inviting their allegiance not so much to anything inherently French as to a model of society associated with advanced international capitalism. In this context, it is not surprising to find that whereas the Gaullist *Union des démocrates pour la République* in the mid-1960s could claim to be a genuinely national 'catch-all' party drawing wide support from all ranks of society, the neo-Gaullist RPR and their allies in the *Union pour la démocratie française* have a more homogeneous class base in which the more privileged groups in society are overrepresented.

The anomaly in this picture is, of course, the dramatic rise of Le Pen's *Front national* from obscurity to prominence in the last six years. Its emphasis on the themes of racism, authoritarianism and the return to traditional French values, ensure that 'nationalism' survives in one section of conservative opinion. It would, of course, be misleading to treat this phenomenon solely as some kind of reaction against the broad evolution of the right described above. Vital contingent factors – the presence of a left-wing government, the impact of immigration, insecurity and unemployment – must be taken into account. It is also true that there is a substantial convergence of attitudes between the FN and the more conservative wing of the RPR and UDF on the themes of law and order, and indeed race, while the FN's wholehearted endorse-ment of economic liberalism represents a major break with the traditions of the extreme right.

However, the parallels with Poujadism are tempting, and not only because Le Pen himself was a Poujadist deputy. Like its predecessor, the FN is preoccupied with a single theme, in this case immigration, but the obsession with the preservation of France's 'pure' national identity reflects the same underlying hostility to the forces of modernisation. If the electorate of the *Front national* is socially more heterogeneous, less distinctively *petit-bourgeois,* more proletarian, than that of Poujadism, then this indicates that the contemporary modernisation process has more far-reaching social consequences than that of the 1950s. Le Pen's hostility to the legacy of De Gaulle is based not just on nostalgia for *Algérie française,* but on resentment at all the forces for change unleashed by the 1960s, which he equates with a process of national degeneration and decline, both at home and abroad. Though he reserves his main barbs for the left, it is the whole 'political class' which stands accused in his eyes of having betrayed the values on which French national identity is based. And while it would be wrong not to recognise that Le Pen is the product of specific historical circumstances and distinctive contemporary problems, the essential 'national' values he invokes are the same conservative, traditionalist ones which underpinned the ideology of Vichy.

NATIONALISM AND THE LEFT SINCE DE GAULLE

The prior condition of any effective challenge to the right's domination of the Fifth Republic was some form of political accommodation between the PCF and the non-communist left, and this was finally achieved in 1972 when the communists signed a Common Programme of Government with the reconstructed Socialist Party (*Parti socialiste*), now led by François Mitterrand. While the PCF had been working towards this end for five or six years, Mitterrand's FGDS alliance (1965–8) was a reluctant partner thanks to the strong anti-communist sentiments of the radicals and many SFIO socialists. It took the shock of the electoral debâcles of 1968 and 1969[12] to reveal the likely price of continuing disunity, and to initiate a process of reorganisation on the non-communist left, which effectively marginalised or excluded the opponents of collaboration with the communists.

It was, of course, Mitterrand's belief that this 'Union of the left' would ultimately work in favour of his rejuvenated and reorganised Socialist Party, and the decade of the 1970s dramatically confirmed his opinion. In successive general and local elections, the PS first caught then outdistanced the PCF, and the latter's growing conviction that it would be the junior partner in any future left government led it finally to break with the alliance in 1977. Mitterrand therefore entered the 1981 presidential elections without the communist support he had enjoyed in his unsuccessful bid of 1974. However, for the first time this disunity proved to be a positive benefit rather than a liability. Freed from suspected communist tutelage, he was now more acceptable to the electoral 'middle ground', while many communist voters, eager for a voice in government, abandoned their own candidate, Georges Marchais, in favour of Mitterrand at the first ballot. Marchais's score of 15 per cent marked the beginning of a chronic communist electoral slide which has continued virtually unabated, and the PCF's acceptance of four minor posts in Mitterrand's new government merely confirmed the party's increasing impotence.

There was, however, a price to be paid for the extraordinary electoral success of Mitterrand's strategy. If the socialists were no longer beholden to the Communist Party, they nonetheless needed to secure the support of their newly-won working-class clientele, whose attitudes and values had so long been shaped ideologically by the PCF. In the key field of economic and social policy, therefore, socialist strategy was still largely based on the Common Programme of 1972, whose underlying philosophy was increasingly anachronistic, as we shall see. Indeed, in a perceptive recent essay George Ross described the 1972 programme as 'Chapter Two of the program of the *Conseil national de la Résistance*,' [13] and the parentage is clear in the proposals for further nationalisations, the restoration of planning, the extension of social welfare and Keynesian demand-stimulation. Ross goes on to argue that this 'left resistance-liberation discourse' had survived on the margins of political life as the main point of potential ideological convergence between the two parties once their 'cold war divisions' [14] had been overcome.

For our own purposes, however, the most striking feature of this discourse was its inherent nationalism. In this respect, it drew on the traditional working-class identification with the 'nation', which the PCF had assiduously cultivated ever since the Liberation, and which persistently equated capitalism with American hegemony and the 'collaborationist' tendencies of the French business community. The communists remained the most strident exponents of this rhetoric, and in their 1978 anti-EEC campaign they accused Giscard and his supporters of promoting 'the uncontrolled domination of multinational companies', and of using foreign support 'to oppose the people of France in the tradition of the *émigrés* of Coblenz; of Thiers allying himself with Bismarck against the Commune; and of the Pétainist collaboration with Hitler.' [15] The socialists were more restrained, but in their pursuit of the working-class vote they too injected a strong dose of nationalism into the intellectual rationale for their economic policies, claiming that the source of France's economic problems lay in her dependent status within the imperialist system of world capitalism, and that the goal of socialism was inseparable from that of national economic liberation.[16]

Paradoxically, however, as George Ross himself points out, by the time the left came to power, the ideological foundations of 'resistance-liberation discourse' had already been profoundly undermined.[17] Collectivist notions of national community and state legitimacy had been weakened by increasing cultural differentiation within civil society, and the decline of national particularism in the face of international influences. Central to this in sociological terms was the dramatic rise of new salaried 'middle strata' – teachers, civil servants, scientists, technicians, managers, communicators – which together came to represent a social bloc as large as the manual working class, while the working class itself was losing its cultural homogeneity under the impact of technology, consumerism and the decline of traditional industries.

Despite efforts to 'bend' traditional left discourse sufficiently to accommodate the aspirations of these new groups, a true ideological synthesis was never achieved, hence the charge that the first two years of socialist government were riddled with contradictions and inconsistencies. Hence also the claim that Mitterrand's subsequent 'modernisation' of the French left drew the inevitable conclusions from the lessons of 1981–3, and embarked on the only possible course – the acceptance of economic liberalism, of Atlanticism, of France's integration into the international capitalist system. In other words, the abandonment of 'heroic' resistance-style nationalism necessarily involved the abandonment of socialism itself.

However, to endorse such arguments is to ignore the fact that, ever since the early 1960s, efforts had been made on the non-communist left to adapt socialist theory to the new cultural and sociological realities wrought by rapid modernisation. Though initially this was largely an intellectual enterprise, the events of May 1968 gave these new themes a deeper popular resonance, and in the 1970s they achieved more substantial organisational expression through the rise of what Alain Touraine has called the 'social movements', through the new dynamism of la vie associative, and through the much vaunted concept of workers' self-management (autogestion). Such initiatives enjoyed sufficient popular appeal for the Socialist Party to take them on board, and its apparent endorsement of feminism, ecology, political decentralisation

185

and community action was as essential to its ideological radicalisation as the more traditional emphasis it placed on state-led economic regeneration. Indeed, its adoption in the mid-1970s of the doctrine of *autogestion* was seen as its distinctive contribution to working-class emancipation, the basis for a democratic socialist alternative to the 'statism' of reformist social democracy and totalitarian communism.

In other words, the abandonment of 'left resistance-liberation discourse' did not necessarily imply the pursuit of the kind of pragmatic consensus which today marks the politics of the PS. The modernist radicalism described above sought to redefine the basis of left-wing politics, and in the process it rejected the nationalist perspectives of workerist, statist left ideology. It shifted the emphasis from the struggle of classes for the exercise of state power to the battleground of 'civil society', which was seen as the crucial domain for the inculcation of new values and for the development of new forms of democratic control. It thus rested on the recognition that the modern state had neither the capacity nor the popular legitimacy to act as a vehicle of social emancipation, and that new decentralised structures of civil action and democratic accountability had to be built at the grass-roots level.

If this alternative was to retain its radical dimension, it had of course to reject the individualism and narrow materialism implicit in the new right-wing doctrines of economic liberalism. The emphasis therefore had to be on collective and communal values, but not those associated with nation and state which had outgrown their progressive potential. Class remained an important dimension in all this, hence the attempt to popularise the concept of 'workers' control', but the shift in the balance of social forces meant that the traditional preoccupations of the working class could no longer be the organising focus of left-wing politics. New themes emerged as a rallying-point for collective interests – women's rights, regional autonomy, municipal action, the concerns of ecologists and Third Worldists.

The rise of the so-called 'social movements' exemplifies many of these trends. First, in general terms, it reflects the fact that the workplace is no longer the organisational and ideological core of radical discourse. Secondly, the social movements are generally characterised by their refusal to adopt the structures and goals of political parties, which are geared of course to the conquest of state power. An examination of their more specific objectives confirms the point. The regionalist movements which achieved such prominence in the 1970s, were driven above all by their rejection of the bureaucratic, alienating centralism of the modern French state, as indeed are the various forms of community action encompassed in the term *vie associative,* whose new vigour testifies to the decline of the old French pattern of passivity in civil society. The ecology movement is equally committed to a more decentralised model of economic and political organisation, while the feminist movement, with its diffuse structures and its emphasis on individual and collective self-discovery, is inevitably geared more to the transformation of popular attitudes than to leverage over the organs of state. Indeed, feminism is deeply subversive of the assumptions on which left-wing nationalism has been constructed through history, for women have until recently been excluded both from citizenship of the Republic and from the national political community of the working class. The concept of nation inevitably lacks historical resonance for many of those who make up half the French population.

It is equally true that the new concerns of radical politics have a strong international dimension, quite explicit in the concerns of Third Worldists but equally prominent in the case of the ecology movement, whose global preoccupations necessarily imply an unprecedented degree of international co-operation and co-ordination. Similarly, the demands of regional autonomists open the prospect of new forms of devolved government which would transcend existing national frontiers. As for the women's movement, by definition it is based on a sense of collective identity whose potential cross-national appeal is more solid than that ever exercised by the notion of class. Indeed, in general terms the exposure of France to outside economic influences has been accompanied by a process of cultural cross-fertilisation which has affected all ranks of society, and the growth of more cosmopolitan perspectives amongst those who were previously denied access to the wider world makes it finally possible for the left to make concrete its internationalist ideals.

It would be churlish not to recognise that the first period of socialist government made some significant contributions to the extension of women's rights and to political decentralisation. However, such reforms were divorced from any overall commitment to genuine social transformation, and the volte face of 1982–3 buried the legacy of 1968 along with that of 1944. Once it was revealed that a national road to economic recovery was no longer viable in the modern world, socialist principles were sacrificed to the logic of international capitalism. The PS now seeks to become the architect of a new moderate consensus, a new catch-all party which, in the words of George Ross, resembles 'nothing more than the American Democratic Party.' [18] The basis of this 'consensus' is the endorsement of a humanised form of economic liberalism, tempered by a technocratic state, and in the field of foreign policy a growing acceptance of Atlanticism and European co-operation.

On the face of it, these latter features would invalidate any comparison with the consensus sought by De Gaulle in the 1960s, and yet significant Gaullist characteristics remain. Mitterrand fills the presidential office with familiar *hauteur,* and France retains her traditional commitment to a 'world role.' And above all, under the socialists as under the right, the word nation is no more than a euphemism for the centralised state, whose pretensions to represent the collective interests of the community today find their best guarantee in growing public apathy and passivity. Indeed, it is tempting to see the extravagant bicentennial celebrations of the French Revolution as an attempt to cloak the state retrospectively in the republican legitimacy it has lost.

Given the blandness of the new Socialist Party, the marginalisation of an ideologically unrepentant PCF, and the retreat of the once *autogestionnaire* CFDT trade-union confederation into 'new realism',[19] there are few signs of any imminent radicalisation of the French left. The success of the PS in recuperating some of the themes of the social movements in the 1970s has had the effect of demobilising them, though the rise of the anti-racist movement, the recent successes of the ecologists, and the burgeoning activity of *la vie associative* testify to the continuing vigour of civil society. For those who, like Daniel Singer, refuse to believe that 'time must have a stop and history end with capitalism,' [20] faith must lie in the capacity of the radical left to reach 'beyond the fragments' [21] and achieve a new synthesis. And in that synthesis there would no longer be any place for nationalism.

CONCLUSION

> Thus today, for domestic and external reasons, the French state no longer defines or crystallises French nationalism, and nationalism in French society no longer serves as a forceful inspiration for the state.
>
> (S. Hoffmann, 1974)

The history of nationalism in France is a complex one, closely interwoven with the country's social and economic evolution and with the tide of political events. For this reason it has not been easy to focus clearly and consistently on the changing forms of nationalism over the last two hundred years, and to indicate the underlying mechanisms of the process involved. We have, however, sought to demonstrate that the phenomenon is primarily political, rather than economic or cultural, and that it is therefore characterised by diversity. The articulation of the idea of nationhood is profoundly different in the ideologies of left and right, reflecting rival class perspectives on the nature and purposes of the political community, and the picture has become more complicated as the class structures of society have evolved. It is not possible to talk of nationalism, only of nationalisms.

THE LEFT AND THE NATION

For the left, the concept of nation developed by the French Revolution was based on the notions of popular sovereignty and self-government. In this sense it was doubly progressive. First, it encouraged subjects to become citizens, to overcome their submissiveness and their parochial horizons and to participate actively in the public affairs of a newly expanded collectivity. Secondly, nationhood was based not on the narrow defence of exclusive interests but on universal principles. All peoples everywhere enjoyed the same rights to free themselves from

189

tyranny, to constitute themselves in self-governing communities, and to become part of a new international order based on the 'equality of nations'.

The concept of democratic nationhood was, of course, based on the notion of an undifferentiated citizenry, who allegedly would enjoy 'equality' by virtue of their common access to certain civil liberties and political rights. The revolutionary potential of this mobilising ideal was however undermined by two parallel historical developments. The first was the process of social differentiation which accompanied the growth of capitalism, and which gradually drove a wedge between the interests and aspirations of an emerging industrial proletariat and those of the property-owning classes. The implications of this new class divide were already apparent in June 1848, and they were decisively confirmed with the crushing of the Paris Commune in 1871. The sentimental unity of the democratic nation foundered on the class antagonisms of modern industrial society.

The second development was the final achievement in the institutions of the Third Republic of the civil liberties and formal political equality envisaged by the Revolution. Nationalism ceased to be a vehicle for social emancipation, and became instead part of the official republican ideology of the established bourgeois state, an agent of consensus and integration imposed from above. In this context it was natural that class rather than nation should become the principal focus for the egalitarian aspirations of the workers' movement. Socialism displaced republicanism on the radical wing of French politics, and sought to transcend the bourgeois nation state, both externally through the ideal of international class solidarity and internally through the creation of its own autonomous organisations in civil society.

There were, however, a number of obstacles to the development of the workers' movement as a fully independent political force – numerical weakness, political division, the need to safeguard the limited democratic rights afforded by the Republic, the difficulty of translating internationalist principles into effective action. As a result, a degree of political collaboration with the rest of the republican left was a powerful strategic option, particularly at crisis points when the regime faced internal subversion (the Dreyfus Affair, the riots of 6 February 1934) or when, as in the run-up to two world wars, national sovereignty itself was threatened.

It would, however, be misleading to interpret this willingness to rally to the defence of the 'nation' and the Republic at such times as proof of the growing integration of the working class into the national political community. The threat of war in the years preceding both 1914 and 1939 involved painful moral and strategic choices in which there was no simple dichotomy between loyalty to class and loyalty to nation, and on both occasions the socialist and workers' movement was chronically and tragically divided by the dilemma. Similarly, as the mass strikes of June 1936 were to show, a strategy of electoral and parliamentary co-operation with the rest of the republican left did not preclude dramatic forms of popular working-class mobilisation and self-organisation.

The decisive change came in the period extending from the Popular Front to the Liberation. The social and economic reforms of 1936 and 1944–5 confirmed a shift in the domestic class compromise, and fostered the illusion the state could be used as an agency for the gradual transformation of capitalism within the republican framework. Similarly, as the onset of the cold war narrowed down the options of socialist internationalism, so the anti-fascist nationalism of the resistance was converted into a central ideological theme of Communist Party discourse, equating capitalism with American imperialism and socialism with the theme of national sovereignty. When in the 1970s the communists and socialists had resolved their cold war antagonisms sufficiently to agree on a common platform, these worker-ist, statist and nationalist themes were an inevitable point of conver-gence.

It is above all in the post-war period, therefore, that the thesis of the working-class integration into the political community becomes con-vincing. The primary importance accorded in both communist and social-democratic discourse to the role of the state as the agent of social and political change has effectively undermined the traditions of autonomous working-class action and self-organisation. It is significant that the Communist Party has been accused by the extreme left of having failed on three separate occasions to appreciate the radical potential of popular movements in civil society – during the mass strikes of 1936, in the liberation period and again during the events of May 1968. Similarly it has been argued that the Socialist Party in the late 1970s successfully demobilised both the trade unions and the social movements by 'recuperating' their aspirations in its electoral manifestos.

At the same time the theme of nationalism, which momentarily during the resistance struggle had appeared to coincide with socialist objectives, has proved since the war to be ideologically incompatible with the traditional egalitarian and democratic demands of the workers' movement. Its opportunistic exploitation by the communists in the 1950s served only to underpin the Gaullist synthesis of the 1960s, and to confirm that in an advanced capitalist system the concept of nation has no concrete significance at the level of civil society. It tends simply to become a euphemism for the interests of the state. It is ironic indeed that the workerist, statist and nationalist perspectives which underpinned both the Resistance Charter and the socialist programme of 1981, had already been called into question by a series of developments that have accompanied the post-war process of economic modernisation – the decomposition of the traditional working class, the rise of the new salaried middle strata, the cultural differentiation of civil society, the subservience of the modern technocratic state to capitalist interests, the profound internationalisation of the French economy. It was not so much socialism itself, but a particular model of socialism, which came to grief in the débâcle of 1981–3.

The radical alternative left which has taken shape since the 1960s has been concerned to address these changes, and its critique has focused precisely on the mainstream left traditions of workerism, statism and nationalism. It has challenged the old notion of 'the leading role of the proletariat' in favour of a new progressive class alliance in which traditional egalitarian demands would be fused with the more recent themes of feminism, anti-racism, ecology and industrial democracy. It has challenged the traditional emphasis on the state as the vehicle for change in favour of a strategy geared to the promotion of democratic action in civil society and the dismantling of the Napoleonic state through political decentralisation. Finally, it has emphasised the international character of contemporary social and cultural change and the growing interdependence of the world economy, and looks to an increasing co-ordination of campaigns across national frontiers.

Significantly, there are strong parallels between these radical alternative perspectives and the original aspirations of the nascent labour movement a century ago, though of course the class bases are substantially different. There is a similar emphasis on the need to transcend the nation state, both through the diffusion of power in civil society and through the promotion of international consciousness. Arguably the climate for such an enterprise has never been more propitious. The capacity of the modern bureaucratic state to fulfil its multiple domestic obligations and to insulate its national sphere of influence against external forces has been decisively called into question. Similarly, the new era of superpower detente, accompanied by dramatic political change in Eastern Europe and in the Soviet Union itself, potentially opens the path to a variety of interchanges between the First and Second worlds, while the pressing concerns of global ecology demand a new relationship between North and South. At the same time, technological progress and economic interdependence have considerably extended cultural horizons in all industrially developed countries. The space thus exists for a new kind of radical inter-nationalism, more diverse, more diffuse, than the institutionalised versions of the past, and free of allegiance to the rigid models of society imposed by the power blocs.

However, such aspirations find little reflection in the current attitudes of the mainstream left, as represented by the French Socialist Party. Here, 'internationalism' involves a pragmatic acceptance of the *force majeure* of international capitalism, with a firmer commitment to Atlanticism than at any time under the Fifth Republic, along with a marked enthusiasm for the single European market of 1992, with all that that implies for the further consolidation of powerful trans-national economic interests. As for nationalism, the radical 'liberation' rhetoric of the PS programme has been abandoned in favour of a more conservative discourse which extols the values of consensus and France's status as a world power, and which above all equates the nation with the state. In this respect, small wonder that so many commentators have drawn the analogy between Mitterrand and De Gaulle.

THE RIGHT AND THE NATION

Historians have variously identified the traditions of the French right with the concepts of 'order' and 'interests', while the left has been associated with 'movement' and 'ideas'. These generalisations, crude though they may be, offer some insight into the relationship between the right and 'nation', which has been rather less complex in ideologi-cal terms than that of the left. The cultivation of national loyalties was above all an instrument of stabilisation and integration in line with the interests of the dominant social classes, and it achieved prominence in right-wing discourse only when more traditional mechanisms of social control had begun to lose their efficacy. It had little to do with the principles of national sovereignty, or indeed with patriotic sentiment, as the 1933–45 period was to prove, and when in more recent times the supra-national structures of the western capitalist bloc became the principal guarantee against social destabilisation, nationalism gradually ceased to be a central pillar of conservative ideology.

For much of the nineteenth century, the mainstream legitimist and Orleanist right had little sympathy for the concept of nationhood, which was deeply associated with the revolutionary doctrines of republicanism and popular sovereignty. The legitimist commitment to divine and hereditary principles of government, to the *ultramontane* authority of the Catholic Church, and to the social order of the *Ancien Régime* which survived beyond French frontiers, left no room for the notion that legitimacy should be rooted in the principle of popular national consent. As for the Orleanists, their attachment to the narrow class interests of the *grande bourgeoisie* and to the principle of government by a propertied elite meant that for them too the word nation had dangerous connotations. When the issue of national sovereignty was raised in its most acute form, during the revolutionary wars and again at the time of the Prussian invasion of 1870, the royalist right gave ample proof of where its interests lay.

Of course, the two Bonapartist interludes presented nationalism in a different form, as an agency of order, discipline and social peace imposed by an authoritarian state. However, while twice in fifty years the classical right found it advantageous to acquiesce in dictatorship, as a rampart against democracy and revolutionary upheaval, it was alarmed by the populist and meritocratic qualities of this nationalism which threatened to disrupt the social hierarchy on which its authority was built. This, and the fact that both the Jacobin and Bonapartist traditions tended to favour an interventionist foreign policy which sought to undermine the stability of the European Old Order, tended to reinforce right-wing suspicions of nationalism in either guise.

The major sea change in right-wing attitudes, which spawned a new and distinctive form of nationalism in the last quarter of the nineteenth century was, as we have indicated, an extremely complex process of ideological synthesis. It fed on anti-German *revanchisme,* on the eagerness of the conservative Third Republic to foster social consensus, on the quest of the old Catholic royalist right for a new political discourse, on the fears of an increasingly isolated and vulnerable *petite bourgeoisie.* There can be no doubt, however, that the new nationalism that emerged was admirably suited to the conservative purpose of internal stabilisation and integration. Membership of the community was defined, not in terms of citizenship, but in terms of race, or in terms of loyalty to Church, army or *raison d'état.* Those whose aspirations were inimical to these establishment principles were presented as enemies of the 'nation'. Such attitudes were to extend their appeal throughout bourgeois society at large when, after the turn of the century, the socialist movement, with its overtly internationalist perspectives, began to pose a threat to capitalism itself.

The Great War was arguably the price that had to be paid for this 'integral' nationalism. The notion of a common external threat, namely Germany, was essential to the achievement of national consensus in an otherwise divided society. However, the international complexities of the inter-war period were to reveal the underlying contradictions of right-wing nationalism, and to confirm that its primary function was that of internal stability. The threat posed to French national sovereignty by the rise of Nazi Germany was a challenge most of the right were unwilling to meet. Not only were they reluctant to face the prospect of another war, but the price of effective resistance was a pact with the Soviet Union and, in their eyes, the risk of domestic social revolution. The tragic sequence of appeasement, Vichy and collaboration confirmed that their 'nationalism' was an internal ideological device, geared to the defence of narrow class interests, rather than to the preservation of national independence.

In this context it is not surprising that in the post-war period much of the right has aligned itself with the principles of Atlanticism and European concertation, which have provided a more stable framework for capitalist consolidation and anti-communism than that offered by the outworn nationalism of the pre-war era. Indeed, under the Fourth Republic right-wing nationalism became the refuge of lost causes, the struggle to preserve France's colonial empire and *petit-bourgeois* resistance to the forces of economic and social modernisation, and the *Front national's* successful promotion of an updated version of this populist discourse in the recessionary climate of the 1980s has drawn on substantially similar psychological reactions.

The phenomenon of Gaullism appears to be something of a hybrid in this context, an attempt to build a new kind of consensual nationalism on the themes of economic and political modernisation and the restoration of France's independent status as a world power. It is, however, important to separate the rhetoric from the reality. The climate of international *détente* and domestic prosperity in the mid-to-late 1960s allowed the French state some freedom to express autonomous ambitions in the field of both economic and foreign policy. However, with the downturn in world economic activity in the 1970s and the renewal of cold war at the end of the decade, the reality of France's economic and diplomatic integration within the western capitalist bloc was progressively confirmed, and policies were adjusted accordingly. The mainstream right's endorsement of neo-liberal economic doctrines, of Atlanticism and European supra-nationalism indicates a declining faith in the role of the state, both internally and externally.

Consequently nationalism has ceased to be the central organising theme of right-wing ideology. Of course, it remains a useful recourse whenever a particular issue makes it opportune to appeal to a sense of national pride, and governments of the left are now prone to the same temptation. However, it is no longer easy to assess precisely what kind of nationalist sentiments are aroused when Chirac refuses the Americans French airspace for their bombing raid on Tripoli, or when a socialist defence minister justifies French terrorist action against Greenpeace. Indeed, the recent academic debate on the nature of contemporary French 'national identity' indicates that, while popular culture is still shaped by the accumulated layers of nationalist rhetoric of the last two hundred years, the ideological foundations of this nationalism are no longer clearly discernible.

On the left, the popular identification of the 'nation' first with an undifferentiated citizenry and later with the vanguard role of the working class is no longer the relevant focus for radical politics. Similarly, on the right, the equation of the 'nation' with the internal conservative apparatus of social control – state, army, Church and capitalist enterprise – is no longer a crucial instrument of ideological stabilisation in the age of international free-market capitalism and military-political supra-nationalism.

It has become fashionable to see the political realignment of recent years in France as marking the end of the French revolutionary tradition. However, it is significant that in the debates that have accompanied the bicentennial celebrations, it is the theme of universal 'human rights' that has been picked out as the key positive historical contribution of the Great Revolution. Could it be that what we are witnessing is not so much the death of radical politics, but the demise of that other great legacy of 1789, the nation state?

NOTES

PREFACE

1 S. Hoffman, 'La nation: pour quoi faire? ', *Essais sur la France: déclin ou renouveau?*, pp. 437–83.
2 'A revolution transcended', *Financial Times*, 14 July 1989.

1 INTRODUCTION: NATION AND NATIONALISM

1 In his remarkable essay on the national question, 'The Modern Janus', Tom Nairn sees Marxism itself as imprisoned by the 'grand universalising tradition' of Enlightenment philosophy, the 'metropolitan fantasy' of 'an even and progressive development of material civilisation and mass culture' (T. Nairn, 'The Modern Janus', *New Left Review*, no. 94, 1975, pp. 3–29).
2 Within the Marxist tradition, cultural definitions of nationhood preoccupied the Austro-Marxists (O. Bauer, *Die Nationalitätenfrage und die Sozialdemokratie*) and later Stalin (J. Stalin, *Der Marxismus und die nationale Frage*). Similarly, non-Marxists have analysed nationalism in economic terms, notably as an ideology of 'modernisation' produced by 'uneven economic development' (E. Gellner, *Thought and Change*).
3 B. Jenkins and G. Minnerup, *Citizens and Comrades: Socialism in a World of Nation-States*.
4 This kind of historical mythology is, of course, above all a by-product of nationalist ideology itself. However, students of nationalism, including Marxists, have often accepted it at face value. Both Otto Bauer (op. cit.) and Josef Stalin (op. cit.) accepted the concept of a common culture and psychological outlook, shaped by a common history, as the chief character-istics of a nation.
5 For example, Stalin (op. cit., pp. 10–11.) defined a nation as 'an historically evolved, stable community of language, territory, economic life and psycho-logical make-up manifested in a community of culture', and insisted that all these criteria had to be met if a given group was to qualify as a 'nation'.
6 Jenkins and Minnerup, op. cit., p. 51.
7 ibid., p. 61.
8 For example, see R. Eccleshall *et al.* (eds), *Political Ideologies*, p. 30: 'The idea

of nation provides malleable raw material from which several ideological perspectives can be manufactured'.

2 THE FRENCH REVOLUTION AND THE BIRTH OF NATIONALISM

1 The theme of nationalism in France has above all been treated in the post-1870 context, and principally as a right-wing phenomenon (see Chapter 7). French socialist perspectives on the 'nation' from the Paris Commune to the First World War are the subject of several essays in E. Cahm and V.-C. Fišera (eds), *Socialism and Nationalism in Contemporary Europe 1848–1945, Vol. 2,* and here the legacy of the Revolution is acknowledged. However, no work offers a sustained analysis of the development of nationalism since the Revolution. (J.-R. Suratteau, *L'Idée nationale de la Révolution à nos jours,* is primarily concerned with the global impact of the concept of nationhood).

2 An illuminating and concise appraisal of this persistent debate is contained in Gwynne Lewis's introduction to a new English edition of Albert Soboul's classic history of the Revolution (A. Soboul, *The French Revolution 1787–1799: From the Storming of the Bastille to Napoleon*).

3 Leaving aside the vast number of specialised studies dealing with particular social categories or localities, general works on this theme are also abundant. Particularly important are: F. Braudel and E. Labrousse, *Histoire économique et sociale de la France, Vol. II. Des derniers temps de l'âge seigneurial aux préludes de l'âge industriel, 1660–1789.* P. Goubert, *L'Ancien Régime, Vol. I: La société.*

4 In the words of Georges Lefebvre, 'at least part of the bourgeoisie shared these hopes. It did not look upon itself as a caste, and even believed that it had suppressed classes by destroying orders and opening its ranks to all'. G. Lefebvre, *The French Revolution from its origins to 1793,* London, Routledge & Kegan Paul, 1962, p. 149. (Originally published in French by Presses Universitaires de France, 1957.)

5 The notion that the abolition of orders, and of venal and hereditary offices, had opened new fields of employment to talented commoners.

6 The Louis-Philippe monarchy (1830–48) is generally regarded as a regime tailored to the interests of the *grande bourgeoisie* (see Chapter 4).

7 These were 'statements of grievances', initially drafted at local assemblies and then passed on to higher bodies, which eventually constituted the agenda of the Estates General.

8 Sutherland, op. cit. p. 60.

9 L. Hunt, *Politics, Culture and Class in the French Revolution.*

10 ibid., p. 27.

11 ibid., p. 20.

12 ibid., p. 20.

13 To quote Sutherland's succinct summary,

The electorate was divided into three groups: passive citizens who paid less than the equivalent of three days' labour in taxes, active citizens who paid more and who had to meet age and residence qualifications, and eligible electors who paid more than the equivalent of ten days' labour in taxes. Active citizens chose a slate of electors from a list of eligibles. The electors in turn chose most government officials ranging from deputies, civil administrators, judges and priests. (D.M.G. Sutherland, *France 1789–1815: Revolution and Counterrevolution*, p. 91).

The number of active citizens may have been as many as 4.3 million, around two-thirds of the adult male population.

14 This gave the state ultimate jurisdiction over the Church. New priests and bishops were elected by the active citizens and electors, episcopal salaries were scaled down and those of the lower clergy raised, and all ranks were required to swear an oath of loyalty to the Civil Constitution.

15 The phrase was used under the July monarchy (1830–48) to describe the 'real world' of the masses who were excluded from the political process, as opposed to the narrow *pays légal* of 200,000 voters who enjoyed political rights.

16 As Anthony Smith puts it, 'more mystical versions of the national ideal became prominent, particularly in Central and Eastern Europe; and it is often thought that this more "romantic" kind of nationalism was caused by the lack of a strong bourgeoisie in these countries, who could support the intelligentsia' (A.D. Smith, *Nationalism in the Twentieth Century*).

17 For a more detailed discussion of the Marxist debate on the 'national question' in this period, see B. Jenkins and G. Minnerup, *Citizens and Comrades: Socialism in a World of Nation States*.

18 This theme has been explored above all in E. Weber, *Peasants into Frenchmen: The Modernisation of Rural France, 1870–1914*.

19 As Lyn Hunt aptly puts it, 'tradition would find its defenders, but, like the other new ideologies, it could never again go unspoken' (Hunt, op. cit., p. 51).

3 STATE AND NATION UNDER NAPOLEON

1 D. Woronoff, *The Thermidorean Regime and the Directory 1794–1799*, p. 20.
2 ibid., p. 30.
3 L. Hunt, *Politics, Culture and Class in the French Revolution*, p. 48.
4 Woronoff, op. cit., p. 131.
5 ibid., p. 153.
6 For a critical summary of Marxist analysis of Bonapartism, see N. Poulantzas, *Fascism and Dictatorship*.
7 K. Marx, *The Eighteenth Brumaire of Louis Bonaparte*, New York, International Publishers, 1963.
8 Woronoff, op. cit., pp. 182–4.
9 ibid., p. 192.
10 H.A.L. Fisher, *Bonapartism: Six Lectures delivered in the University of London*, p. 9.
11 ibid., p. 46. 'He made the fusion of opposites the cardinal feature in his system.'
12 M. Weber, *On Charisma and Institution-Building*.
13 F. Bluche, *Le Bonapartisme*, p. 28 (author's translation).
14 ibid., p. 25 (author's translation).
15 The *livret* was the passbook which workers were obliged to carry with them, and which gave details of their employment record.

16 Hunt, op. cit., p. 48.
17 Fisher, op. cit., p. 49.
18 Bluche, op. cit., p. 27 (author's translatio
19 ibid., p. 13.
20 Fisher, op. cit., p. 47.
21 Quoted in Fisher, op. cit., p. 45.
22 The 'Mémorial de Saint-Hélène' was transcribed from conversations with Napoleon by his companion in exile, the French historian Las Cases, and was published in 1823.
23 As Fisher put it (op. cit., p. 46), 'Emigrants served in the household, the senate and the armies; Girondins, Jacobins, and royalists sat together in the law courts, in the departmental councils, and in the Council of State.'
24 Hunt, op. cit., p. 233.

4 THE NATION DENIED: FRANCE 1815–48

1 R. Magraw, *France 1815–1914: The Bourgeois Century*, p. 26. Magraw's book is an invaluable survey of a century of French history, providing an admirable synthesis and summary of recent historiography in the field.
2 ibid., p. 49.
3 ibid., p. 49.
4 A. Jardin and A.J. Tudesq, *Restoration and Reaction 1815–1848*, p. 110.
5 The argument that France was economically retarded in the nineteenth century, above all by the lack of an entrepreneurial spirit, has been put most forcefully by David Landes, especially in his famous article 'French entrepreneurship and industrial growth in the nineteenth century', *Journal of Economic History*, IX, pp. 45–61. Such views have been challenged by, among others, Rondo Cameron (*France and the Economic Development of Europe, 1800–1914*, and François Caron (*An Economic History of Modern France*).
6 Magraw, op. cit., p. 58.
7 ibid., p. 54.
8 Forty-four per cent of deputies were nobles at the end of the Restoration period, compared with only 14 per cent in 1831. T. Beck, *French Legislators 1800–34: A Study in Quantitative History*.
9 Magraw, op. cit., p. 68.
10 R. Rémond, *La Droite en France de la Première Restauration à la Vᵉ République, Vol. I 1815–1940*, p. 67.
11 Jardin and Tudesq, op. cit., p. 126.
12 See S. Citron, *Le Mythe national: l'histoire de France en question*, pp. 18–22.

5 NATION, BONAPARTISM AND SOCIALISM: FRANCE 1848–71

1 M. Agulhon, *The Republican Experiment 1848–52*, pp. 187–92.
2 R. Magraw, *France 1815–1914: The Bourgeois Century*, p. 124.
3 G. Duveau, *La vie ouvrière sous le Second Empire*, Paris, Gallimard, 1946.
4 M. Agulhon, *The Republic in the Village: The people of the Var from the French Revolution to the Second Republic*.
5 See Nicos Poulantzas discussion of the work of Auguste Thalheimer and

Antonio Gramsci on the concept of Bonapartism in N. Poulantzas, *Fascism and Dictatorship*, pp. 57–64.

6 Quoted by Poulantzas, op. cit., pp. 60–1.

7 Alain [Emile Chartier], *Eléments d'une doctrine radicale*.

8 Magraw, op. cit., p. 155.

9 J. Lhomme, *La Grande Bourgeoise au pouvoir 1830–1880*, pp. 155–63.

10 H.A.L. Fisher, *Bonapartism: Six Lectures delivered in the University of London*, p. 47.

11 See E. Cahm, 'French socialist theories of the nation to 1889' in E. Cahm and V. Fišera (eds), *Socialism and Nationalism in Contemporary Europe, 1848–1945*, Vol. 2, pp. 2–9.

12 Blanquists were the largest group on the elected governing body of the Commune, with Proudhonists making up a sizeable minority. Those directly influenced by Marx's First International were relatively few.

13 Decree of the Commune, 12 April 1871. Quoted by R.D. Thomas, 'French revolutionary socialists and the revolutionary tradition 1789–1871', in Cahm and Fišera (eds) op. cit., pp. 10–21.

6 THE THIRD REPUBLIC AND THE NATION

1 R. Girardet, *Le Nationalisme français, 1871–1914*. H. Guillemin, *Nationalistes et nationaux 1870–1940*. S. Hoffmann, 'La nation; pour quoi faire?', *Essais sur la France: déclin ou renouveau?*, pp. 437–83.

2 A compromise between the two monarchist factions appeared to have been agreed in 1873, whereby the legitimist Comte de Chambord, who was childless, would be succeeded on his death by the Orleanist pretender. However, Chambord eventually refused to make any move unless on his own terms and under the *fleur de lys* flag.

3 J. Lhomme, *La Grande Bourgeoisie au pouvoir, 1830–1880*.

4 R. Magraw, *France 1815–1914: The Bourgeois Century*, p. 230.

5 M. Rébérioux, *La République radicale? 1898–1914*, is the best survey of the period of radical ascendancy.

6 Magraw, op. cit., p. 212.

7 L. Hunt, *Politics, Culture and Class in the French Revolution*, p. 86.

8 Magraw, op. cit., p. 212.

9 ibid., p. 212.

10 E. Weber, *Peasants into Frenchmen: The Modernisation of Rural France, 1870–1914*.

11 Quoted in C. Nicolet, *L'Idée républicaine en France: essai d'histoire critique*, pp. 99–100 (author's translation).

12 S. Citron, *Le Mythe national: l'Histoire de France en question*, p. 68 (author's translation).

13 J.-J. Chevallier, *Histoire des institutions politiques de la France moderne, 1789–1958*, p. 410.

14 S. Hoffmann, *Essais sur la France: déclin ou renouveau*, p. 442.

15 J. Bainville, *Histoire de France*.

16 'G. Bruno' (Mme Alfred Fouillée), *Le Tour de la France par deux enfants*.

17 M. Ozouf, *L'Ecole de France*.

18 Citron, op. cit., p. 37 (author's translation).

7 THE RIGHT AND THE NATION 1870–1914

1 R. Magraw, *France 1815–1914: The Bourgeois Century*, p. 259.
2 The battle of Valmy against Prussian forces on 20 September 1792 was the first great victory of the revolutionary armies.
3 Z. Sternhell, 'Paul Déroulède and the origins of French nationalism', in J.C. Cairns (ed.), *Contemporary France: Illusion, Conflict and Regeneration*, p. 11.
4 The importance of Rochefort as a political leader in Paris has been underlined by Eric Cahm, 'Socialism and the nationalist movement at the time of the Dreyfus Affair', in E. Cahm and V.C. Fišera (eds), *Socialism and Nationalism in Contemporary Europe, 1848–1945*, Vol. 2, pp. 48–64.
5 ibid., p. 52.
6 R. Rémond, *La Droite en France de la Première Restauration à la Ve République*.
7 D. Thomson, *Democracy in France since 1870*, p. 33.
8 Sternhell, op. cit., p. 16.
9 'This excessively cosmopolitan, or rather excessively German, socialism which would undermine the defence of the fatherland' (M. Barrès, *Scènes et doctrines du nationalisme,* vol. 2, p. 161, (author's translation).)
10 Investigations into the bankruptcy of the Panama Canal Company in 1888 revealed that around 150 members of Parliament, including Clemenceau and several cabinet ministers, had been bribed by the company in an effort to avert financial collapse. The three main financial promoters involved were all Jews, and this fuelled the anti-semitism of the 1890s.
11 Magraw, op. cit., pp. 269–70.
12 J.-J. Chevallier, *Histoire des institutions politiques de la France moderne, 1789–1958,* p. 445 (author's translation).
13 Barrès, op. cit., Vol. I, p. 219 (author's translation).
14 Sternhell, op. cit., p. 22.
15 H. Rogger and E. Weber, *The European Right: A Historical Profile,* p. 97.
16 Magraw, op. cit., p. 282.
17 Thomson, op. cit., p. 72.

8 THE LEFT AND THE NATION 1870–1914

1 S. Hoffmann, 'La nation; pour quoi faire? ', *Essais sur la France: déclin ou renouveau?*
2 J. Schwarzmantel, 'Nationalism and the French working-class movement 1905–14', in E. Cahm and V.C. Fišera, *Socialism and Nationalism in Contemporary Europe, 1848–1945*, vol. 2, p. 68.
3 For the evolution of Jaurès's attitudes in this respect, see E. Cahm, 'Socialism and the nationalist movement in France at the time of the Dreyfus Affair', in Cahm and Fišera, op. cit., pp. 48–64.
4 R. Magraw, *France 1815–1914: The Bourgeois Century*, pp. 266–7.
5 See Cahm, op. cit.
6 G. Lefranc, *Le Mouvement socialiste sous la Troisième République (1875–1940),* p. 101.
7 ibid., p. 102.
8 Quoted by Magraw, op. cit., p. 300.

9 Quoted in J.-J. Chevallier, *Histoire des institutions politiques de la France moderne, 1789–1958,* p. 429.

10 Cahm, op. cit., p. 48.

11 ibid., p. 48.

12 ibid., p. 59

13 ibid., p. 49.

14 Schwarzmantel, op. cit., p. 69.

15 See in particular G. Haupt, *Socialism and the Great War. The Collapse of the Second International.*

16 Quoted in Lefranc, op. cit., p. 198 (author's translation).

17 His speech at Lyon-Vaise on 25 July 1914 (author's translation).

18 Magraw, op. cit., p. 361.

19 Quoted in J. Howorth, 'The left in France and Germany, internationalism and war: a dialogue of the deaf 1900–14', in Cahm and Fišera, op. cit., p. 81.

20 ibid., p. 95.

9 PERSPECTIVES AND USES OF NATIONALISM 1918–40

1 G. Dupeux, *La Société française 1789–1970,* p. 198.

2 In 1931, half the total farming population owned their own land, and the ratio of paid farm labour to tenants and owners was 645:1,000.

3 S. Hoffmann, *Essais sur la France: déclin ou renouveau?.* See also M. Crozier, *La Société bloquée.*

4 The *Confédération générale de la production française* was established on 31 July, 1919.

5 As William Shirer put it, 'the selfishness of the moneyed class in avoiding any financial sacrifice to help put the country back on its feet later struck many French historians as shocking' (W. Shirer, *The Collapse of the Third Republic,* p. 136.)

6 France's financial difficulties throughout the 1920s were linked in public opinion with Germany's failure to meet war reparation payments. This theme was a constant backdrop to the agitation of the right-wing leagues from the demonstrations that accompanied the fall of the Herriot government in July 1926 to those that greeted the resignation of another Herriot cabinet in December 1932.

7 The Hoover moratorium, which cancelled reparations, did not cancel the payment of French war debts to the United States. Prime Minister Herriot's insistence that France should honour the next instalment of war debts led to anti-American riots in Paris and the defeat of his government.

8 The Paris riots of 6 February, 1934, came in the aftermath of the 'Stavisky Affair', a politico-financial scandal implicating members of the governing Radical Party. The right-wing leagues seized the opportunity to demonstrate against the incoming Daladier Government, and in the ensuing confrontation seventeen demonstrators were killed by police fire. The left viewed the riots as an attempted fascist coup, and the events were instrumental in the construction of the Popular Front. (See B. Jenkins, *The Paris Riots of February 6th, 1934: The Crisis of the Third French Republic.*)

9 The *Croix de feu* was founded in 1928 as an elite veterans' association for ex-officers, but it soon widened its recruitment, set up a youth organisation,

and developed a political line. By 1934 it claimed 140,000 members, but it reached its height in 1938 when, as the *Parti social français,* its membership may realistically be assessed at 750,000.

10 See note 8. Alexandre Stavisky was a financial swindler who had apparently enjoyed the protection of Radical Party politicians and members of the judicial and police apparatus. His alleged 'suicide' when on the point of arrest in early January 1934 was widely interpreted as a 'convenient' solution to prevent embarrassing disclosures. The exploitation of the affair by the right-wing press paved the way for the riots of 6 February 1934.

11 The mainstream right had only a skeletal national organisation. Around a dozen separate parliamentary groupings sat to the right of the Radical Party in the Chamber of Deputies, and for electoral purposes these were loosely co-ordinated under two umbrella structures outside Parliament, the conservative *Union républicaine démocratique* and the more moderate *Alliance démocratique.*

12 J.-J. Chevallier, *Histoire des institutions politiques de la France moderne 1789–1958,* p. 299. Chevallier contrasts those who were republicans out of 'reason' or 'resignation' with those who were so by conviction.

13 The moderate right politician, Raymond Poincaré, was President of the Republic during the Great War, and as prime minister was responsible for sending troops to occupy the Ruhr in January 1923. He was recalled to office in July 1926, when the parliamentary alliance between the radicals and the socialists collapsed, and headed a government of National Union (excluding only the SFIO and the communists), which succeeded in restoring business confidence.

14 Right-wing fears centred on the decision of the new prime minister, the radical Edouard Daladier, to sack the fiercely anti-communist Paris Prefect of Police, Jean Chiappe. This was interpreted as a move designed to win socialist support for the new government and as the precursor of more 'sinister' developments.

15 The Matignon agreements brought an end to the mass strikes which celebrated and supported the Popular Front election victory in June 1936. The key reforms were the introduction of a forty-hour working week, two weeks annual paid holidays and new collective bargaining rights for workers.

16 Tardieu hoped to reconcile the moderate right with the pragmatic wing of the Radical Party, and during his terms as prime minister between 1929 and 1931 he advanced a policy of social reform and economic modernisation which he saw as a potential basis for such a *rapprochement.* When his plans foundered, he turned to proposals for constitutional reform as the sole means of breaking the political mould.

17 Doumergue's proposals, largely inspired by Tardieu, sought to strengthen the office of the President of the Republic by empowering him to dissolve the Chamber of Deputies without the authorisation of the Senate.

18 For a detailed and fascinating discussion of these dissident intellectual groups in the 1930s, see J. Loubet del Bayle, *Les Non-conformistes des années 30.*

19 Ernest Mercier, a leading capitalist in the electrical power industry, founded the anti-parliamentary right-wing movement *Redressement français* in 1926. Jean Coutrot, an economist and graduate of the *Ecole polytechnique,*

was associated in the 1930s with a series of shadowy groups with corporatist and technocratic aims.

20 Ironically, the reason for Doriot's dispute with the party leadership was his advocacy of an anti-fascist alliance with the socialists in early 1934, some six months before the Third International and the PCF decided to move precisely in this direction. For a balanced recent assessment of the affair, see E. Mortimer, *The Rise of the French Communist Party 1920–47.*

21 P. Burrin, *La Dérive fasciste: Doriot, Déat, Bergéry, 1933–45,* p. 312 (author's translation).

22 This typology closely follows that proposed by C. Micaud, *The French Right and Nazi Germany 1933–39.*

23 Louis Marin was the leading figure in the conservative *Union Républicaine démocratique* throughout the inter-war period.

24 Micaud, op. cit., p. 201.

25 Micaud, op. cit.

26 The other significant leagues of the early 1930s were Taittinger's *Jeunesses patriotes,* and *Solidarité française,* founded in 1933 by the perfume tycoon François Coty and modelled on the paramilitary fascist formations of Italy and Germany. Both were wound up when the Popular Front government banned such organisations in 1936.

27 For an interesting study of ex-communist Doriot, the neo-socialist Déat and the dissident radical Gaston Bergéry, see P. Burrin, op. cit.

28 Flandin, one of the leaders of the *Alliance démocratique,* had been prime minister in 1934, and repeated the experience briefly under the Vichy regime (December 1940–February 1941).

29 The timid attempts of the radicals in 1924–6 to introduce a degree of fiscal reform and exchange control had led to such concerted resistance from the financial and industrial establishments that they never again dared to challenge the so-called *Mur d'argent* (Wall of Money).

30 Electoral agreements between the SFIO and the radicals were concluded for the elections of 1924, 1932 and, of course, 1936, when the communists were also involved. Such arrangements proved much more advantageous than the situations in 1919 and 1928, when the radicals lacked a clear electoral identity and were 'squeezed' between right and left.

31 R. Manévy, *Histoire de la presse, 1914–1939,* p. 199.

32 State intervention was limited to some nationalisation (the railways, sections of the armaments industry, public control of the Bank of France) and an attempt to regulate the grain market. The social reforms of the Matignon accords (see note 15) were part of a wider Keynesian strategy to boost domestic demand by raising popular living standards and purchasing power. For a recent assessment, see J. Kergoat, *La France du Front Populaire.*

33 France's 'sister' Popular Front government in Spain was challenged in July 1936 by Franco's military rebellion. The subsequent civil war, with Italy and Germany supporting and supplying the rebels and the Soviet Union backing the Spanish republicans, inevitably raised the issue of potential intervention by France.

34 See N. Greene, *Crisis and Decline. The French Socialist Party in the Popular Front Era.*

35 Besides Blum's fear that French involvement in Spain would drag her into a

general European war, he knew he would not receive British backing, and he also argued that intervention would fatally divide the nation. It was certainly true that the Popular Front alliance would have been deeply split by such a move, given the attitude of the radicals and many socialists.

36 In his speech at the Seventh World Congress of the Comintern in 1935, the PCF leader Maurice Thorez announced

> We claim the intellectual and revolutionary tradition of the Encyclopaedists who paved the way for the great revolution of 1789 . . . of the Jacobins . . . and the Commune. We present ourselves to the masses of the people as the champions of the liberty and the independence of the country.
>
> Jane Degras (ed.), *The Communist International 1919–43: Documents,* Vol. III, p. 358.

10 NATIONALISM FROM LIBERATION TO DE GAULLE

1 M. Larkin, *France since the Popular Front 1936–86,* p. 108.
2 ibid., pp. 108–9.
3 ibid., p. 130.
4

> For it is a revolution, the greatest in its history, that France, betrayed by its ruling elites and its privileged classes, has begun to undertake . . . Those who expect to find, after the last gunshot, a France that, politically, socially, morally, resembles the country they once knew, will be seriously mistaken.
>
> (Charles de Gaulle, speech in London, 1 April 1942, author's translation)

5 The nationalisations affected the coal, electricity and gas industries, the four largest clearing banks, 60 per cent of insurance companies, air transport and merchant shipping, the Renault car firm and the Gnôme et Rhône aeronautical company. Paris urban transport was brought under municipal control.

6 The *comités d'entreprise,* established by ordinance in February 1945, were designed to give workers a permanent voice in matters concerning welfare and working conditions, and allowed them access to the firm's accounts. However, their powers were purely consultative and their views were often ignored.

7 'In the decade following the 1957 Treaty of Rome . . . the share of commercial exchanges with former colonies dropped from over a quarter to well under a tenth.' (W. Rand Smith, 'We can make the Ariane but we can't make washing-machines: the state and industrial performance in post-war France', J. Howorth and G. Ross, *Contemporary France: A Review of Interdisciplinary Studies, Vol. 3,* London and New York, Pinter, 1989, p. 179.)

8 J.-P. Rioux, *The Fourth Republic 1944–58,* p. 122.

9 Mendès France's energetic and decisive approach to government won him genuine public popularity, but failed to break the parliamentary mould. He was invested in June 1954 by an unprecedented majority of 419 votes to 47,

but despite the relative success of his administration, he was toppled eight months later by 319 votes to 273.

10 M. Newman, *Socialism and European Unity: The Dilemma of the Left in Britain and France*, p. 15.

11 Rioux, op. cit., p. 85.

12 ibid., p. 85.

13 Socialist ambiguities on the colonial question were endemic. The political team of Marius Moutet, Minister for Colonies in Blum's Popular Front government, produced a document on 'socialist colonial policy' in 1936 which warned against exporting socialist ideas to the native population of the colonies, for fear of unleashing 'uncontrollable forces'. It warned that 'ill-digested notions of class struggle' might be corrupted by 'religious fanaticism, the emotional nature of the African people, the dissimulation of the Islamic and Asiatic temperament' (quoted in J. Kergoat, *La France du Front Populaire*, p. 233, author's translation).

14 Newman, op. cit., p. 40.

15 The modern CFDT is the descendant of the Catholic *Confédération française des travailleurs chrétiens* (CFTC), founded in 1919. Between the wars it was still inspired by social Catholic ideals of class collaboration, but it was radicalised by the resistance experience, and in 1964 was transformed into the CFDT, thereafter adopting democratic socialist perspectives and a more combative position.

16 In February 1956, a poll indicated that 49 per cent wanted Algeria to remain a *département* of France, while 25 per cent would accept a looser tie. By September 1957 the balance of opinion had been reversed, with 40 per cent against 36 per cent willing to accept a changed relationship (quoted in Rioux, op. cit., p. 298).

17 The PCF, in its campaign against the EDC from mid-1953, changed its attitude to De Gaulle, calling him a 'good Frenchman' (Newman, op. cit., p. 46.), while as Rioux records, the Party avoided condemning the Poujadists until the autumn of 1955 (Rioux, op. cit., p. 248).

18 Newman, op. cit., p. 51

11 THE SWANSONG OF THE NATION STATE?

1 Charles de Gaulle, *Le Fil de l'épée*, pp. 41–6.

2 The electoral college of 80,000 was made up of parliamentarians, and delegates from the departmental and municipal councils.

3 The Senate is renewed by one-third every three years, each senator sitting for nine years. Furthermore, the electoral colleges for the Senate are composed largely of municipal councillors, themselves only elected every six years. As a result the composition of the Senate always lags behind the state of electoral opinion, and it takes a long time for a new political party to establish a presence there.

4 An IFOP poll of August 1958 revealed that, in the electorates of the major political parties, 79 per cent of radicals, 68 per cent of socialists, 85 per cent of MRP, and 93 per cent of moderates placed their confidence in De Gaulle's government first and foremost because of its constitutional proposals (quoted in J.-P. Rioux, *The Fourth Republic 1944–58*, p. 313).

5 'All my life I have cherished a certain idea of France' (*'une certaine idée de la France'*, author's translation). Charles de Gaulle, *Mémoires de guerre, I: L'Appel 1940–42*, p. 5.

6 Z. Sternhell, 'Paul Déroulède and the origins of modern French nationalism', in J.C. Cairns (ed.), *Contemporary France: Illusion, Conflict and Regeneration*, p. 22.

7 ibid., p. 8.

8 In his famous speech at Bayeux in June 1946, De Gaulle talked of 'our old Gallic propensity for division and dispute' and argued that 'party rivalries' were allowed to jeopardise the 'higher interests of the country' (Charles de Gaulle, *Mémoires de guerre, III: Le Salut 1944–6*, pp. 647–52). Elsewhere, in the famous passage on 'a certain idea of France' he went on; 'if on occasions her behaviour smacks of mediocrity, this always seems to me an absurd anomaly, attributable to the failings of the French rather than to the spirit of France itself' (ibid., p. 5, author's translation).

9 D.L. Hanley, A.P. Kerr and N.H. Waites, *Contemporary France: Politics and Society since 1945*, p. 220.

10 ibid., p. 243.

11 See S. Hoffmann, 'France and Europe: the dichotomy of autonomy and cooperation', in J. Howorth and G. Ross (eds), *Contemporary France: A Review of Interdisciplinary Studies, Vol. I*, pp. 46–54.

12 At the general elections of June 1968, both the SFIO (down from 19 per cent to 16.5 per cent) and the PCF (down from 22.5 per cent to 20 per cent) lost electoral ground, but the lack of electoral agreements for the second ballot made the result even worse in terms of seats. At the presidential elections of 1969 the left vote was split four ways at the first ballot (Michel Rocard and the Trotskyist Alain Krivine being the minor candidates), with the communist Duclos scoring a creditable 21.5 per cent, but the socialist Defferre recording a disastrous 5.1 per cent. Consequently the left was unrepresented at the second round, with the centrist Alain Poher contesting the run-off with Pompidou.

13 G. Ross, 'Adieu vieilles idées: the middle strata and the decline of resistance-liberation left discourse in France', in Howorth and Ross (eds), op. cit., p. 65.

14 ibid., p. 64.

15 Quoted in M. Newman, *Socialism and European Unity: The Dilemma of the Left in Britain and France*, p. 88.

16 See D.L. Hanley, ' "Les variables de Solferino" or thoughts on steering the socialist economy: an analysis of the economic discourse of the French *Parti socialiste*', in S. Williams (ed.), *Socialism in France from Jaurès to Mitterrand*, pp. 136–54.

17 Ross, op. cit.

18 Ross, op. cit., p. 78.

19 In the aftermath of May 1968 the CFDT fell under the influence of its radical left wing, and began to advance doctrines of workers' self-management. This remained its distinctive ideological contribution to French trade unionism until the late 1970s, when the CFDT moved towards a more pragmatic position.

20 D. Singer, *Is Socialism Doomed? The Meaning of Mitterrand*, p. 294.

21 The phrase is borrowed from the title of an influential book on the reconstruction of the socialist left in Britain (S. Rowbotham, L. Segal and H. Wainwright, *Beyond the Fragments: Feminism and the making of socialism*).

BIBLIOGRAPHY

GENERAL

The following sources are relevant to more than one chapter of this work.

Beaune, C., *Naissance de la nation française,* Paris, Gallimard, 1985.

Cahm, E., *Politics and Society in Contemporary France, 1789–1970,* London, Harrap, 1972.

Cahm, E. and Fišera, V.-C., *Socialism and Nationalism in Contemporary Europe, 1848–1945* (3 vols), Nottingham, Spokesman, 1978–80.

Cameron, R., *France and the Economic Development of Europe, 1800–1914,* Princeton, Princeton University Press, 1961.

Campbell, P., *French Electoral Systems and Elections since 1789,* 2nd edition, London, Faber & Faber, 1965.

Chevallier, J.-J. *Histoire des institutions politiques de la France moderne, 1789–1958,* Paris, Librairie Dalloz, 3ᵉ édition, 1967.

Citron, S., *Le Mythe national: l'histoire de France en question,* Paris, Les Editions ouvrières – Etudes et documentations internationales, 1987.

Crozier, M., *La Société bloquée.*

Dossiers de Sèvres, Les, *Certaines Idées de la France,* Sèvres, Centre International d'Etudes Pédagogiques de Sèvres, 1980.

Dupeux, G., *La Société française, 1789–1970,* Paris, Armand Colin, 7ᵉ édition, 1974.

Gallie, D., *Social Inequality and Class Radicalism in France and Britain,* Cambridge, Cambridge University Press, 1983.

Gerard, A., *La Révolution française, mythes et interprétations 1789–1970,* Paris, Flammarion, 1970.

Girardet, R., *Le nationalisme français, 1871–1914,* Paris, Armand Colin, 1966.

Girardet, R., 'Introduction à l'histoire du nationalisme français', *Revue française de science politique,* vol. VIII, no. 3, September 1958.

Goguel, F., *La Politique des partis sous la IIIᵉ République,* Paris, Editions du Seuil, 1946.

Guillemin, H., *Nationalistes et nationaux, 1870–1940,* Paris, Gallimard, 1974.

Guiomar, J.-Y., *L'idéologie nationale: nation, représentation, propriété,* Paris, Champ Libre, 1974.

Hanley, D.L., Kerr, A. and Waites, N.H., *Contemporary France: Politics and Society since 1945,* 2nd edition, London, Routledge & Kegan Paul, 1984.

Hoffmann, S., *Essais sur la France: déclin ou renouveau?*, Paris, Editions du Seuil, 1974.

Hunt, L., *Politics, Culture and Class in the French Revolution*, London, Methuen, 1986.

Jenkins, B. and Minnerup, G., *Citizens and Comrades: Socialism in a World of Nation States*, London, Pluto Press, 1984.

Kemp, T., *Economic Forces in French History*, London, Dobson, 1971.

Larkin, M., *France since the Popular Front 1936–86*, Oxford, Clarendon Press, 1988.

Lestocquoy, J., *Histoire du patriotisme en France*, Paris, Albin Michel, 1968.

Lhomme, J., *La Grande Bourgeoisie au pouvoir 1830–1880*, Paris, Presses Universitaires de France, 1960.

McMillan, J., *Dreyfus to De Gaulle: Politics and Society in France 1898–1969*, London, Edward Arnold, 1985.

Magraw, R., *France 1815–1914: The Bourgeois Century*, London, Fontana, 1983.

Martelli, R., *Comprendre la nation*, Paris, Editions sociales, 1979.

Newman, M., *Socialism and European Unity: The Dilemma of the Left in Britain and France*, London, Junction Books, 1983.

Nicolet, C., *L'Idée républicaine en France: essai d'histoire critique*, Paris, Gallimard, 1982.

Noiriel, G., *Les Ouvriers dans la société française, XIXe–XXe siècle*, Paris, Editions du Seuil, 1986.

Pernoud, R., *Histoire de la bourgeoisie en France II: Les Temps modernes*, Paris, Editions du Seuil, 1962.

Perrot, M., *Le Mode de vie des familles bourgeoises 1873–1953*, Paris, Armand Colin, 1961.

Portis, L., *Les Classes sociales en France: un débat inachevé (1789–1989)*, Paris, Les Editions ouvrières, 1988.

Rémond, R., *Les Droites en France*, Paris, Aubier-Montaigne, 4e édition, 1982.

Shorter, E. and Tilly, C., *Strikes in France 1830–1968*, London, Cambridge University Press, 1974.

Sorlin, P., *La Société française, vol. I, 1840–1914*, Paris, Arthaud, 1969.

Suratteau, J.-R., *L'Idée nationale de la Révolution à nos jours*, Paris, Presses Universitaires de France, 1972.

Sutherland, D., *France 1789–1815: Revolution and Counter-revolution*, London, Fontana Press, 1985.

Thomson, D., *Democracy in France Since 1870*, London, Oxford University Press, 1964.

Tint, H., *The Decline of French Patriotism 1870–1940*, London, Weidenfeld & Nicolson, 1964.

Weber, E., *Peasants into Frenchmen: The Modernisation of Rural France 1870–1914*, Stanford, Stanford University Press, 1976.

Wright, G., *France in Modern Times*, 4th edition, London and New York, W.W. Norton, 1987.

Wright, G., *Rural Revolution in France: the Peasantry in the Twentieth Century*, Stanford, Stanford University Press, 1964.

Zeldin, T., *France 1848–1945*, Oxford, Clarendon Press, 1973.

1 INTRODUCTION: NATION AND NATIONALISM

Alter, P., *Nationalism,* London, Edward Arnold, 1985.

Anderson, B., *Imagined Communities,* London, Verso, 1983.

Bauer, O., *Die Nationalitätenfrage und die Sozialdemokratie,* Vienna, 1907.

Eccleshall, R. *et al.* (eds), *Political Ideologies,* London, Hutchinson.

Gellner, E., *Thought and Change,* London, Weidenfeld & Nicolson, 1964.

Hayes, C., *The Historical Evolution of Modern Nationalism,* New York, Smith, 1931.

Hobsbawm, E., 'Some reflections on "The Break-up of Britain" ', *New Left Review,* 105, 1977.

Kohn, H., *Prelude to Nation-States: the French and German Experience, 1789–1815,* Princeton, Van Nostrand, 1967.

Lowy, M., 'Marxists and the national question', *New Left Review,* 96, 1976.

Nairn, T., 'The modern Janus', *New Left Review,* 94, 1975.

Smith, A.D., *Nationalism in the Twentieth Century,* Oxford, Martin Robertson, 1979.

Smith, A.D., *Theories of Nationalism,* London, Duckworth, 1971.

Stalin, J., *Der Marxismus und die nationale Frage,* Vienna, 1913.

Strasser, J., *Die Arbeiter und die Nation,* Vienna, Junius, 1982.

2 THE FRENCH REVOLUTION AND THE BIRTH OF NATIONALISM

Aulard, A., *Histoire politique de la Révolution française,* 4 vols, Paris, Armand Colin, 1901.

Bouloiseau, M., *La République jacobine,* Paris, Editions du Seuil, 1972.

Braudel, F. and Labrousse, E., *Histoire économique et sociale de la France, Vol. II: Des derniers temps de l'âge seigneurial aux préludes de l'âge industriel, 1660–1789,* Paris, Presses Universitaires de France, 1970.

Brinton, C., *A Decade of Revolution, 1789–1799,* New York, Harper, 1934.

Cobban, A., *The Social Interpretation of the French Revolution,* Cambridge, Cambridge University Press, 1964.

Doyle, W., *The Origins of the French Revolution,* Oxford, Oxford University Press, 1988.

Doyle, W., *The Oxford History of the French Revolution,* Oxford, Clarendon Press, 1989.

Furet, F., *Interpreting the French Revolution,* Cambridge, Cambridge University Press, 1981.

Furet, F. and Ozouf, M., *Dictionnaire critique de la Révolution française,* Paris, Flammarion, 1988.

Furet, F. and Richet, D., *La Révolution française,* 2 vols, Paris, Hachette-Réalités, 1965–6.

Godechot, J., *La Grande Nation: L'Expansion révolutionnaire de la France dans le monde,* 2 vols, Paris, Aubier, 1956.

Goubert, P., *L'Ancien régime, Vol. I: La société,* Paris, Armand Colin, 1969.

Guérin, D., *Les Luttes de classes sous la Première République: Bourgeois et 'bras nus', 1793–1797,* Paris, Gallimard, 1968.

Hampson, N., *A Social History of the French Revolution,* London and Toronto, University of Toronto Press, 1963.

Jaurès, J., *Histoire socialiste de la Révolution française,* Paris, Editions sociales, 1968.

Lefebvre, G., *Etudes sur la Révolution française,* Paris, Presses Universitaires de France, 1954.

Lefebvre, G., *The French Revolution from its Origins to 1793,* London, Routledge & Kegan Paul, 1962.

Mathiez, A., *La Révolution française,* Paris, Armand Colin, 1922–7.

Palmer, R., *The Age of the Democratic Revolution,* 2 vols, Princeton, Princeton University Press, 1962–4.

Rudé, G., *The Crowd in the French Revolution,* Oxford, Clarendon Press, 1964.

Soboul, A., *The French Revolution 1787–1799: From the Storming of the Bastille to Napoleon,* London, Unwin Hyman, 1989.

Talmon, J., *The Origins of Totalitarian Democracy,* London, Secker & Warburg, 1952.

Tocqueville, A. de, *The Old Regime and the French Revolution,* New York, Doubleday, 1955.

Vovelle, M., *La Chute de la monarchie, 1789–1792,* Paris, Editions du Seuil, 1972.

3 STATE AND NATION UNDER NAPOLEON

Bergeron, L., *France under Napoleon,* Princeton, Princeton University Press, 1981.

Bluche, F., *Le Bonapartisme,* Paris, Presses Universitaires de France, 1981.

Fisher, H.A.L., *Bonapartism: Six Lectures delivered in the University of London,* London, Oxford University Press, 1908.

Geyl, P., *Napoleon: For and Against,* New Haven, Yale University Press, 1949.

Guyot, R., *Le Directoire et la paix de l'Europe,* Paris, Alcan, 1911.

Hutt, M., *Napoleon,* London, Oxford University Press, 1965.

Holtman, R., *The Napoleonic Revolution,* Baton Rouge and London, Louisiana University Press, 1967.

Lefebvre, G., *Napoleon,* 2 vols, London, Routledge & Kegan Paul, 1969.

Lefebvre, G., *The Thermidoreans,* London, Routledge & Kegan Paul, 1965.

Lefebvre, G., *The Directory,* London, Routledge & Kegan Paul, 1965.

Lyons, M., *France under the Directory,* London, Cambridge University Press, 1975.

Markham, F., *Napoleon and the Awakening of Europe,* London, English Universities Press, 1954.

Marx, K., *The Eighteenth Brumaire of Louis Bonaparte,* New York, International Publishers, 1963.

Poulantzas, N., *Fascism and Dictatorship,* London, New Left Books, 1974.

Tulard, J., *Le Grand Empire, 1804–1815,* Paris, Fayard, 1982.

Weber, M., *On Charisma and Institution-building* (selected Papers edited by S.N. Eisenstadt), Chicago, University of Chicago Press, 1968.

Woronoff, D., *The Thermidorean Regime and the Directory, 1794–1799,* Cambridge, Cambridge University Press, 1984 (first published in French by Editions du Seuil, 1972).

4 THE NATION DENIED: FRANCE 1815–48

Beck, T., *French Legislators 1800–34: A Study in Quantitative History,* Berkeley, University of California Press, 1974.

Bertier de Sauvigny, G., *La Restauration*, Paris, Flammarion, 1955.

Braudel, F. and Labrousse, E., *Histoire économique et sociale de la France*, III, 2 vols, Paris, Presses Universitaires de France, 1976.

Caron, F., *An Economic History of Modern France*, New York, Columbia University Press, 1979.

Jardin, A. and Tudesq, A.-J., *Restoration and Reaction, 1815–1848*, Cambridge, Cambridge University Press, 1983 (first published in French in two volumes by Editions du Seuil, 1973).

Johnson, D., *Guizot: Aspects of French History*, London, Routledge, 1963.

Landes, D., 'French entrepreneurship and industrial growth in the nineteenth century', *Journal of Economic History*, IX, 1949.

Pinkney, D., *The French Revolution of 1830*, Princeton, Princeton University Press, 1972.

Sewell, W., *Work and Revolution in France: The Language of Labour from the Old Regime to 1848*, Cambridge, Cambridge University Press, 1980.

Vigier, P., *La Monarchie de juillet*, Paris, Presses Universitaires de France, 1969.

5 NATION, BONAPARTISM AND SOCIALISM: FRANCE 1848–71

Agulhon, M., *The Republic in the Village: The people of the Var from the French Revolution to the Second Republic*, New York, Cambridge University Press, 1982 (originally published in French by Plon, 1970).

Agulhon, M., *The Republican Experiment 1848–52*, Cambridge, Cambridge University Press, 1983 (originally published in French by Editions du Seuil, 1973).

Alain [Emile Chartier], *Eléments d'une doctrine radicale*, Paris, Gallimard, 1925.

Blanc, L., *Organisation du travail*, 5th edition, Paris, Au Bureau de la Société de l'Industrie Fraternelle, 1848.

Bruhat, J., *La Commune de 1871*, Paris, Editions sociales, 1970.

Bury, J., *Napoleon III and the Second Empire*, London, English Universities Press, 1965.

Campbell, S., *The Second Empire Revisited*, New Brunswick, Rutgers University Press, 1978.

Duveau, G., *La Vie ouvrière sous le Second Empire*, Paris, Gallimard, 1946.

Edwards, S., *The Paris Commune 1871*, London, Eyre & Spottiswoode, 1971.

Guillemin, H., *Le Coup d'état du 2 décembre*, Paris, Gallimard, 1951.

Lefebvre, H., *La Proclamation de la Commune*, Paris, Gallimard, 1965.

Margadant, T., *French Peasants in Revolt: The Insurrection of 1851*, Princeton, Princeton University Press, 1980.

Marx, K., *The Class Struggles in France 1848–1850*, New York, International Publishers, 1964.

Marx, K., *The Civil War in France*, Moscow, Progress Publishers, 1974.

Merriman, J., *The Agony of the Republic*, New Haven, Yale University Press, 1978.

Plessis, A., *De La Fête impériale au mur des fédérés*, Paris, Editions du Seuil, 1973.

Poulantzas, N., *Fascism and Dictatorship*, London, New Left Books, 1974 (originally published in French by François Maspéro, 1970).

Price, R., *The French Second Republic: A Social History*, Ithaca, Cornell University Press, 1972.

Tudesq, A.-J., *L'Election présidentielle de Louis-Napoléon Bonaparte (10 décembre 1848)*, Paris, Armand Colin, 1965.

Zeldin, T., *The Political System of Napoleon III*, London, Macmillan, 1978.

6 THE THIRD REPUBLIC AND THE NATION

Anderson, R., *France 1870–1914: Politics and Society*, London, Routledge & Kegan Paul, 1984.

Azema, J.-P. and Winock, M., *La IIIe République*, Paris, Calmann-Lévy, 1970.

Bainville, J., *Histoire de France*, Paris, Fayard, 1924.

G. Bruno (Mme Alfred Fouillée), *Le Tour de la France par deux enfants*, Paris, Eugène Belin, 1877.

Chastenet, J., *Histoire de la Troisième République*, 7 vols, Paris, Hachette, 1952–63.

Elwitt, S., *The Making of the Third Republic: Class and Politics in France 1868–1884*, Baton Rouge, Louisiana University Press, 1975.

Girardet, R., *L'Idée coloniale en France*, Paris, La Table Ronde, 1972.

Mayeur, J., *Les Débuts de la Troisième République*, Paris, Editions du Seuil, 1973.

Nora, P., 'Ernest Lavisse: son rôle dans la formation du sentiment national', *Revue historique*, July–September 1962.

Ozouf, M., *L'Ecole, l'église et la République 1871–1914*, Paris, Armand Colin, 1963.

Ozouf, M., *L'Ecole de France*, Paris, Gallimard, 1984.

Prost, A., *L'Enseignement en France 1800–1967*, Paris, Armand Colin, 1968.

Rébérioux, M., *La République radicale? 1898–1914*, Paris, Editions du Seuil, 1973.

Siegfried, A., *Tableau des partis en France*, Paris, Grasset, 1930.

7 THE RIGHT AND THE NATION: 1870–1914

Anderson, R., *Conservative Politics in France*, London, Allen & Unwin, 1974.

Barrès, M., *Scènes et doctrines du nationalisme*, Vol. 2, Paris, Plon, 1925.

Bredin, J.-D., *The Affair: The Case of Alfred Dreyfus*, New York, Braziller, 1986.

Burns, M., *Rural Society and French Politics: Boulangism and the Dreyfus Affair 1886–1900*, Princeton, Princeton University Press, 1984.

Buthman, W., *The Rise of Integral Nationalism in France*, New York, Columbia University Press, 1939.

Johnson, D., *France and the Dreyfus Affair*, New York, Walker, 1967.

Kedward, R., *The Dreyfus Affair*, London, Longman, 1965.

Rogger, H. and Weber, E., *The European Right: A Historical Profile*, London, Weidenfeld & Nicolson, 1965.

Soucy, R., *Fascism in France: The Case of Maurice Barrès*, London, University of California Press, 1972.

Sternhell, Z., 'Paul Déroulède and the origins of modern French nationalism', in J.C. Cairns (ed.), *Contemporary France: Illusion, Conflict and Regeneration*, New York, New Viewpoints, 1978 (originally published in *Journal of History* no. 4, 1971, pp. 46–70).

Sternhell, Z., *La Droite révolutionnaire 1885–1914: Les Origines françaises du fascisme*, Paris, Editions du Seuil, 1978.

Weber, E., *Action française: Royalism and Reaction in Twentieth Century France*, Stanford, Stanford University Press, 1962.

Weber, E., *The Nationalist Revival in France, 1905–1914,* Berkeley, University of California Press, 1959.

8 THE LEFT AND THE NATION: 1870–1914

Brécy, R., *Le Mouvement syndical en France, 1871–1921,* Paris, Mouton, 1963.
Bron, J., *Histoire du mouvement ouvrier français,* 2 vols, Paris, Editions ouvrières, 1968.
Collinet, M., *L'Ouvrier français. Essai sur la condition ouvrière (1900–1950),* Paris, Editions ouvrières, 1951.
Droz, J. (ed.), *Histoire générale du socialisme, Vol. II, 1875–1918,* Paris, Presses Universitaires de France, 1975.
Dubief, H., *Le Syndicalisme révolutionnaire,* Paris, Armand Colin, 1969.
Haupt, G., *Socialism and the Great War. The Collapse of the Second International,* Oxford, Clarendon Press, 1972.
Lefranc, G., *Le Mouvement socialiste sous la Troisième République (1875–1940),* Paris, Payot, 1963.
Lefranc, G., *Le Mouvement syndical sous la Troisième République,* Paris, Payot, 1967.
Ligou, D., *Histoire du socialisme en France 1871–1961,* Paris, Presses Universitaires de France, 1962.
Lorwin, V., *The French Labor Movement,* Harvard, Harvard University Press, 1954.
Perrot, M., *Les Ouvriers en grève: France 1871–1890,* Paris, Mouton, 1974.
Willard, C., *Socialisme et communisme français,* Paris, Armand Colin, 1967.

9 PERSPECTIVES AND USES OF NATIONALISM: 1918–40

Bernard, P., *La Fin d'un monde (1914–1929),* Paris, Editions du Seuil, 1973.
Bloch, M., *Strange Defeat,* New York, Oxford University Press, 1949.
Brower, D., *The New Jacobins: the French Communist Party and the Popular Front,* Ithaca, Cornell University Press, 1968.
Burrin, P., *La Dérive fasciste: Doriot, Déat, Bergéry, 1933–45,* Paris, Editions du Seuil, 1986.
Degras, J. (ed.), *The Communist International 1919–43: Documents,* Vol. III, 1956.
Dubief, H., *Le Déclin de la Troisième République (1929–1938),* Paris, Editions du Seuil, 1973.
Duroselle, J.B., *La Décadence 1932–1939,* Paris, Imprimerie Nationale, 1979.
Duroselle, J.B., *Les Relations franco-allemandes de 1914 à 1939,* Paris, Armand Colin, 1977.
Fohlen, C., *La France d l'entre-deux-guerres,* Paris, Casterman, 1966.
Frederix, P., *Etat des forces en France,* Paris, Gallimard, 1935.
Greene, N., *Crisis and Decline: The French Socialist Party in the Popular Front Era,* New York, Cornell University Press, 1969.
Jackson, J., *The Politics of Depression in France 1932–1936,* Cambridge, Cambridge University Press, 1985.
Jenkins, B., *The Paris Riots of February 6th 1934: The Crisis of the Third French Republic,* published PhD thesis, University of London, 1979.
Kemp, T., *The French Economy 1919–1939: The History of a Decline,* London, Longman, 1972.

Kergoat, J., *La France du Front Populaire*, Paris, Editions la Découverte, 1986.

Larmour, P., *The French Radical Party in the 1930s*, Stanford, Stanford University Press, 1964.

Lefranc, G., *Histoire du Front Populaire*, Paris, Payot, 1974.

Loubet del Bayle, J., *Les Non-conformistes des années 30*, Paris, Editions du Seuil, 1969.

Machefer, P., *Ligues et fascismes en France, 1918–1939*, Paris, Presses Universitaires de France, 1974.

Manévy, R., *Histoire de la presse, 1914–1939*, Paris, Correa, 1945.

Marcus, J., *French Socialism in the Crisis Years (1933–1936)*, New York, Praeger, 1958.

Micaud, C., *The French Right and Nazi Germany 1933–1939*, Durham, North Carolina, University of North Carolina Press, 1943.

Mortimer, E., *The Rise of the French Communist Party 1920–47*, London, Faber & Faber, 1984.

Plumyène, J. and Lasierra, R., *Les Fascismes français*, Paris, Editions du Seuil, 1963.

Shirer, W., *The Collapse of the Third Republic*, London, Heinemann/Secker & Warburg, 1970.

Soucy, R., *French Fascism: The First Wave 1924–1933*, New Haven, Yale University Press, 1986.

10 NATIONALISM FROM LIBERATION TO DE GAULLE

Andrieu, C., Le Van, L. and Prost, A., *Les Nationalisations de la libération*, Paris, Presses de la Fondation Nationale des Sciences Politiques, 1987.

Azéma, J.-P., *De Munich à la Libération (1938–1944)*, Paris, Editions du Seuil, 1979.

Bleton, P., *Les Hommes des temps qui viennent*, Paris, Editions ouvrières, 1956.

Carmoy, G. de, *Les Politiques étrangères de la France (1944–1966)*, Paris, La Table Ronde, 1967.

Dupeux, G., *La France de 1945 à 1965*, Paris, Armand Colin, 1969.

Duroselle, J.-B., *Histoire diplomatique de 1919 à nos jours*, Paris, Dalloz, 1978.

Elgey, G., *La République des illusions (1945–51)*, Paris, Fayard, 1965.

Elgey, G., *La République des contradictions (1951–1954)*, Paris, Fayard, 1968.

Fauvet, J., *La IVe République*, Paris, Fayard, 1959.

Graham, B., *The French Socialists and Tripartism, 1944–1947*, London, Weidenfeld & Nicolson, 1965.

Hoffmann, S., *France: Change and Tradition*, London, Gollancz, 1963.

Julliard, J., *La IVe République (1947–1958)*, Paris, Calmann–Lévy, 1968.

Kedward, R., *Resistance and Vichy France*, Oxford, Oxford University Press, 1978.

Kuisel, R., *Capitalism and the State in Modern France*, Cambridge, Cambridge University Press, 1981.

Laroque, P., *Succès et faiblesses de l'effort social français*, Paris, Armand Colin, 1961.

Mendras, H., *Les Paysans et la modernisation de l'agriculture*, Paris, CNRS, 1958.

Noguères, H., *Histoire de la résistance en France de 1940 à 1945*, 5 vols, Paris, Laffont, 1967–1976.

Paxton, R., *Vichy France: Old Guard and New Order*, New York, Knopf, 1972.

Parodi, M., *L'Economie et la société française de 1945 à 1970*, Paris, Armand Colin, 1971.

Rioux, J.-P., *The Fourth Republic 1944–58*, Cambridge, Cambridge University Press, 1987 (first published in French in 2 vols by Editions du Seuil, 1980 and 1983.)

Williams, P., *Crisis and Compromise: Politics in the Fourth Republic*, London, Longman, 1964.

Williams, P., *War, Plots and Scandals in Post-War France*, Cambridge, Cambridge University Press, 1970.

11 THE SWANSONG OF THE NATION STATE?

Andrews, W. and Hoffmann, S. (eds), *The Fifth Republic at Twenty*, Albany, State University of New York, 1981.

Andrieux, A. and Lignon, J., *L'Ouvrier d'aujourd'hui*, Paris, Rivière, 1960.

Ardagh, J., *France in the 1980s*, London, Penguin, 1983.

Avril, P., *La Ve République: Histoire politique et constitutionnelle*, Paris, Presses Universitaires de France, 1987.

Bell, D. (ed.), *Contemporary French Political Parties*, London, Croom Helm, 1981.

Berstein, S., *La France de l'expansion: I. La république gaullienne 1958–1969*, Paris, Editions du Seuil, 1989.

Birnbaum, P., Barucq, C. and Bellaide, M., *La Classe dirigeante*, Paris, Presses Universitaires de France, 1978.

Cerny, P., *The Politics of Grandeur*, Cambridge, Cambridge University Press, 1980.

Chapsal, J., *La Vie politique sous la Ve République*, Paris, Presses Universitaires de France, 1987.

Charlot, J., *Le Phénomène gaulliste*, Paris, Fayard, 1970.

De Gaulle, C., *Le Fil de l'épée*, 2nd edition, Paris, Berger-Levrault, 1944.

De Gaulle, C., *Mémoires de guerre, I: L'Appel 1940–1942*, Paris, Plon, 1954.

De Gaulle, C., *Mémoires de guerre, III: Le Salut 1944–1946*, Paris, Plon, 1959.

Hamon, H. and Rotman, P., *Génération: I. Les Années de rêve. II. Les Années de poudre*, Paris, Editions du Seuil, 1987–88.

Hanley, D.L., ' "Les variables de Solferino" or thoughts on steering the socialist economy: An analysis of the economic discourse of the French *Parti socialiste*', in S. Williams (ed.) *Socialism in France from Jaurès to Mitterrand*, London, Frances Pinter, 1983.

Hayward, J., *Governing France: The One and Indivisible French Republic*, London, Weidenfeld & Nicolson, 1983.

Howorth, J. and Ross, G. (eds), *Contemporary France: A Review of Interdisciplinary Studies, Vol. I*, London, Frances Pinter, 1987.

Mallet, S., *La Nouvelle Classe ouvrière*, Paris, Editions du Seuil, 1969.

Marceau, J., *Class and Status in France*, London, Oxford University Press, 1977.

Morin, E., *L'Esprit du temps*, Paris, Grasset, 1962.

Mouriaux, R., *Syndicalisme et politique*, Paris, Editions ouvrières, 1985.

Ross, G., *Workers and Communists in France: From Popular Front to Eurocommunism*, Berkeley, University of California Press, 1982.

Rowbotham, S., Segal, L. and Wainwright, H., *Beyond the Fragments: Feminism and the making of socialism*, London, Merlin Press, 1979.

BIBLIOGRAPHY

Singer, D., *Is Socialism Doomed? The Meaning of Mitterrand,* New York, Oxford University Press, 1988.

Viansson-Ponté, P., *Histoire de la république gaullienne,* 2 vols, Paris, Fayard, 1970–1.

Wright, V. (ed.), *Continuity and Change in France,* London, Allen & Unwin, 1984.

INDEX